D1528075

Utility and Production Functions

To Soojun, Caroline, and Edward

Utility and
Production Functions

Theory and Applications

Jae Wan Chung

BLACKWELL
Oxford UK & Cambridge USA

First published 1994

Blackwell Publishers
238 Main Street
Cambridge, Massachusetts 02142
USA

108 Cowley Road
Oxford OX4 1JF
UK

Library of Congress Cataloging-in-Publication Data
Chung, Jae Wan.
   Utility and production functions: theory and applications / Jae Wan Chung.
      p. cm.
   Includes bibliographical references and index.
   ISBN 1–55786–417–9 (acid-free paper)
   1. Utility theory – Mathematical models. 2. Production functions (Economic theory) I. Title.
HB201.C5498 1994
338.6–dc20   93-5451
                                                                                 CIP

British Library Cataloguing in Publication Data
A CIP catalogue record for this book is available from the British Library.

Typeset in 10 on 12 pt Times
by Photo·graphics, Honiton, Devon
Printed in Great Britain by T.J. Press (Padstow) Ltd, Padstow, Cornwall.

This book is printed on acid-free paper

Contents

List of Figures

Preface

Economists have been developing utility functions and production functions for many decades. Given the massive number of writings on the subject, most of which are highly mathematical, it is a formidable task for students to comprehend systematically the economic rationale behind them. This book intends to provide readers easy access to these hard-core areas in microeconomics. The book illustrates explicitly in chronological order the major utility functions and production functions developed so far. It focuses on the main arguments of each function and economists' attempts to resolve the problems that each function has.

This book has been written over several years. I did the preliminary work while I was a visiting professor at Seoul National University a number of years ago and the details were worked out after I returned to my regular position at George Mason University. I would like to thank Richard E. Wagner, Chair, Department of Economics, for his support of the project. I have accumulated a significant amount of intellectual debts to many people. First of all, I am indebted to my colleagues for their general support and encouragement. Michael Alexeev, Roger D. Congleton, and Willem Thorbecke read the entire manuscript and gave me valuable comments. Detailed reviews of part of the manuscript by Kevin B. Grier have contributed greatly to clarifying some remaining problems and ambiguities. I would like to thank Ronald A. Heiner for his advice and suggestions. I received helpful comments from my graduate assistants, past and present. I owe much gratitude to Mark Lynner and Kurt Schuler. Also, I gratefully acknowledge a significant contribution made by Anthony de Carvalho and

Peter J. Kunzel, two undergraduate students, and my 1990 graduate class in microeconomics.

Needless to say, preparation of a manuscript requires a considerable amount of patience as well as skill. I wish to thank the entire staff of the Office Support Services of George Mason University. I extend my special thanks to Anne G. Bonanno, Rolf A. Janke, Executive Editor, and anonymous reviewers who have given me helpful comments and suggestions. G. Sharrock of Omega Scientific, the copy editor, has helped me greatly improve the entire manuscript.

Finally, I am grateful to authors (or estates)/editors/publishers of journals and books listed in the acknowledgment section for permissions to adapt articles used partially in this book.

Jae Wan Chung
Fairfax, Virginia

Acknowledgments

Among many articles and books used in this book as references, the following are the ones that I have adapted or reprinted partially. I gratefully acknowledge permissions of authors (or estates)/editors/ publishers for adaptations and partial reprints.

Theory of Utility

Barten, A. P. 1964: Consumer demand functions under conditions of almost additive preferences. *Econometrica*, 32, 1–38.

Brown, M. and Heien, D. 1972: The S-branch utility tree: a generalization of the linear expenditure system. *Econometrica*, 40, July, 737–47.

Christensen, L. R., Jorgenson, D. W. and Lau, L. J. 1975: Transcendental logarithmic utility function. *American Economic Review*, LXV, June, 367–83.

Christensen, L. R. and Manser, M. E. 1977: Estimating U.S. consumer preferences for meat with a flexible utility function. *Journal of Econometrics*, 5, January, 37–53.

Deaton, A. and Muellbauer, J. 1980: An almost ideal demand system. *American Economic Review*, 70, June, 312–26.

Houthakker, H. S. 1960: Additive preferences. *Econometrica*, 28, April, 244–57.

Samuelson, P. A. 1947–8: Some implications of "linearity." *Review of Economic Studies*, 15 (2), 88–90.

Stone, R. 1954: Linear expenditure systems and demand analysis: an application to the pattern of British demand. *Economic Journal*, 64, September, 511–27.

Theil, H. 1967: *Economics and Information Theory*. Amsterdam: North-Holland.

Theory of Production

Arrow, K. J., Chenery, H. B., Minhas, B. S. and Solow, R. M. 1961: Capital–labor substitution and economic efficiency. *Review of Economics and Statistics*, 63, August, 225–50.

Berndt, E. R. and Wood, D. O. Technology, prices, and the derived demand for energy. *Review of Economics and Statistics*, 57, August, 259–68.

Christensen, L. R., Jorgenson, D. W. and Lau, L. J. 1973: Transcendental logarithmic production function frontiers. *Review of Economics and Statistics*, 55, February, 29–45.

Cobb, C. W. and Douglas, P. H. 1928: A theory of production. *American Economic Review*, 18, 139–65.

Diewert, W. E. 1971: An application of the Shepard duality theorem: a generalized Leontief production function. *Journal of Political Economy*, 79, 481–507. © 1971 by the University of Chicago. All rights reserved.

Jones, R. W. 1965: The structure of simple general equilibrium models.[1] *Journal of Political Economy*, LXXII, December, 557–72. © 1965 by the University of Chicago. All rights reserved.

Pollak, R. A., Sickles, R. C. and Wales, T. J. 1984: The CES–translog: specification and estimation of a new cost function. *Review of Economics and Statistics*, 66, November, 602–7.

Sato, K. 1967: A two-level constant-elasticity of substitution production function. *Review of Economic Studies*, 34, 201–18.

Uzawa, H. 1962: Production function with constant elasticities of substitution. *Review of Economic Studies*, 29, 291–9.

Introduction

The theory of consumer behavior and the theory of the firm are the foundations of modern economic analysis. Both theories have advanced in concert with the various utility and production functions that have been developed over the past several decades. During this period, the primary objective of economists has been to find *flexible* functions that establish correctly specified behavioral models.

The purpose of this book is to retrace footprints left behind by earlier economists in their search for flexible forms of utility and production functions. These functions are compiled systematically in this volume. I explicitly show how and why a specific function is applied in analyzing the optimal behavior of consumers and producers. There has been a tendency in applied economics to neglect theory. Many economists have relied on *ad hoc* models that lack a solid basis in economic theory. It is hoped that rigorous yet illustrative discussions of the functions will stimulate readers of this book to develop an analytical mode of thought that is properly grounded in theory and to use it to expound adequately the actual operation of economic processes.

Economists have two major concerns in identifying a flexible function. First of all, a particular function should be *well behaved*. A function is well behaved if it is monotonic and convex. These characteristics are often called the *regulatory conditions*. Without them, the function fails to rest on standard economic reasoning. Second, the function should be free from restrictive assumptions as much as possible. *Additivity* (separability) and/or *homotheticity* (homogeneity) are two assumptions that have been traditionally imposed on utility and production functions. If a function is "homothetic," the commodity shares of the consumer's budget or the input shares of the producer's cost are "independent" of the total budget or total output, respectively. If the function is both "additive and homothetic," elasticities of substitution are constant and identical for all pairs of commodities or inputs (Christensen et al., 1975, p. 367). Homotheticity yields unitary income elasticity and separability, which allows a pairwise analysis (the microeconomic foundation for the value-added specification that requires use of aggregate indices of capital and labor), precludes the roles played by related goods or inputs in the demand function. Although these two assumptions have played a significant role in applied economics, they have generated considerable controversy among economists over policy relevance of the corresponding results. Many economists today believe that actual data conflict with these assumptions.

This book is divided into two parts: one on utility functions and the other on production functions. The functions will be presented in a chronological order. Most of the chapters are divided in a uniform manner. Each chapter presents a function, examines its underlying properties, derives the system of expenditure share functions (for commodities) or the system of cost share functions (for inputs), and investigates their behavior. It also derives and discusses various elasticities, including the so-called Allen–Uzawa partial elasticities of substitution. The dual approach to the theory of utility and the theory of the firm plays an important role throughout the book. Each chapter contains a section of empirical remarks which deal with empirical results selected from references, if available. The primary objective in this section is not to discuss econometric procedures and problems but to provide readers with an opportunity to ascertain the main point addressed in the theoretical sections. Of course, the central theme maintained throughout the book is not always uniform in every study because the intent of each researcher is different and theories are advancing.

Chapter 1 examines the linear logarithmic utility function and its expenditure system. As an additive and homogeneous utility function, it is highly restrictive. Chapters 2 and 3 discuss two utility functions that retain only the assumption of additivity: the Stone–Geary utility function and Hendrik Houthakker's additive logarithmic (addilog) utility function. They are more flexible than the linear logarithmic function. The expenditure system of the Stone–Geary utility function includes parameters such as the marginal budget shares and the subsistence levels of commodity consumption. In the case of the addilog function, Houthakker discusses a duality between the direct and indirect forms of the utility function and consequences of additivity. Roy's identity, applied to the indirect form of the addilog function, yields expenditure share equations. However, the Stone–Geary function and Houthakker's addilog function, being additive, are far from being fully flexible. Chapter 4 is concerned with the Rotterdam system of demand functions which is based on the *almost* additive utility function. Chapter 5 deals with the constant-elasticity-of-substitution (CES) utility function and expenditure system. This function is homogeneous and weakly separable. Although it is more flexible than the linear logarithmic function, the assumptions underlying it are still quite restrictive. This chapter also investigates the S-branch utility function that generalizes the functions mentioned earlier. This function takes an approach that combines the CES and Stone–Geary functions, hence broadening the range of flexibility. However, the range is still narrow. Chapter 6 analyzes the so-called translog utility function. This function does not have to be additive and homothetic, although these conditions can be imposed as testable hypotheses. The translog function allows budget shares to vary with total expenditure and also permits a wide range of variation in elasticities of substitution. As a special case of the translog function, the almost ideal demand system will be discussed here. Chapter 7 introduces the CES–translog utility function, which admits even greater variability in elasticities of substitution than the translog function.

Chapter 8 is concerned with the Cobb–Douglas production function. As a linearly homogeneous and weakly separable function, its elasticity of substitution is restricted to unity. In chapters 9 and 10, we discuss the CES production function and a multi-factor generalized version of the CES production function, respectively. These are also homogeneous and separable functions, in which the elasticity of substitution is an arbitrary constant, rather than unity. Their flexibility is greater than that of the Cobb–Douglas production function although it is still limited. Chapter 11 examines the two-level CES production function. Each level has its own elasticity of substitution: the intra-class elasticity of substitution between any pair of inputs within the same group at the lower level and the inter-class elasticity of substitution between aggregate inputs in different groups at the upper level. Elasticities of substitution between any pair of inputs within the same group are constant, but those between inputs in different groups are not. Chapter 12 deals with the translog production function, which does not require any additivity or homotheticity assumptions, and hence the translog specification is superior to others. In the translog function, input shares of total cost are not independent of output and elasticities of substitution are not restricted to any constant number. If the function is separable, however, the translog may be broken down into a Cobb–Douglas function of translog subaggregates or a translog function of Cobb–Douglas subaggregates. The CES–translog production function, explored in chapter 13, remedies this problem. The combination of the CES and translog forms provides a wider range of variation of elasticities than the translog function by itself.

Chapter 14 covers the Leontief production function. This function is based on the Walras–Leontief assumption of fixed-input coefficients and exhibits a zero elasticity of substitution. A generalized Leontief production function is examined in chapter 15. The generalized Leontief function is much more flexible than the original Leontief function, but reduces to the regular Leontief form under certain conditions. Finally, the appendices at the end of the book summarize some essential concepts, definitions, and theorems. Readers should be familiar with them before they read the main part of the book.

Each of the functions has enjoyed a period of popularity. The Cobb–Douglas function and its variants predominated during the 1950s and 1960s; the CES function and its variants rose to prominence during the 1960s and 1970s; and the translog function became ascendant in the 1970s and 1980s. At present, economists are continuing to search for more flexible functions by generalizing the translog and Leontief functions.

This book is written chiefly for upper-level undergraduate students and graduate students. It will also be useful for professional economists who have not had the opportunity to stay in touch with the recent developments in the theories of utility and production. A background in elementary calculus and matrix algebra is recommended.

Part I

Utility Functions

1 The Linear Logarithmic Utility Function

The modern theory of consumer behavior began with the linear logarithmic utility function. It was the most popular function in the 1960s and the 1970s and is still widely used by economists. Of the many studies conducted with this function, those by Allen and Bowley (1935), Schultz (1938), Working (1943), Wold (1953), Stone (1954a), Frish (1959), Leser (1963), Houthakker and Taylor (1970), and Prais and Houthaker (1971) are frequently cited as major references.

The linear logarithmic function has the simplest form of all the utility functions examined in this book. It is a well-behaved function in the sense that it satisfies the regularity conditions – monotonicity and convexity. However, it requires restrictive assumptions – additivity and homotheticity. Demand models based on such assumptions severely distort estimated price and income elasticities. In general, (1) commodity shares of the consumer's budget are independent of the total budget if the utility function is homothetic and (2) the Allen–Uzawa partial elasticities of substitution (AES) are restricted to a constant that is identical for all pairs of commodities when the utility function is homothetic and additive. As an additive and homothetic utility function, the usefulness of the linear logarithmic utility function is questionable in empirical work.

Section 1.1 presents the function and examines its basic properties. Section 1.2 derives the demand function. We discuss limitations of the demand system by examining various elasticities and the expenditure (or budget) share functions in section 1.3. Section 1.4 derives the Engel curve. Section 1.5 takes the dual approach to utility theory. The main result of the dual approach is the Allen–Uzawa partial elasticities of substitution. Section 1.6 presents empirical results. Section 1.7 summarizes the chapter.

1.1   The Function and its Properties

The linear logarithmic function is written as

$$u = \ln U = \sum_{i=1}^{n} \beta_i \ln q_i \qquad (1.1)$$

where u is the index of utility, q_i is the quantity of good i, and $0 < \beta_i < 1$.

Note that equation (1.1) is a version of the function that amounts to a logarithmic (hence monotonically increasing) transformation on term utility U. It is a monotonically increasing function because

$$\frac{\partial u}{\partial q_i} = \frac{\beta_i}{q_i} > 0 \qquad (1.2)$$

for $\beta_i > 0$ and $q_i > 0$. That implies that the marginal utility of good i (MU_i) is positive. In addition, the function satisfies the law of diminishing marginal utility, i.e.

$$\frac{\partial^2 u}{\partial q_i^2} = -\frac{\beta_i}{q_i^2} < 0. \qquad (1.3)$$

Convexity prevails. Assuming that there are two goods i and j, the rate of change of the slope of the indifference curve, $d^2 q_j / dq_i^2$, is positive. Equivalently, the second-order bordered Hessian $|\overline{H}_2|$ is positive, the second-order total differential of the utility function is negative definite ($d^2 u < 0$), the utility function is strictly *quasi-concave*, or the indifference curve is *convex*. Substituting equations (1.2), (1.3), and (1.6) below into equation (B.4) in appendix B, we have

$$|\overline{H}_2| = \left(\frac{\beta_i}{q_i}\right)^2 \frac{\beta_j}{q_j^2} + \frac{\beta_i}{q_i^2}\left(\frac{\beta_j}{q_j}\right)^2 > 0 \qquad (i \neq j). \qquad (1.4)$$

A strictly (or strictly quasi) concave utility function in the two-good case has the shape of an igloo, which is shown in figure 1.1. Note that the concave utility surface yields the convex indifference curves on the floor (in $q_1 q_2$, space). Economists assume monotonicity and convexity. These assumptions flow naturally from standard economic reasoning.

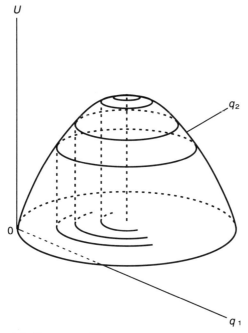

Figure 1.1 Concave utility function and indifference curve.

If the indifference curves are monotonically decreasing but concave, the best attainable position is a corner solution, implying that the consumer spends his income only on one commodity at the optimum.

The underlying assumptions of this utility function are homotheticity and additivity.[1] The function is homothetic because utility rises by the scalar or a scalar proportion if each commodity is multiplied by scalar θ, i.e.

$$u + \ln \theta \sum_i \beta_i = \sum_i \beta_i \ln(\theta q_i). \tag{1.5}$$

Also, it is *strongly additive* because the cross-partial derivative of the utility function is zero, i.e.

$$\frac{\partial^2 u}{\partial q_i \partial q_j} = 0. \tag{1.6}$$

Equation (1.6) implies that the marginal utility of good i is independent of the quantity of good j. For more than two goods, the additivity condition can be equivalently stated as implying that the marginal rate of substitution between any pair of goods is independent of the quantity of a third good. This condition will be discussed in detail in chapters 6 and 12.

1.2   Consumer Demand Function

Maximizing the utility function (equation (1.1)) subject to the budget constraint yields the demand function.

Given the consumer's budget constraint

$$m = \sum_{i=1}^{n} p_i q_i \tag{1.7}$$

the augmented objective function is

$$\mathcal{L}(q; \lambda) = \sum_i \beta_i \ln q_i + \lambda \left(m - \sum_i p_i q_i \right) \tag{1.8}$$

where m is income, p_i is the price of good i, and λ is the Lagrange multiplier (or the marginal utility of income).

The first-order conditions for maximization are

$$\frac{\partial \mathcal{L}}{\partial q_i} = \frac{\beta_i}{q_i} - \lambda p_i = 0 \tag{1.9}$$

$$\frac{\partial \mathcal{L}}{\partial \lambda} = m - \sum_i p_i q_i = 0. \tag{1.10}$$

Substituting equation (1.9) into equation (1.10) yields the demand function:

$$q_i = \frac{\beta_i}{\Sigma_j \beta_j} \frac{m}{p_i} \qquad (i \in j). \tag{1.11}$$

For a given set of prices $(p_1, p_2, \ldots, p_n)$ included in equations (1.9) and (1.10), this procedure implies that $MU_i/MU_j = p_i/p_j$. There are $n - 1$ such independent marginal rate of substitution (MRS) equations. Together with the budget constraint, we have n equations with n variables to solve for q_i ($i = 1, 2, \ldots, n$). Note that the demand function is homogeneous of degree zero in prices and income, by which we mean that if all the prices in MU equations and income increase in the same proportion, the quantity demanded is unaffected. This feature implies that a typical consumer is not fooled by his higher nominal income if prices increase in the same proportion. It is often referred to as the absence of money illusion in the classical context of the theory of demand. Also note that the demand function is (locally) linear in income.

1.3 Price and Income Elasticities

Differentiating equation (1.11) with respect to prices and income, we obtain own-price (ϵ_{ii}), cross-price (ϵ_{ij}), and income (ϵ_{im}) elasticities. They are as follows:[2]

$$\epsilon_{ii} = \frac{\partial q_i}{\partial p_i}\frac{p_i}{q_i} = -\frac{\beta_i}{\Sigma\,\beta_j}\frac{m}{p_i\,q_i} = -1 \qquad (1.12)$$

$$\epsilon_{ij} = \frac{\partial q_i}{\partial p_j}\frac{p_j}{q_i} = 0 \qquad (i \neq j) \qquad (1.13)$$

$$\epsilon_{im} = \frac{\partial q_i}{\partial m}\frac{m}{q_i} = \frac{\beta_i}{\Sigma_j\,\beta_j}\frac{m}{p_i\,q_i} = 1. \qquad (1.14)$$

Let us discuss the above results.

1 The own-price elasticities are negative and hence confirm the law of demand. However, the unitary elasticity is restrictive.

2 The cross-price elasticities are zero, implying that goods i and j are *grossly* independent. Note that the gross concept is based on the cross-price elasticity being equivalent to the total effect in the Slutsky equation.[3] In contrast to the gross concept, the net concept is based on the Hicks–Allen substitution effect. If the net substitution effect is positive, goods i and j are called net substitutes or substitutes in the Hicks–Allen sense. If the net substitution effect is negative, the goods are called net complements. The Slutsky equation expressed in terms of elasticities is

$$\epsilon_{ij} = \eta_{ij} - S_j\epsilon_{im} \qquad (1.15)$$

where

$$\eta_{ij} = \frac{\partial q_i}{\partial p_j}\frac{p_j}{q_i}\bigg|_{u\,=\,\text{constant}}$$

and $S_j = p_jq_j/m$ is the expenditure share of good j.[4]

Given that the total effect (ϵ_{ij}) is equal to zero and part of the income effect (ϵ_{im} in equation (1.14)) is equal to unity, we know that η_{ij} (the Hicks–Allen substitution effect) equals $S_j > 0$, implying that goods i and j are net substitutes.

3 The income elasticities are positive ($\epsilon_{im} = 1 > 0$), so all goods are normal goods. The linear logarithmic utility function does not permit inferior goods.

Results 1–3 show clearly the limitations of the linear logarithmic utlity function, unless they are empirically true.

1.4 Engel Expenditure System

The *Engel curve* relates quantity q_i to income m.[5] Given p_i as a constant, equation (1.11) shows that the Engel curve is a straight line through the origin. The income elasticity is the ratio of the slope of (or the tangent line to) the Engel curve (dq_i/dm for the marginal function) to the slope of a ray radiating from the origin to the curve (q_i/m for the average function). Given the Engel curve EC in figure 1.2, note that the magnitude of the marginal function (M) is less than the magnitude of the average function (A) at point a (and point b), that the value for the income elasticity of the Engel curve is less than

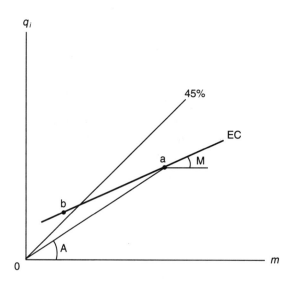

Figure 1.2 Income elasticity.

unity, and thus that Engel's law prevails if this is the case of a smaller food consumption of the typical household.

If, however, the Engel curve passes through the origin, the values for M and A are the same. Therefore the magnitude of the income elasticity of the Engel curve derived from equation (1.11) is unity whether the curve is the 45° line itself or is steeper or flatter than the 45° line. Among four possible Engel curves exhibited in figure 1.3, equation (1.11) corresponds to curve B. Readers should also note that a nonlinear Engel curve (such as the broken curve) can also have unitary income elasticity locally in the neighborhood of the tangent point if the tangent line passes through the origin.

The *Engel expenditure curve* relates expenditure $p_i q_i$ to income m. Multiplying through the demand functions (equation (1.11)) by p_i yields the Engel expenditure function

$$E_i = p_i q_i = \frac{\beta_i}{\Sigma_j \beta_j} m. \qquad (1.16)$$

Note that the equation is linear in income and is sloped upward. It passes through the origin. These graphical features confirm that the linear logarithmic utility function eliminates inferior goods.

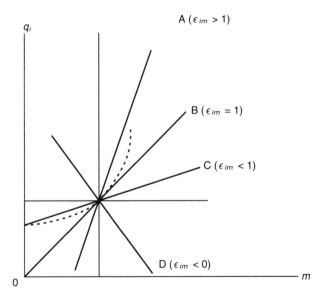

Figure 1.3 Engel curves.

The *expenditure share function* is obtained by dividing through equation (1.16) by m, i.e.

$$S_i = \frac{p_i q_i}{m} = \frac{\beta_i}{\Sigma_j \beta_j}.$$ (1.17)

The share function is constant. Note that it is independent of the total expenditure. The result follows from the assumption that the linear logarithmic utility function is homothetic.

It is notable that, if two goods are perfect (gross) substitutes, the indifference curve is a straight line with slope -1. The optimal choice takes place usually on the boundary. The demand curve is fragmentary. Depending on the prices of the two goods, it may be vertical or horizontal. It may also be a curve with a negative slope. The Engel curve is linear and passes through the origin. Therefore the income elasticity is unity. If two goods are perfect complements, the indifference curve is L-shaped. The optimal choice takes place on the diagonal line, yielding the demand curve with a negative slope and the Engel curve with the unitary income elasticity. The features associated with the right-angled curve will be extensively discussed in chapter 14.

1.5   Duality, Expenditure Shares, and Elasticities

To find the expenditure share function and the Allen–Uzawa partial elasticities of substitution, economists have recently employed the *dual* approach to utility theory.[6] In accordance with Houthakker (1960), duality permits us to find the indirect utility function corresponding to the direct utility function in equation (1.1).[7] The indirect utility function is

$$\ln \nu = -\ln U = \zeta + \sum_i \beta_i \ln\left(\frac{p_i}{m}\right)$$ (1.18)

where

$$\zeta = -\sum_i \beta_i \ln\left(\frac{\beta_i}{\Sigma_j \beta_j}\right).$$

The rationale for duality will be discussed in detail in chapter 3.

First-order and second-order partial derivatives of the indirect utility function are, respectively,

$$\frac{\partial v}{\partial p_i} = \beta_i \frac{v}{p_i} \tag{1.19}$$

$$\frac{\partial v}{\partial m} = -(\beta_i + \beta_j)\frac{v}{m} \quad (i \neq j) \tag{1.20}$$

$$\frac{\partial^2 v}{\partial p_i^2} = \beta_i\, v\, \frac{\beta_i - 1}{p_i^2} \tag{1.21}$$

$$\frac{\partial^2 v}{\partial p_i\, \partial p_j} = \beta_i\, \beta_j\, \frac{v}{p_i p_j} \quad (i \neq j)$$

$$\left(= \frac{\partial^2 v}{\partial p_j\, \partial p_i}\, \text{by Young's theorem} \right). \tag{1.22}$$

Substituting equations (1.19) and (1.20) into Roy's identity yields the expenditure share function:[8]

$$S_i \equiv -\frac{(\partial v/\partial p_i)(p_i/v)}{(\partial v/\partial m)(m/v)} = \frac{\beta_i}{\Sigma_j\, \beta_j} \quad (i = 1, \ldots, n). \tag{1.23}$$

Substituting equations (1.19) and (1.20) into the definition for the Allen–Uzawa own elasticity of substitution and equations (1.19) and (1.21) into the definition for the Allen–Uzawa cross-partial elasticity of substitution yields[9]

$$\sigma_{ii} = \frac{v\, \partial^2 v/\partial p_i^2}{(\partial v/\partial p_i)(\partial v/\partial p_i)} = -\frac{1 - \beta_i}{\beta_i} \tag{1.24}$$

$$\sigma_{ij} = \frac{v\, \partial^2 v/\partial p_i\, \partial p_j}{(\partial v/\partial p_i)(\partial v/\partial p_j)} = 1. \tag{1.25}$$

Equation (1.25) implies that the Allen–Uzawa cross-partial elasticities of substitution are constant ($=1$) and identical *a priori* for all pairs of commodities. This feature stems from the underlying assumptions that the utility function is not only additive but also homothetic. Allen (1938, p. 512) shows the Slutsky equation expressed in terms of the partial elasticity of substitution. It is

$$\epsilon_{ij} = S_j(\sigma_{ij} - \epsilon_{im}). \tag{1.26}$$

Note that the Allen–Uzawa partial elasticity of substitution is a component of the net substitution effect. Given $0 < S_j < 1$, the unitary cross-partial elasticity of substitution ($\sigma_{ij} = 1$) implies that all goods included in this utility function are invariably pairwise substitutes to each other in the net concept. This feature is a severe limitation of the linear logarithmic utility function.

1.6   Empirical Remarks[10]

A linear demand function used by earlier economists is basically one of various econometric specifications of equation (1.11) generalized by prices of two or three related goods (substitutes or complements) to reflect a higher degree of economic realism. A typical form of the function is a double-logarithmic linear demand function of constant elasticities, the form used frequently by Marshall in his exposition of demand theory. Frisch (1959) also advocated using this form. Schultz (1938) and Wold and Juréen (1953) are two important references.

Schultz (1938), one of the pioneering econometric studies on consumer demand, sets out both the linear demand function and the log linear demand function and gives a time-series analysis of the structure of consumer demand for disaggregated agricultural goods in the United States. Wold and Juréen derived interesting restrictions on demand functions, particularly on cross-price elasticities.

There are also various functional forms for the Engel curve from equation (1.16). Allen and Bowley (1935) is the first major analysis of cross-sectional data based on the linear Engel curve. A semilogarithmic specification with the adding-up criterion was estimated by Working (1943) and was used later by Leser (1963). It is often referred to as the Working–Leser model. Double-logarithmic, semilogarithmic, hyperbolic, and log-reciprocal versions have been tested by Prais and Houthakker (1971).

Since I do not attempt to provide a historical survey of empirical work on demand functions or Engel curves in this book, this section briefly examines only the work done by Schultz. Schultz was a student of Moore at Columbia University and spent his entire career (1926–38) at Chicago, where he demonstrated his intellectual power in economic theory and empirical demand analysis until he died in a tragic automobile accident at age 45.[11] In light of the central question revolving around various elasticities discussed in the earlier sections, it suffices to exemplify the theoretical concerns by the results of the log linear demand function involving a few items. I take the case of beef in connection with pork and mutton.

The results are various elasticities demands in the United States, 1922–33. The own-price elasticity of beef is −0.8576, which is statistically significant in terms of the *t* statistic. The law of demand prevails. The cross-price elasticity of beef with respect to pork is 0.0955; the cross-price elasticity of beef with respect to mutton is 0.2010. However, the cross-price elasticities are statistically insignificant. The income elasticity of beef is 0.4810, which is statistically significant.

Estimated values of the own-price elasticity and the cross-price elasticities are roughly consistent with the values given *a priori* by equations (1.12) and (1.13). However, the estimated value of income elasticity is not consistent with the value given by equation (1.14). There is no information available for the Allen–Uzawa partial elasticities of substitution.

1.7 Summary

The linear logarithmic utility function is a well-behaved function. The demand functions derived from it uphold the classical law of demand, as characterized by the own-price elasticities. The cross-price elasticities and the income elasticity suggest that the utility function permits only Hicks–Allen substitutes and normal goods. Under the restrictive assumptions imposed on the utility function, homotheticity and additivity, the Engel expenditure share function is constant and independent of the total expenditure and the Allen–Uzawa cross-partial elasticities of substitution are equal to unity and are identical for any pairs of commodities.

The demand function and the Engel curve derived in this chapter have been elaborated in various ways. The logarithmic linear form was a popular function employed frequently by earlier economists. I briefly discuss only the work done by Schultz. Although estimated values of the own-price elasticity and the cross-price elasticities are consistent with the values given *a priori* in theoretical propositions, the income elasticity is not. The concept of the Allen–Uzawa partial elasticities of substitution did not exist when the linear logarithmic utility function was popular. There is no information on those elasticities in Schultz's work.

The linear logarithmic utility function has been popular among economists. However, consumer behavior cannot be adequately analyzed with the demand function derived from the linear logarithmic utility function.

Notes

1 Homotheticity or homogeneity and additivity or separability are the concepts used extensively throughout the book. In general, homogeneity is a special case of homotheticity and additivity is a special case of separability. For their definitions, see appendices C and D.

2 As shown in equation (1.17), the term in parentheses is equal to $p_i q_i/m$ and thus $\epsilon_{ii} = -1$ and $\epsilon_{im} = 1$, respectively.

3 For the net and gross concepts, see appendix F.

4 See equation (F.28) in appendix F.

5 The Engel curve, the Engel expenditure curve, and the expenditure share function are the related concepts. Since prices are held constant for the first two concepts, the consumer's expenditure on the product is proportional to quantity demanded. Therefore it makes no difference whether we use expenditure or quantity. However, we use the three concepts distinctively in this book.

6 The dual approach to the theory of utility did not exist at the time when the linear logarithmic utility function was popular. For the rationale, see appendix G.

7 Hotelling (1932) introduced the concept of indirect utility function first. For details, see chapter 3.

8 For Roy's identity, see appendix H.

9 See appendix L. For details, see Allen (1964, pp. 340-3, 369-74, and 503-13) and Uzawa (1962).

10 The primary objective of this section and empirical sections in subsequent chapters is to provide readers with an opportunity to confirm the main points addressed in theoretical sections, not to discuss econometric procedures and problems in detail or to assess them. Economists have found certain utility functions and production functions more appealing than others for empirical studies. Depending on when a particular function was introduced, the amount of empirical research done on each function varies. Some functions have been the subject of a large number of empirical studies, others of only a limited number of studies, and still others of no studies. Frequently studied functions are the Stone–Geary utility function, the CES production function, and the translog production function. The generalized CES production function (chapter 10) and the Leontief production function (chapter 14) have been the subject of no empirical studies. Other utility and production functions have been studied to a limited degree. I shall confine myself to a discussion of the results most relevant to the main themes of each chapter. They are selected not necessarily for their superiority to other studies but for their illustrative value. Readers should keep in mind that the empirical sections do not always fully substantiate theoretical claims because empirical studies are motivated by authors'

perspectives at that time, whereas theories are always advancing. It is notable that Seale and Theil (1991, pp. 141–74) have recently emphasized the empirical importance of the selection of a functional form of the demand system for the behavior of income and price elasticities.

11   See Kaul and Sengupta (1991, p. 5).

Recommended Reading

Frisch, R. 1959: A complete scheme for computing all direct and cross demand elasticities in a model with many sectors. *Econometrica*, 27, 177–96.

Hotelling, H. 1932: Edgeworth's taxation paradox and the nature of demand and supply functions. *Journal of Political Economy*, 40, October, 577–616.

Houthakker, H.S. and Taylor, L.D. 1970: *Consumer Demand in the United States 1929–70*, second edition. Cambridge, MA: Harvard University Press.

Leser, C.E.V. 1963: Forms of Engel functions. *Econometrica*, 31, 694–703.

Prais, S.J. and Houthakker, H.S. 1971: *Analysis of Family Budgets*. Cambridge: Cambridge University Press.

Schultz, H. 1938: *The Theory and Measurement of Demand*. Chicago, IL: University of Chicago Press.

Stone, R. 1954: *The Measurement of Consumers' Expenditure and Behavior in the United Kingdom, 1920–1938*, vol. I. Cambridge: Cambridge University Press.

Wold, H.O.A. and Juréen, L. 1953: *Demand Analysis*. New York: Wiley.

Working, H. 1943: Statistical laws of family expenditure. *Journal of the American Statistical Association*, 38, 43–56.

2 The Stone–Geary Utility Function

In this chapter, we examine the Stone–Geary utility function, which is also frequently referred to as the Klein–Rubin utility function. Samuelson (1947–8) and Geary (1949) found that the expenditure system presented by Klein and Rubin (1947) implied the Stone–Geary form of utility function. Stone (1954a,b) developed and extensively applied the expenditure system. Later, Goldberger (1967), Parks (1969), Pollak and Wales (1969), Brown and Deaton (1972), Christensen and Manser (1976), and Deaton and Muellbauer (1980a) rigorously examined the theoretical features of the system. Its expenditure system is linear and is often referred to as the Stone–Geary linear expenditure system.

The Stone–Geary utility function assumes that utilities are additive. It is less restrictive than the linear logarithmic function discussed in chapter 1, which assumes both homotheticity and additivity. The Stone–Geary function can be reduced to the linear logarithmic utility function under certain conditions. The function offers an interesting approach to demand analysis. Two parameters highlight the function: the marginal budget share and the subsistence level.

Section 2.1 presents the basic properties of the Stone–Geary utility function. We derive its demand function and examine various elasticities and classical features associated with the demand function in section 2.2. Section 2.3 discusses the Engel linear expenditure function and expenditure share function and shows the major limitation imposed by the additivity assumption. Section 2.4 employs the dual approach to the expenditure system and to the Allen–Uzawa partial elasticities of substitution. Section 2.5 examines Stone's empirical results and gives empirical remarks on several other studies. Section 2.6 summarizes the chapter.

2.1 The Function and its Properties

The Stone–Geary utility function is written as

$$u = \ln U = \sum_{i=1}^{n} \beta_i \ln(q_i - \gamma_i) \tag{2.1}$$

where q_i is commodity i, $0 < \beta_i < 1$, $\Sigma_i \beta_i = 1$, $\gamma_i > 0$, and $q_i - \gamma_i > 0$.
The significance of parameters β_i and γ_i will be examined in the next section. Note that the Stone–Geary utility function reduces to the linear logarithmic utility function introduced in chapter 1 if $\gamma_i = 0$.
    To examine the properties of the Stone–Geary utility function, we differentiate it twice with respect to q_i. The first- and second-order derivatives are as follows:

$$\frac{\partial u}{\partial q_i} = \frac{\beta_i}{q_i - \gamma_i} > 0 \tag{2.2}$$

$$\frac{\partial^2 u}{\partial q_i^2} = \frac{-\beta_i}{(q_i - \gamma_i)^2} < 0 \tag{2.3}$$

$$\frac{\partial^2 u}{\partial q_i \partial q_j} = 0 \qquad (i \neq j). \tag{2.4}$$

    Unlike the linear logarithmic utility function, the Stone–Geary function assumes only additivity. This is because the cross-partial derivatives equal zero, as shown in equation (2.4), implying that the marginal utility of each commodity only depends upon the quantity of that commodity. The Stone–Geary function is nonhomothetic because scalar multiplication of each commodity in the function does not increase the utility exactly by the scalar θ or by any scalar proportion, i.e.

$$\theta^r u \neq \sum_i \beta_i \ln(\theta q_i - \gamma_i) \tag{2.5}$$

where r is an arbitrary constant. The implications associated with nonhomotheticity are discussed in the subsequent section.
    The Stone–Geary utility function satisfies the classical properties of consumer theory. First, the marginal utility of good i is positive. This is seen from equation (2.2). The value of equation (2.2) is positive

because $0 < \beta_i < 1$ and $q_i - \gamma_i > 0$, as the restrictions in equation (2.1) require. Positive marginal utility implies that the corresponding total utility is a monotonically increasing function. Second, the law of diminishing marginal utility holds for each good. This is because, given the above restrictions imposed on equation (2.1), equation (2.3) is negative. Third, strict convexity prevails. Given the additivity assumption (i.e. equation (2.4) = 0), the convexity condition in appendix B for two goods i and j yields

$$|\overline{H}_2| = \frac{\beta_i}{(q_i - \gamma_i)^2}\left(\frac{\beta_j}{q_j - \gamma_j}\right)^2 + \frac{\beta_j}{(q_j - \gamma_j)^2}\left(\frac{\beta_i}{q_i - \gamma_i}\right)^2 > 0 \qquad (i \neq j)$$

(2.6)

which gives the graphical configuration of the Stone–Geary utility function as illustrated in figure 1.1.

Since it is monotonic and convex, the Stone–Geary function is certainly a well-defined function.

2.2 Consumer Demand Function

We will derive the consumer demand function in basically the same way as we did in the previous chapter by maximizing the consumer's utility function subject to a budget constraint. There is a slight difference, however, in the procedure for derivation.

Given the utility function of equation (2.1) and the budget constraint, which is written as

$$m = \sum_{i=1}^{n} p_i q_i \qquad (i = 1, \ldots, n),$$ (2.7)

the augmented objective function is

$$\mathscr{L}(q; \lambda) = \sum_i \beta_i \ln(q_i - \gamma_i) + \lambda\left(m - \sum_i p_i q_i\right)$$ (2.8)

where m is consumer's income, p_i is the price of good i, and λ is the Lagrangian multiplier.

Income and the price of good i are assumed to be constant. The first-order condition (the necessary condition) for utility maximization is given by

$$\frac{\partial \mathscr{L}}{\partial q_i} = \frac{\beta_i}{q_i - \gamma_i} - \lambda p_i = 0$$ (2.9)

$$\frac{\partial \mathcal{L}}{\partial \lambda} = m - \sum_i p_i\, q_i = 0. \tag{2.10}$$

Summing up (2.9) over i we obtain

$$\lambda = \frac{1}{m - \Sigma_i\, p_i\, \gamma_i}. \tag{2.11}$$

Recall that equation (2.10) gives $m = \Sigma\, p_i q_i$ and the βs add up to unity. Substituting equation (2.11) into equation (2.9) gives the demand function

$$q_i = \gamma_i + \beta_i\, \frac{m - \Sigma_j p_j\, \gamma_j}{p_i} \qquad (i \in j). \tag{2.12}$$

This demand function has two interesting properties.

1   The consumer first sets aside his budget for the minimum necessary purchases of goods in accordance with parameters γ at their prices. This amounts to $\Sigma p_j \gamma_j$ for all j. Stone (1954a, b) refers to γ_i as the *subsistence level* of good i.
2   The consumer then allocates his remaining budget, i.e. $m - \Sigma p_j \gamma_j$, to good i in proportion to parameter β_i. For this reason, parameter β is referred to as the *marginal budget share* and $m - \Sigma p_j \gamma_j$ as the *supernumerary income*. It is the supernumerary income that the consumer distributes optimally in response to the market price of good i.

Various elasticities of the Stone–Geary demand function are as follows. The own-price elasticity is

$$\epsilon_{ii} = \frac{\partial q_i}{\partial p_i}\frac{p_i}{q_i} = -\frac{\beta_i\,[1 - (p_j\,\gamma_j/m)]}{S_i} < 0 \tag{2.13}$$

where $S_i = p_i q_i/m$ (the budget share of good i). The Stone–Geary function thus confirms the law of demand ($\epsilon_{ii} < 0$) but permits only an inelastic demand ($|\epsilon_{ii}| < 1$). The cross-price elasticity is

$$\epsilon_{ij} = \frac{\partial q_i}{\partial p_j}\frac{p_j}{q_i} = -\frac{\beta_i\,(p_j\,\gamma_j/m)}{S_i} < 0 \qquad (i \neq j). \tag{2.14}$$

This suggests that all goods are complements in the gross concept. The income elasticity of good i is

$$\epsilon_{im} = \frac{\partial q_i}{\partial m}\frac{m}{q_i} = \frac{\beta_i}{S_i} > 0. \tag{2.15}$$

Note that the Stone–Geary utility function does not impose any explicit restriction on the income elasticity, i.e. $\epsilon_{im} \neq 1$. But it rules out inferior goods, i.e. $\epsilon_{im} > 0$. The above three elasticities imply that the Stone–Geary function is fairly restrictive.

We now turn our attention to the general features of the Stone–Geary demand function: the Engel aggregation condition, the Cournot aggregation condition, the symmetry condition, and the homogeneity condition. They are restrictions on the utility function itself or income and price elasticities. Appendix E derives the formula for each condition. They are utilized here to verify the conditions.

The Engel aggregation condition associated with the demand function (2.12) is

$$\sum_i p_i \frac{\beta_i}{p_i} = 1. \tag{2.16}$$

This suggests that equation (E.3) in appendix E holds for the Stone–Geary utility function. Then the weighted average of income elasticities of goods (where the weight is the budget share) is unity, implying that an increase in income and the average percentage increase in the demand for goods are the same. In other words, as the consumer's income increases by 1 percent, his demand for goods increases by 1 percent on the average.

The Cournot aggregation condition (equation (E.5) in appendix E) holds for the following reason. Given goods i and j, we have

$$p_i \left[\frac{-\beta_i(m - p_j \gamma_j)}{p_i^2} \right] + p_j \left(\frac{-\beta_j \gamma_j}{p_j} \right) = -q_i \qquad (i \neq j). \tag{2.17}$$

Note that the first and second terms on the left are always negative and the sum of the two terms equals $-q_i$. Equation (2.17) suggests that equations (E.6) and (E.7) hold for the Stone–Geary function. The weighted average of the percentage changes in demand for two goods i and j with respect to an increase in the price of good i is negative, implying that the demand for good j decreases when the price of good i increases.

The symmetry condition (equation (E.9) in appendix E) states that Slutsky symmetry exists between two Hicks–Allen net substitution effects: one for a change in the ith good for a compensated change in the jth price and the other for a change in the jth good for a compensated change in the ith price. Utilizing the gross substitution effect and the income effect, it is possible to verify the symmetry between them, i.e.

$$\frac{\beta_i}{p_i}\frac{\beta_j}{\lambda p_j} = \frac{\beta_j}{p_j}\frac{\beta_i}{\lambda p_i}. \tag{2.18}$$

This result implies that increases in the demand for good i in response to an increase in price j are equivalent to increases in the demand for good j in response to an increase in price i.

The homogeneity condition (equation (E.11) in appendix E) is written as

$$p_i \frac{\beta_i(m - p_j\,\gamma_j)}{p_i^2} + p_j \frac{\beta_i\,\gamma_j}{p_i} + \frac{\beta_i\,m}{p_i} = 0 \qquad (i \neq j). \tag{2.19}$$

Equation (2.19) implies that equations (E.12) and (E.13) hold for the Stone–Geary function. Equi-proportional increases in prices and income leave the quantity of good i demanded invariant. Intuitively, an increase in prices overall is equivalent to a decrease in the consumer's real income, so that nothing happens in the demand function. This situation is often referred to as the *absence of money illusion*; it occurs when the demand function is homogeneous of degree zero. Note that equation (2.12) is homogeneous of degree zero.

2.3   Stone–Geary Linear Expenditure System

The Engel expenditure function is obtained by multiplying equation (2.12) by p_i. It is written as follows:

$$p_i\,q_i = p_i\gamma_i + \beta_i\left(m - \sum_j p_j\,\gamma_j\right) \qquad (i \neq j). \tag{2.20}$$

Note that the expenditure equation is a linear function of income and prices.[1] Because of this feature, equation (2.20) is often called the Stone–Geary linear expenditure system. Parameter β_i represents portions of the supernumerary income spent on good i, i.e.

$$\beta_i = \frac{\partial(p_i\,q_i)}{\partial N} = \frac{\partial(p_i\,q_i)}{\partial m} \tag{2.21}$$

where N is the supernumerary income.

Note that the marginal budget share is identical to the average budget share when $\gamma_i = 0$.

We now divide through equations (2.20) by the total expenditure, $m = \sum_i p_i q_i$, to obtain

$$\frac{p_i\, q_i}{m} = \frac{p_i\, \gamma_i}{m} + \frac{\beta_i\, (m - \Sigma_j p_j\, \gamma_j)}{m} \qquad (i \in j). \qquad (2.22)$$

Equation (2.22) is called the expenditure share function. It is important to compare equation (2.22) with equations (1.17) in chapter 1. Clearly, the Stone–Geary expenditure share function is not independent of the total expenditure. Unless $\gamma = 0$, the Stone–Geary function is not homothetic.

2.4   Dual Approach to the Expenditure Share Functions and Allen–Uzawa Partial Elasticities of Substitution

The dual approach to consumer behavior suggests that we can substitute equation (2.12) into equation (2.1) to obtain the indirect utility function corresponding to the Stone–Geary (direct) utility function. The result is as follows:

$$\ln v = -\ln U = -\sum_i \beta_i \ln \beta_i + \sum_i \beta_i \ln \left(\frac{p_i}{m - \Sigma_j p_j\, \gamma_j} \right) \qquad (i \in j).$$
$$(2.23)$$

This equation enables us to find the expenditure share functions and the Allen–Uzawa partial elasticities of substitution. To find the expenditure share functions, take the first-order partial derivatives of the indirect utility function with respect to price p_i and income m. They are

$$\frac{\partial v}{\partial p_i} = \left(\frac{\beta_i}{p_i} + \frac{\gamma_i}{m - \Sigma_j p_j\, \gamma_j} \right) v \qquad (2.24)$$

$$\frac{\partial v}{\partial m} = - \left(\frac{1}{m - \Sigma_j p_j\, \gamma_j} \right) v. \qquad (2.25)$$

In accordance with Roy's identity (equation (2.26) below), substitute equations (2.24) and (2.25) into

$$S_i = - \frac{(\partial v/\partial p_i)\, (p_i/v)}{(\partial v/\partial m)\, (m/v)} \qquad (2.26)$$

to get the expenditure share function of good i:

$$S_i = \gamma_i \frac{p_i}{m} + \beta_i \left[1 - \sum_j \gamma_j \left(\frac{p_j}{m} \right) \right]$$

where $S_i = p_i q_i/m$. Observe that equation (2.26) is the same as equation (2.22).

It is necessary to have the second-order partial derivatives of the indirect utility function with respect to prices p_i and p_j to get the Allen–Uzawa partial elasticities of substitution. The second-order partial derivatives are

$$\frac{\partial^2 v}{\partial p_i^2} = -\left[\frac{\beta_i}{p_i^2} + \frac{\gamma_i^2}{(m - \Sigma_j p_j \gamma_j)^2}\right] v + \left(\frac{\beta_i}{p_i} + \frac{\gamma_i}{m - \Sigma_j p_j \gamma_j}\right)^2 v \quad (2.27)$$

$$\frac{\partial^2 v}{\partial p_i \partial p_j} = \frac{-\gamma_i \gamma_j}{(m - \Sigma_h p_h \gamma_h)^2} v + \prod_k \left(\frac{\beta_k}{p_k} + \frac{\gamma_k}{m - \Sigma_h p_h \gamma_h}\right) v \quad (2.28)$$

$$(i, j = 1, \ldots, n; i, j \in h, k; i \neq j).$$

Substituting equations (2.24) and (2.27) into

$$\sigma_{ii} = \frac{v \left(\partial^2 v/\partial p_i^2\right)}{(\partial v/\partial p_i)^2}$$

yields the Allen–Uzawa own-partial elasticity of substitution:

$$\sigma_{ii} = 1 - \frac{p_i^2 \gamma_i^2 + \beta_i (m - \Sigma_j p_j \gamma_j)^2}{S_i^2 m^2} \quad (i \in j). \quad (2.29)$$

Finally, substitute equations (2.24) and (2.28) into

$$\sigma_{ij} = \frac{v \left(\partial^2 v/\partial p_i \partial p_j\right)}{(\partial v/\partial p_i)(\partial v/\partial p_j)}$$

to get the Allen–Uzawa cross-partial elasticity of substitution:

$$\sigma_{ij} = 1 - \frac{\Pi_h p_h \gamma_h}{S_i S_j m^2} \quad (i \neq j; i, j \in h). \quad (2.30)$$

Note that the Allen–Uzawa cross-partial elasticities of substitution are positive and thus all goods included in the Stone–Geary utility function are Hicks–Allen net substitutes.[2] If the γs are zero, the Stone–Geary utility function reduces to the linear logarithmic utility function (equation (1.1)) and the Allen–Uzawa cross-partial elasticities of substitution become unity.

2.5 Empirical Remarks

There are numerous applications of the Stone–Geary linear expenditure system. Among them are Stone (1954a, b), an application to the pattern of British demand, which is discussed in detail below; Stone and Rowe (1957), an analysis of the market demand for durable goods; Stone et al. (1964), a study analyzing and projecting the demand pattern in Britain during 1900–70; Pollak and Wales (1969), an estimation of the habit-augmented linear expenditure system, fitted to US data, 1948–65; Powell (1974), an application to Australian data, 1966–7; and Deaton and Muellbauer (1980a), a recent study done for five food items. I examine a work done by Stone.

In a 1954 study, Stone (1954b) analyzes the pattern of demand for consumer's goods using this new system of expenditure (equation (2.20)) for the United Kingdom during the period 1920–38. He assesses the results with respect to the actual state of demand in 1900 and compares the post-war structure of demand with what might have been expected from the inter-war relationships under free-market conditions.

Stone considers three different models arising from equation (2.20): a naive model, a sophisticated model, and their combination. In each case, the expenditure system conforms to certain conditions. The first condition is additivity: the sum of expenditures on individual goods must equal the total expenditure. The second condition is homogeneity: the sum of income and price elasticities equals zero. The third condition is symmetry of the substitution matrix.[3] Stone estimates the three models to analyze consumers' expenditure on six commodity groups together rather than their expenditure on individual commodities or even groups of commodities in isolation. The six commodity groups are (1) meat, fish, dairy products, and fats; (2) fruits and vegetables; (3) drink and tobacco; (4) household expenses; (5) durable goods; and (6) all other consumers' goods and services.

Stone uses the correlations between the actual and the estimated expenditures to decide how good the system is. He uses the least squares method to estimate model 1 and the two-step iterative estimation procedure to estimate models 2 and 3.[4] Stone finds that the sophisticated model is, in general, superior to the naive model. The sophisticated model provides higher correlations between the actual and estimated expenditures for commodity groups 1, 2, and 4, but a lower correlation for group 3. Both models have high correlation for commodity groups 5 and 6, without any significant difference between them. Stone decides to use the naive model for commodity groups 3, 5, and 6. The results suggest that consumers in the United Kingdom spend certain fixed *proportions* of their total expenditure on commodity groups 3, 5, and 6, while they purchase certain fixed *quantities* of commodity groups 1, 2, and 4 and then allocate the balance of their expenditure over groups 1, 2, and 4 in certain fixed proportions. The results for groups 1, 2, and 4 suggest that actual data conform to the Stone–Geary linear expenditure system.

Next, Stone tests the validity of his estimation method by projecting backward to 1900 and forward to 1952. Given values of m and p for 1900, he assumes that the value of $p_i q_i$ is the same for 1900 as for 1920–38. He compares the calculated values with the actual values. Most values yield slight differences with the exception of values for groups 3 and 5. In the case of group 5, however, Stone believes that there are some durable goods available from 1920–38 that were unavailable in 1900. Stone also believes that there are good reasons to suppose that in the case of group 3, changes in tastes and habits are important. He notes the major shifts of consumption habits in alcoholic consumption during the inter-war period from those over the time period in 1900. Stone makes similar projections for 1952: estimating quantity adjustments on the basis of 1952 values of m and p and estimating price adjustments on the basis of 1952 values of m and q. Assuming *elastic* supplies under the 1952 income and prices, consumers purchase more of groups 1 and 4, substantially less of group 3, and moderately less of group 6. The quantity adjustments on groups 2 and 5 were moderately high. Assuming supplies are perfectly *inelastic* at 1952 prices, the prices for groups 1 and 4 are considerably high to balance 1952 quantities and expenditures. The price adjustments for groups 2, 3, and 6 are exceedingly low to balance 1952 quantities and expenditures.

2.6 Summary

The Stone–Geary function and its system of consumer demand satisfy various classical properties. As a nonhomothetic function, it does not restrict the income elasticity to unity. It yields a linear expenditure system that is easy to deal with theoretically and econometrically. The system is characterized by the marginal budget-share and subsistence-level parameters. The Stone–Geary system offers a convincing argument that the consumer's optimal behavior for allocation of his budget takes place only after he secures the minimum necessary amount of each good.

However, the function still requires the additivity assumption. Given this assumption, the permissible ranges for the own-price elasticity, the cross-price elasticities, and the income elasticity are limited. The linear nature of the expenditure system is also a weakness of this utility function.

Among many applications of the Stone–Geary linear expenditure system, a study by Stone himself is discussed in the empirical section. Stone analyzes patterns of demand for goods in Great Britain according to his system of demand equations. He discusses estimated results, examines statistical implications, and projects the estimated results backwards and forwards to compare them with actual demand. Stone concludes that his system is a workable set of demand equations that conform to economic theory.

Appendix

Derivation of the Demand Function[5]

Given two goods, 1 and 2, equation (2.8) is written as

$$\mathcal{L}(q_1, q_2; \lambda) = \beta_1 \ln(q_1 - \gamma_1) + \beta_2 \ln(q_2 - \gamma_2) + \lambda(m - p_1 q_1 - p_2 q_2). \tag{1}$$

The first-order derivatives yield

$$\frac{\partial \mathcal{L}}{\partial q_1} = \frac{\beta_1}{q_1 - \gamma_1} - \lambda p_1 = 0 \tag{2}$$

$$\frac{\partial \mathcal{L}}{\partial q_1} = \frac{\beta_2}{q_2 - \gamma_2} - \lambda p_2 = 0 \tag{3}$$

$$\frac{\partial \mathcal{L}}{\partial \lambda} = m - p_1 q_1 - p_2 q_2 = 0. \tag{4}$$

Solving equations (2) and (3) with respect to β_1 and β_2 gives

$$\beta_1 = \lambda p_1 (q_1 - \gamma_1) \tag{5}$$

$$\beta_2 = \lambda p_2 (q_2 - \gamma_2). \tag{6}$$

Add equations (5) and (6) in order to obtain

$$1 = \lambda [p_1 (q_1 - \gamma_1) + p_2 (q_2 - \gamma_2)]. \tag{7}$$

Recall that $\beta_1 + \beta_2 = 1$. Equation (7) is rewritten as

$$1 = \lambda (m - p_1 \gamma_1 - p_2 \gamma_2) \tag{8}$$

yielding

$$\lambda = \frac{1}{m - p_1\gamma_1 - p_2\gamma_2}. \tag{9}$$

Substituting equation (9) into equations (5) and (6), we get

$$\beta_1 = \frac{p_1(q_1 - \gamma_1)}{m - p_1\gamma_1 - p_2\gamma_2} \tag{10}$$

$$\beta_2 = \frac{p_1(q_2 - \gamma_2)}{m - p_1\gamma_1 - p_2\gamma_2}. \tag{11}$$

It is possible to derive demand functions from equations (10) and (11). They are

$$q_1 = \gamma_1 + \beta_1 \frac{m - p_1\gamma_1 - p_2\gamma_2}{p_1} \tag{12}$$

$$q_2 = \gamma_2 + \beta_2 \frac{m - p_1\gamma_1 - p_2\gamma_2}{p_2}. \tag{13}$$

Notes

1 Pollak (1971a, p. 405) has proved that an additive utility function yields demand functions locally linear in income.
2 See appendix L.
3 For homogeneity and symmetry conditions, see appendix E.
4 Stone's two-step iterative procedure is discussed in detail in Stone (1954b).
5 See Goldberger (1967, p. 46).

Recommended Reading

Brown, A. and Deaton, A. 1972: Surveys in applied economics: models of consumer behavior. *Economic Journal*, December, 1145–234.
Deaton, A. and Muellbauer, J. 1980: *Economics and Consumer Behavior*, Cambridge: Cambridge University Press, 60–7.
Geary, R.C. 1949–50: A note on "a constant utility index of the cost of living". *Review of Economic Studies*, 18, 65–6.
Goldberger, A.S. 1967: Functional form and utility: a review of consumer demand theory. Social Systems Research Institute, University of Wisconsin, Workshop Paper SFMP 6703, October, 1–122.
Goldman, S.M. and Uzawa, H. 1964: A note on separability in demand analysis. *Econometrica*, 32, 387–98.

Gorman, W.M. 1959: Separable utility and aggregation. *Econometrica*, 27, 469–81.

Klein, L.R. and Rubin, H. 1947–8: A constant utility index of the cost of living. *Review of Economic Studies*, XV (2), 84–7.

Parks, R.W. 1969: Systems of demand equations: an empirical comparison of alternative functional forms. *Econometrica*, 37, October, 629–50.

Pollak, R.A. and Wales, T.J. 1969: Estimation of the linear expenditures system. *Econometrica*, 37, October, 611–28.

Powell, A.A. 1974: *Empirical Analytics of Demand System*, Lexington, MA: D.C. Heath, 43–57.

Samuelson, P.A. 1947–8: Some implications of "linearity". *Review of Economic Studies*, 15 (2), 88–90.

Stone, R. 1954: *The Measurement of Consumers' Expenditure and Behaviour in the United Kingdom, 1920–1938*, vol. I, Cambridge: Cambridge University Press.

—— 1954: Linear expenditure systems and demand analysis: an application to the pattern of British demand. *Economic Journal*, 64, September, 511–27.

—— and Rowe, D.A. 1957: The market demand for durable goods. *Econometrica*, 25, 423–43.

——, Brown, J.A.C. and Rowe, D.A. 1964: Demand analysis and projections for Britain 1900–70: a study in method. In J. Sandee (ed.), *Europe's Future Consumption*. Amsterdam: North-Holland.

Strotz, R.H. 1959: The utility tree – a correction and future appraisal. *Econometrica*, 27, 482–8.

3 The Houthakker Addilog Utility Function

This chapter examines the additive logarithmic (*addilog*) utility function that Hendrik S. Houthakker (1960) devised. The addilog utility function to be discussed in this chapter and the Stone–Geary utility function discussed in the previous chapter are different from the linear logarithmic utility function discussed in chapter 1, in that the addilog and Stone–Geary functions assume additivity only. The addilog function is not homothetic and thus expenditure shares must vary with income.

As we saw in earlier chapters, to assume that a utility function is additive severely restricts the roles of related goods as substitutes or complements in demand or expenditure share functions and therefore narrows substantially the scope of the theory of consumer behavior. However, Houthakker argues that there are still reasons for studying observable consequences of additivity. He suggests that additivity may be chosen as an adequate assumption because of its simplicity and analytical efficiency in examining the case for large aggregates (food, clothing, etc.), in which their interrelations follow largely from competition for the consumer's dollar, and that nonadditive systems do not mesh with empirical results.[1]

Houthakker begins his analysis by showing two different ways of representing consumer's utility – the direct utility function f and the indirect utility function g:[2]

$$f_1(q_1) + f_2(q_2) + \cdots + f_n(q_n) \tag{3.1}$$

$$g_1\left(\frac{p_1}{m}\right) + g_2\left(\frac{p_2}{m}\right) + \cdots + g_n\left(\frac{p_n}{m}\right) \tag{3.2}$$

where q_i is commodity i, p_i is the price of commodity i, and m is income.

Houthakker derives the demand functions from explicit forms of direct and indirect double logarithmic utility functions (called the direct addilog utility function and the indirect addilog utility function, respectively). For the latter, he employs Roy's identity. He compared empirically the relative demand functions derived from the two addilog functions and suggests that the direct addilog utility function is more realistic.

Section 3.1 discusses three theorems proposed by Houthakker under additivity. Section 3.2 presents the direct addilog utility function and derives the expenditure share functions by maximizing the direct utility function with given prices and income. Section 3.3 deals with the indirect addilog utility function and shows how to get the expenditure share functions by minimizing the indirect addilog utility function with given quantities. Section 3.4 derives various elasticities, including the Allen–Uzawa elasticities of substitution. Section 3.5 compares empirical performance of directly additive and indirectly additive preference systems in accordance with the criteria that Houthakker proposed. Section 3.6 summarizes the chapter.

3.1   Additivity and its Consequences

Houthakker derives the necessary and sufficient conditions for direct and indirect additivity. He proposes three theorems relating prices, income, and quantities on the basis of the conditions.

Given the utility function of three goods q_1, q_2, and q_3, and the corresponding budget constraint

$$u = f(q_1, q_2, q_3) \qquad (3.3)$$

$$m = p_1 q_1 + p_2 q_2 + p_3 q_3 \qquad (3.4)$$

the augmented objective function we wish to maximize is

$$\mathscr{L}(q; \lambda) = f(q_1, q_2, q_3) + \lambda(m - p_1 q_1 - p_2 q_2 - p_3 q_3). \qquad (3.5)$$

The number of goods is restricted to three to illustrate the system.

The first-order conditions for maximizing the constrained utility are

$$f_1 - \lambda p_1 = 0 \qquad (3.6)$$

$$f_2 - \lambda p_2 = 0 \qquad (3.7)$$

$$f_3 - \lambda p_3 = 0 \tag{3.8}$$

$$m - p_1 q_1 - p_2 q_2 - p_3 q_3 = 0 \tag{3.9}$$

where $f_i = \partial u/\partial q_i$ $(i = 1, 2, 3)$.

Equations (3.6)–(3.9) yield the complete set of demand functions:

$$q_1 = q_1(m, p_1, p_2, p_3) \tag{3.10}$$

$$q_2 = q_2(m, p_1, p_2, p_3) \tag{3.11}$$

$$q_3 = q_3(m, p_1, p_2, p_3) \tag{3.12}$$

$$\lambda = \lambda(m, p_1, p_2, p_3). \tag{3.13}$$

Total differentials of the first-order conditions (equations (3.6)–(3.9)) and demand functions (equations (3.10)–(3.13)) yield, respectively,

$$f_{11}dq_1 + f_{12}dq_2 + f_{13}dq_3 - p_1 d\lambda = \lambda dp_1 \tag{3.14}$$

$$f_{21}dq_1 + f_{22}dq_2 + f_{23}dq_3 - p_2 d\lambda = \lambda dp_2 \tag{3.15}$$

$$f_{31}dq_1 + f_{32}dq_2 + f_{33}dq_3 - p_3 d\lambda = \lambda dp_3 \tag{3.16}$$

$$p_1 dq_1 + p_2 dq_2 + p_3 dq_3 = dm - q_1 dp_1 - q_2 dp_2 - q_3 dp_3 \tag{3.17}$$

where $f_{ij} = \partial^2 u/\partial q_i \partial q_j$ $(i, j = 1, 2, 3)$ and

$$dq_1 = \frac{\partial q_1}{\partial m} dm + \frac{\partial q_1}{\partial p_1} dp_1 + \frac{\partial q_1}{\partial p_2} dp_2 + \frac{\partial q_1}{\partial p_3} dp_3 \tag{3.18}$$

$$dq_2 = \frac{\partial q_2}{\partial m} dm + \frac{\partial q_2}{\partial p_1} dp_1 + \frac{\partial q_2}{\partial p_2} dp_2 + \frac{\partial q_2}{\partial p_3} dp_3 \tag{3.19}$$

$$dq_3 = \frac{\partial q_3}{\partial m} dm + \frac{\partial q_3}{\partial p_1} dp_1 + \frac{\partial q_3}{\partial p_2} dp_2 + \frac{\partial q_3}{\partial p_3} dp_3 \tag{3.20}$$

$$d\lambda = -\frac{\partial \lambda}{\partial m} dm - \frac{\partial \lambda}{\partial p_1} dp_1 - \frac{\partial \lambda}{\partial p_2} dp_2 - \frac{\partial \lambda}{\partial p_3} dp_3. \tag{3.21}$$

It is convenient to write the two different sets of equations above in matrix notation, respectively, as follows:

$$\begin{bmatrix} f_{11} & f_{12} & f_{13} & p_1 \\ f_{21} & f_{22} & f_{23} & p_2 \\ f_{31} & f_{32} & f_{33} & p_3 \\ p_1 & p_2 & p_3 & 0 \end{bmatrix} \begin{bmatrix} dq_1 \\ dq_2 \\ dq_3 \\ -d\lambda \end{bmatrix} = \begin{bmatrix} 0 & \lambda & 0 & 0 \\ 0 & 0 & \lambda & 0 \\ 0 & 0 & 0 & \lambda \\ 1 & -q_1 & -q_2 & -q_3 \end{bmatrix} \begin{bmatrix} dm \\ dp_1 \\ dp_2 \\ dp_3 \end{bmatrix} \tag{3.22}$$

and

$$
\begin{bmatrix} dq_1 \\ dq_2 \\ dq_3 \\ -d\lambda \end{bmatrix}
=
\begin{bmatrix}
\dfrac{\partial q_1}{\partial m} & \dfrac{\partial q_1}{\partial p_1} & \dfrac{\partial q_1}{\partial p_2} & \dfrac{\partial q_1}{\partial p_3} \\[2ex]
\dfrac{\partial q_2}{\partial m} & \dfrac{\partial q_2}{\partial p_1} & \dfrac{\partial q_2}{\partial p_2} & \dfrac{\partial q_2}{\partial p_3} \\[2ex]
\dfrac{\partial q_3}{\partial m} & \dfrac{\partial q_3}{\partial p_1} & \dfrac{\partial q_3}{\partial p_2} & \dfrac{\partial q_3}{\partial p_3} \\[2ex]
-\dfrac{\partial \lambda}{\partial m} & -\dfrac{\partial \lambda}{\partial p_1} & -\dfrac{\partial \lambda}{\partial p_2} & -\dfrac{\partial \lambda}{\partial p_3}
\end{bmatrix}
\begin{bmatrix} dm \\ dp_1 \\ dp_2 \\ dp_3 \end{bmatrix}
\tag{3.23}
$$

Substituting equation (3.23) into equation (3.22) gives

$$
\begin{bmatrix}
f_{11} & f_{12} & f_{13} & p_1 \\
f_{21} & f_{22} & f_{23} & p_2 \\
f_{31} & f_{32} & f_{33} & p_3 \\
p_1 & p_2 & p_3 & 0
\end{bmatrix}
\begin{bmatrix}
\dfrac{\partial q_1}{\partial m} & \dfrac{\partial q_1}{\partial p_1} & \dfrac{\partial q_1}{\partial p_2} & \dfrac{\partial q_1}{\partial p_3} \\[2ex]
\dfrac{\partial q_2}{\partial m} & \dfrac{\partial q_2}{\partial p_1} & \dfrac{\partial q_2}{\partial p_2} & \dfrac{\partial q_2}{\partial p_3} \\[2ex]
\dfrac{\partial q_3}{\partial m} & \dfrac{\partial q_3}{\partial p_1} & \dfrac{\partial q_3}{\partial p_2} & \dfrac{\partial q_3}{\partial p_3} \\[2ex]
-\dfrac{\partial \lambda}{\partial m} & -\dfrac{\partial \lambda}{\partial p_1} & -\dfrac{\partial \lambda}{\partial p_2} & -\dfrac{\partial \lambda}{\partial p_3}
\end{bmatrix}
$$

$$
=
\begin{bmatrix}
0 & \lambda & 0 & 0 \\
0 & 0 & \lambda & 0 \\
0 & 0 & 0 & \lambda \\
1 & -q_1 & -q_2 & -q_3
\end{bmatrix}.
\tag{3.24}
$$

Now, suppose that the utility function is additive such that $f_{12} = f_{13} = f_{21} = f_{23} = f_{31} = f_{32} = 0$. In other words, the marginal utility of each good is independent of the quantities of all the other goods. The Hessian matrix of the additive utility function is then diagonal. Equation (3.24) can be rewritten as

$$
\left[
\begin{array}{c|ccc}
\dfrac{\partial q_1}{\partial m} & \dfrac{\partial q_1}{\partial p_1} & \dfrac{\partial q_1}{\partial p_2} & \dfrac{\partial q_1}{\partial p_3} \\[2ex]
\dfrac{\partial q_2}{\partial m} & \dfrac{\partial q_2}{\partial p_1} & \dfrac{\partial q_2}{\partial p_2} & \dfrac{\partial q_2}{\partial p_3} \\[2ex]
\dfrac{\partial q_3}{\partial m} & \dfrac{\partial q_3}{\partial p_1} & \dfrac{\partial q_3}{\partial p_2} & \dfrac{\partial q_3}{\partial p_3} \\[2ex]
\hline
-\dfrac{\partial \lambda}{\partial m} & -\dfrac{\partial \lambda}{\partial p_1} & -\dfrac{\partial \lambda}{\partial p_2} & -\dfrac{\partial \lambda}{\partial p_3}
\end{array}
\right]
$$

$$
= \begin{bmatrix} f_{11} & 0 & 0 & p_1 \\ 0 & f_{22} & 0 & p_2 \\ 0 & 0 & f_{33} & p_3 \\ p_1 & p_2 & p_3 & 0 \end{bmatrix}^{-1} \begin{bmatrix} 0 & \lambda & 0 & 0 \\ 0 & 0 & \lambda & 0 \\ 0 & 0 & 0 & \lambda \\ 1 & -q_1 & -q_2 & -q_3 \end{bmatrix}
$$

$$
= \frac{1}{\Delta} \begin{bmatrix} -a_{41} & \lambda a_{11} + a_{41}q_1 & -\lambda a_{21} + a_{41}q_2 & \lambda a_{31} + a_{41}q_3 \\ a_{42} & -\lambda a_{12} - a_{42}q_1 & \lambda a_{22} - a_{42}q_2 & -\lambda a_{32} - a_{42}q_3 \\ -a_{43} & \lambda a_{13} + a_{43}q_1 & -\lambda a_{23} + a_{43}q_2 & \lambda a_{33} + a_{43}q_3 \\ \hline a_{44} & -\lambda a_{14} - a_{44}q_1 & \lambda a_{24} - a_{44}q_2 & -\lambda a_{34} - a_{44}q_3 \end{bmatrix} \quad (3.25)
$$

where Δ is the determinant of the Hessian matrix of the utility function ($\neq 0$).

$(-1)^{i+j}a_{ij}$ is the element of the ith row and jth column in the cofactor matrix of the Hessian. Beginning with the fourth row and fourth column in the above matrix, it is immediately clear that the element is

$$
\frac{\partial \lambda}{\partial p_3} = -\left(\lambda \frac{\partial q_3}{\partial m} + \frac{\partial \lambda}{\partial m} q_3 \right)
$$

$$
= -\frac{\partial \lambda}{\partial m}\left(\phi \frac{\partial q_3}{\partial m} + q_3 \right) \quad (3.26)
$$

where $\phi = \lambda/(\partial \lambda/\partial m)$. Houthakker calls the parameter ϕ *income flexi-bility*.[3]

Meanwhile, we know that

$$
\frac{\partial q_1}{\partial p_3} = \frac{p_1}{f_{11}} \frac{d\lambda}{dp_3} \quad (3.27)
$$

$$
\frac{\partial q_2}{\partial p_3} = \frac{p_2}{f_{22}} \frac{d\lambda}{dp_3} \quad (3.28)
$$

under the assumption of additivity and $dp_1/dp_3 = dp_2/dp_3 = 0$. We also know that

$$
\frac{\partial q_1}{\partial m} = \frac{p_1}{f_{11}} \frac{d\lambda}{dm} \quad (3.29)
$$

$$
\frac{\partial q_2}{\partial m} = \frac{p_2}{f_{22}} \frac{d\lambda}{dm} \quad (3.30)
$$

under the assumptions of additivity and $dp_1/dm = dp_2/dm = 0$. Combining equations (3.26), (3.27), and (3.29) and equations (3.26), (3.28), and (3.30) yields

$$\frac{\partial q_1}{\partial p_3} = -\frac{\partial q_1}{\partial m}\left(\phi\frac{\partial q_3}{\partial m} + q_3\right) \tag{3.31}$$

$$\frac{\partial q_2}{\partial p_3} = -\frac{\partial q_2}{\partial m}\left(\phi\frac{\partial q_3}{\partial m} + q_3\right). \tag{3.32}$$

It follows then that

$$\frac{\partial q_1/\partial p_3}{\partial q_2/\partial p_3} = \frac{\partial q_1/\partial m}{\partial q_2/\partial m}. \tag{3.33}$$

Equation (3.33) suggests that the cross-price derivatives $\partial q_1/\partial p_3$ and $\partial q_2/\partial p_3$ on the left-hand side of the Slutsky equation are proportional to the income derivatives $\partial q_1/\partial m$ and $\partial q_2/\partial m$.

Substituting equation (3.31) into the Slutsky equation (see equation (F.24) in appendix F)[4]

$$\left.\frac{\partial q_1}{\partial p_3}\right|_{u = \text{constant}} = \frac{\partial q_1}{\partial p_3} + q_3\frac{\partial q_1}{\partial m}$$

yields

$$\left.\frac{\partial q_1}{\partial p_3}\right|_{u = \text{constant}} = -\frac{\partial q_1}{\partial m}\left(\phi\frac{\partial q_3}{\partial m} + q_3\right) + q_3\frac{\partial q_1}{\partial m}$$

$$= -\phi\frac{\partial q_1}{\partial m}\frac{\partial q_3}{\partial m}. \tag{3.34}$$

Similarly, we can have

$$\left.\frac{\partial q_2}{\partial p_3}\right|_{u = \text{constant}} = -\phi\frac{\partial q_2}{\partial m}\frac{\partial q_3}{\partial m}. \tag{3.35}$$

Note that, under the assumption of additivity, the substitution effects (the terms on the left-hand side of equations (3.34) and (3.35)) are proportional to the income derivatives, where the proportionality factor is the income flexibility (ϕ on the right-hand side). Houthakker suggests that the direct utility function is additive if and only if equations (3.34) and (3.35) hold. The results are Houthakker's theorem 1, the necessary and sufficient condition for the direct utility function to be additive.

Suppose that the indirect utility function corresponding to the direct utility function (equation (3.3)) is

$$v = g\left(\frac{p_1}{m}, \frac{p_2}{m}, \frac{p_3}{m}\right). \tag{3.36}$$

Roy's identity applied to equation (3.36) yields

$$q_1 \equiv -\frac{\partial v/\partial p_1}{\partial v/\partial m}. \tag{3.37}$$

Taking the partial derivative of equation (3.37) with respect to p_3 yields

$$\frac{\partial q_1}{\partial p_3} = \frac{-(\partial v/\partial m)(\partial^2 v/\partial p_1 \partial p_3) + (\partial v/\partial p_1)(\partial^2 v/\partial m \partial p_3)}{(\partial v/\partial m)^2}. \tag{3.38}$$

Under the additivity assumption we impose on the indirect utility function, i.e. $\partial^2 v/\partial p_1 \partial p_3 = 0$, equation (3.38) reduces to

$$\frac{\partial q_1}{\partial p_3} = \frac{-q_1(\partial^2 v/\partial p_3 \partial m)}{\partial v/\partial m}. \tag{3.39}$$

Similarly, we can have

$$\frac{\partial q_2}{\partial p_3} = \frac{-q_2(\partial^2 v/\partial p_3 \partial m)}{\partial v/\partial m}. \tag{3.40}$$

Hence we have

$$\frac{\partial q_1/\partial p_3}{\partial q_2/\partial p_3} = \frac{q_1}{q_2}. \tag{3.41}$$

Equation (3.41) suggests that the cross-price derivatives are proportional to the quantities involved with equations (3.39) and (3.40). It is contrasted with equation (3.33). We can rewrite equation (3.41) as

$$\frac{(\partial q_1/\partial p_3)(p_3/q_1)}{(\partial q_2/\partial p_3)(p_3/q_2)} = \frac{q_1 \, p_3/q_1}{q_2 \, p_3/q_2} = 1. \tag{3.42}$$

Equation (3.42) suggests that the indirect utility function is additive if and only if the cross-price elasticities are the same for all related commodities. It is Houthakker's theorem 2.

Combining equations (3.33) and (3.41), we have

$$\frac{\partial q_1/\partial m}{\partial q_2/\partial m} = \frac{q_1}{q_2} \tag{3.43}$$

which we can rewrite as

$$\frac{(\partial q_1/\partial m)\,(m/q_1)}{(\partial q_2/\partial m)\,(m/q_2)} = 1. \tag{3.44}$$

Equation (3.44) indicates that income elasticities for all goods are the same and hence their ratio is unity. It implies that the Engel curve of an additive utility function, direct or indirect, can be a straight line passing through the origin. This result is Houthakker's theorem 3.

3.2   The Direct Addilog Utility Function and the Expenditure Share Functions

Houthakker calls the utility function expressed in terms of commodities the direct utility function. His direct addilog utility function is

$$u = \sum_{i=1}^{n} a_i\, q_i^{b_i}. \tag{3.45}$$

where $0 < a_i < 1$ ($\Sigma_i\, a_i = 1$) and $0 < b_i < 1$.[5] Since the function is a sum of double-logarithmic functions, it is described as *additive logarithmic* or *addilog* for short. Though preliminary, he uses it for an empirical verification of the theorems.

The first-order derivative is

$$\frac{\partial u}{\partial q_i} = a_i\, b_i\, q_i^{b_i-1} > 0. \tag{3.46}$$

The marginal rate of substitution is then

$$\frac{\partial u/\partial q_i}{\partial u/\partial q_j} = \frac{a_i\, b_i\, q_i^{b_i-1}}{a_j\, b_j\, q_j^{b_j-1}} \qquad (i \neq j). \tag{3.47}$$

Equation (3.46) implies that the marginal utility is positive. Therefore, the direct addilog utility function is monotonic. The second-order derivatives are

$$\frac{\partial^2 u}{\partial q_i^2} = a_i\, b_i\, (b_i - 1)\, q_i^{b_i-2} < 0 \tag{3.48}$$

$$\frac{\partial^2 u}{\partial q_i \partial q_j} = 0 \qquad (i \neq j). \tag{3.49}$$

Equation (3.48) implies that the law of diminishing marginal utility holds. The bordered Hessian, $(-1)^n\,|\overline{H}_n|$, formed from equations (3.46),

(3.48), and (3.49), is positive. This result suggests that Houthakker's direct addilog function is strictly quasi-concave. Its monotonicity and convexity suggest that the direct addilog utility function meets the regularity conditions.

The direct addilog utility function is *strongly additive* because the cross-partial derivative (equation (3.49)) is zero in the case of two goods.[6] The direct addilog utility function is not homothetic because scalar multiplication does not amplify the utility level by the scalar θ or a scalar proportion, i.e.

$$\theta^r u \neq \sum_i a_i (\theta q_i)^{b_i}. \tag{3.50}$$

where r is any constant. Note, however, that the utility function is homogeneous in each commodity and that the degree of homogeneity is different from commodity to commodity. If the parameter values b are the same, the addilog utility function becomes an additive and homothetic function, as was the function we examined in chapter 1.

We now derive the demand function from the direct utility function. As usual, the augmented objective function is

$$\mathcal{L}(q; \lambda) = \sum_i a_i q_i^{b_i} + \lambda \left(m - \sum_i p_i q_i \right). \tag{3.51}$$

The consumer maximizes the function, given prices and income. The first-order conditions for a maximum are

$$\frac{\partial \mathcal{L}}{\partial q_i} = a_i b_i q_i^{b_i - 1} - \lambda p_i = 0 \tag{3.52}$$

$$\frac{\partial \mathcal{L}}{\partial \lambda} = m - \sum_i p_i q_i = 0. \tag{3.53}$$

From equations (3.52) and (3.53), we get

$$\frac{p_i q_i}{m} = \frac{a_i b_i q_i^{b_i}}{\sum_j a_j b_j q_j^{b_j}} \qquad (i \in j). \tag{3.54}$$

As Houthakker suggests, the direct addilog preference ordering is less tractable. Therefore I do not attempt to discuss various elasticities associated with the direct utility function in this section. However, the duality between the direct utility function and the indirect utility function permits us to examine them. We will investigate them in section 3.4.

3.3   Indirect Addilog Utility Function and the Expenditure Share Functions

The indirect addilog utility function corresponding to the direct addilog utility function (equation (3.45)) is

$$v(\boldsymbol{p}, m) = \sum_{i=1}^{n} a_i \left(\frac{m}{p_i}\right)^{\beta_i}. \tag{3.55}$$

The parameter restrictions imposed on equation (3.45) are applicable. See appendix G for its rationale and properties. To generate the expenditure share function, we first differentiate the indirect addilog utility function with respect to p_i and m. Note that we minimize the indirect utility function with given quantities. Differentiating it, we get

$$\frac{\partial v}{\partial p_i} = -a_i \beta_i m^{\beta_i} p_i^{-(1+\beta_i)} \tag{3.56}$$

$$\frac{\partial v}{\partial m} = \sum_i a_i \beta_i m^{\beta_i - 1} p_i^{-\beta_i}. \tag{3.57}$$

Following Houthakker, we substitute equations (3.56) and (3.57) into Roy's identity (see appendix H for its rationale) to get the demand function:

$$q_i = -\frac{\partial v/\partial p_i}{\partial v/\partial m} = \frac{a_i \beta_i (m/p_i)^{1+\beta_i}}{\sum_j a_j \beta_j (m/p_j)^{\beta_j}} \qquad (i \in j; i, j = 1, ..., n). \tag{3.58}$$

Equation (3.58) yields the expenditure share function:

$$S_i = \frac{p_i q_i}{m} = \frac{a_i \beta_i (m/p_i)^{\beta_i}}{\sum_j a_j \beta_j (m/p_j)^{\beta_j}}. \tag{3.59}$$

It is interesting to note that, if $\beta_i = \beta_j$ for all i and j, equation (3.59) is equivalent to equation (5.9), the expenditure share function for the CES utility function in chapter 5. The Engel expenditure function is then

$$p_i q_i = \frac{a_i \beta_i (m/p_i)^{\beta_i} m}{\sum_j a_j \beta_j (m/p_j)^{\beta_j}}. \tag{3.60}$$

Observe that the budget share is not independent of income. Readers should keep in mind that this flexibility stems from dropping the assumption of homotheticity that was imposed on the utility function discussed in chapter 1.

3.4 Elasticities

To get price elasticities and income elasticities of demand for q_i, differentiate equation (3.58) with respect to p_i, p_j, and m. The derivatives are

$$\frac{\partial q_i}{\partial p_i} = [-(1 + \beta_i) + \beta_i S_i] \frac{q_i}{p_i} \tag{3.61}$$

$$\frac{\partial q_i}{\partial p_j} = \beta_j S_j \frac{q_i}{p_j} \qquad (i \neq j) \tag{3.62}$$

$$\frac{\partial q_i}{\partial m} = \left[\beta_i + \sum_j (1 - \beta_j) q_j \frac{p_j}{m} \right] \frac{q_i}{m} \qquad (i \in j). \tag{3.63}$$

The own-price elasticity, the cross-price elasticity, and the income elasticity are[7]

$$\epsilon_{ii} = \frac{\partial q_i}{\partial p_i} \frac{p_i}{q_i} = -[1 + \beta_i (1 - S_i)] < 0 \tag{3.64}$$

$$\epsilon_{ij} = \frac{\partial q_i}{\partial p_j} \frac{p_j}{q_i} = \beta_j S_j > 0 \qquad (i \neq j) \tag{3.65}$$

$$\epsilon_{im} = (1 + \beta_i) - \sum_j \beta_j S_j > 0 \qquad (i \in j). \tag{3.66}$$

The law of demand prevails (equation (3.64)), goods are substitutes in the gross concept (equation (3.65)), and they are normal goods (equation (3.66)). Equation (3.66) implies that the difference between two income elasticities of goods i and j is constant $(\beta_i - \beta_j)$. By theorem 3 (equation (3.44)), the difference is expected to be zero, so that $\beta_i = \beta_j$.

To get Allen–Uzawa elasticities of substitution, differentiate equation (3.55) with respect to p_i and p_j. The results are

$$\frac{\partial v}{\partial p_i} = -a_i \beta_i m^{\beta_i} p_i^{-(1 + \beta_i)} \tag{3.67}$$

$$\frac{\partial^2 v}{\partial p_i^2} = a_i \beta_i (1 + \beta_i) p_i^{-2} \left(\frac{m}{p_i} \right)^{\beta_i} \tag{3.68}$$

$$\frac{\partial^2 \nu}{\partial p_i^2 \, p_j} = 0. \tag{3.69}$$

Substituting equations (3.56) and (3.68) into the definition for the Allen–Uzawa own elasticity of substitution and equations (3.56) and (3.69) into the definition for the Allen–Uzawa cross-partial elasticity of substitution gives

$$\sigma_{ii} = \frac{\nu(\partial^2 \nu/\partial p_i^2)}{(\partial \nu/\partial p_i)\,(\partial \nu/\partial p_i)} = (1 + \beta_i)\left[1 + \frac{a_j\,(m/p_j)^{\beta_j}}{a_i\,\beta_i\,(m/p_i)^{\beta_i}}\right] \quad (i \neq j) \tag{3.70}$$

$$\sigma_{ij} = \frac{\nu\,(\partial^2 \nu/\partial p_i \partial p_j)}{(\partial \nu/\partial p_i)\,(\partial \nu/\partial p_j)} = 0 \quad (i \neq j). \tag{3.71}$$

Note that the cross Allen–Uzawa elasticity of substitution is zero, implying that goods i and j are independent in the net concept.

3.5   Empirical Remarks

To study the consequences of additivity in connection with consumer expenditure, Houthakker (1960) takes the ratios of equations (3.54) and (3.59), respectively, for any two goods, converts them into double-logarithmic form, and employs the resulting equations for cross-sectional as well as time-series data for British household budget expenditure. No other reference is available.

For the cross-sectional analysis, he compares the direct addilog, indirect addilog, and the ordinary double-log utility functions. The method he follows is the analysis of variance. A lower value of the residual sum of squares suggests a higher degree of conformity between actual data and fitted values. He analyzes aggregates of food, housing, clothing, and other goods. The ordinary double-log function gives the best results for housing and clothing, while the direct addilog function is best for food and other goods. The indirect addilog function, however, produces the largest residuals in all cases.

For the time-series analysis, Houthakker's categories are food, rent, clothing, durables, and all other goods. He looks at these five series for Sweden and Canada over a long period, and one series for thirteen countries of the OECD over a short period. Houthakker compares coefficients for different pairs of commodities. He finds that the coefficients are fairly similar throughout for both the direct and indirect addilog functions. Considering results for both the cross-section and time-series data, he asserts that the direct addilog function is more realistic than the indirect addilog function.

Houthakker implicitly suggests that the cross-price derivatives are proportional to the income derivatives under the direct addilog function; that the cross-price derivatives are proportional to the quantities affected under the indirect addilog, implying that cross-price elasticities are the same for all affected commodities; and that the Engel curve is a straight line through the origin for direct and indirect addilog preferences, i.e. that the ratios between income elasticities are constant under the direct addilog function whereas the differences are constant under the indirect addilog function.

3.6   Summary

Houthakker's addilog utility function retains only the assumption of additivity. Houthakker discusses the duality between direct and indirect utility functions and various features of additivity. He proves theorems for the direct and indirect utility functions to be additive and for the Engel curve to be linear. Using Roy's identity, he derives the expenditure share function. As an additive (but not homothetic) utility function, the addilog function yields the expenditure share function that is dependent upon the consumers income. The Allen–Uzawa cross-partial elasticities of substitution are zero. This result is a severe restriction.

Houthakker makes empirical comparisons of directly additive and indirectly additive preference systems and suggests that the directly additive preference system is more realistic.

Notes

1   Stone and Croft-Murray (1959) report that the substitution effect is small in their study which deals with broad aggregates of goods. Allen and Bowley (1935), Stone (1954b), and Stone and Croft-Murray (1959) suggest that nonadditive systems are not always satisfactory from an empirical standpoint.

2   The indirect addilog system was developed originally by Leser (1941).

3   Frisch (1932, 1959) calls it money flexibility or flexibility of the marginal utility of money.

4   For the Slutsky equation of two goods, see appendix F.

5   Houthakker did not impose any restrictions on the parameters.
6   See note 7.
7   For any two goods ($i = h, k$), the ratio of two cross-price elasticities with respect to the price of good j equals 1 (equation (3.42)). Thus the indirect utility function (equation (3.55)) is additive.

Recommended Reading

Frisch, R. 1932: *New Methods of Measuring Marginal Utility*. Tübingen: Mohr.
—— 1959: A complete scheme for computing all direct and cross demand elasticities in a model with many sectors. *Econometrica*, 27, 177–96.
Houthakker, H.S. 1960: Additive preferences. *Econometrica*, 28, April, 244–57.
Leser, C.E.V. 1941: Family budget data and price elasticities of demand. *Review of Economic Studies*, IX, 40–59.
Stone, R. 1954: Linear expenditure systems and demand analysis: an application to the pattern of British demand. *Economic Journal*, 64, September, 511–27.
—— and Croft-Murray, G. 1959: *Social Accounting and Economic Models*. London: Bowes and Bowes.

4 The Rotterdam System of Demand Functions

The additivity assumption of the linear logarithmic utility function, the Stone–Geary utility function and the Houthakker's addilog utility function is a severe restriction for an adequate specification of the behavior of consumers' demand.

The Rotterdam system of consumer demand functions, developed by Barten (1964) and Theil (1965a, b, 1967), is a double-logarithmic system of infinitesimal changes.[1] It does not use or propose any explicit form of utility function but rests on *almost* additive preferences. It allows specific interactions between different types of consumers' expenditures. The system collapses to the demand function of the linear logarithmic utility function if the utility function is additive. Therefore, the linear additive logarithmic system is a special case of the Rotterdam system.

Section 4.1 begins with the utility function stated in a general form. This is the form used throughout the chapter. We shall assume that the law of diminishing marginal utility prevails and that the Hessian determinant is negative definite. Section 4.2 analyzes the *fundamental matrix equation of the theory of consumer demand*. It shows that the substitution effect in the Cournot price slope equation (the net effect in the Slutsky equation) is composed of the *specific substitution effect* and the *general substitution effect*. Section 4.3 derives demand equations in infinitesimal changes. Section 4.4 deals with empirical results obtained by Barten and Parks, respectively. Section 4.5 summarizes the chapter.

4.1   General Features of the Utility Function

The utility function of two goods is given by

$$u = f(q_1, q_2) \tag{4.1}$$

where u is utility, q_1 is commodity 1, and q_2 is commodity 2. The number of goods is restricted to two to illustrate the system. Assume that the function is repeatedly differentiable. Classical demand theory claims that the marginal utilities are positive, i.e. $\partial u/\partial q_1 > 0$ and $\partial u/\partial q_2 > 0$, and that the law of diminishing marginal utility prevails, i.e. $\partial^2 u/\partial q_1^2 < 0$ and $\partial^2 u/\partial q_2^2 < 0$. The Hessian matrix is

$$U = \begin{bmatrix} f_{11} & f_{12} \\ f_{21} & f_{22} \end{bmatrix} \tag{4.2}$$

where $f_{11} = \partial^2 u/\partial q_1^2$, $f_{22} = \partial^2 u/\partial q_2^2$, and $f_{12} = \partial^2 u/\partial q_1 \partial q_2$. Its inverse matrix is

$$U^{-1} = \begin{bmatrix} f_{11} & f_{12} \\ f_{21} & f_{22} \end{bmatrix}^{-1} = \frac{1}{D} \begin{bmatrix} f_{22} & -f_{12} \\ -f_{21} & f_{11} \end{bmatrix} = \begin{bmatrix} u^{11} & u^{12} \\ u^{21} & u^{22} \end{bmatrix} \tag{4.3}$$

where D is the determinant of matrix U: $f_{11}f_{22} - f_{12}f_{21} \neq 0$, and $u^{12} = u^{21}$. We assume that matrix U (equation (4.2)) is symmetric ($f_{12} = f_{21}$) and negative definite everywhere. Note that the diagonal elements are negative. However, we do not assume additivity for the time being, i.e. $f_{12} \neq f_{21} \neq 0$.

4.2   The "Fundamental Matrix Equation of the Theory of Consumer Demand" under "Almost" Additive Preferences

For readers' convenience, we now reproduce equation (3.25) from the previous chapter. Given two goods 1 and 2, if utility is not additive, then

$$\begin{bmatrix} \dfrac{\partial q_1}{\partial m} & \dfrac{\partial q_1}{\partial p_1} & \dfrac{\partial q_1}{\partial p_2} \\[2ex] \dfrac{\partial q_2}{\partial m} & \dfrac{\partial q_2}{\partial p_1} & \dfrac{\partial q_2}{\partial p_2} \\[2ex] -\dfrac{\partial \lambda}{\partial m} & -\dfrac{\partial \lambda}{\partial p_1} & -\dfrac{\partial \lambda}{\partial p_2} \end{bmatrix} = \begin{bmatrix} f_{11} & f_{12} & p_1 \\ f_{21} & f_{22} & p_2 \\ p_1 & p_2 & 0 \end{bmatrix}^{-1} \begin{bmatrix} 0 & \lambda & 0 \\ 0 & 0 & \lambda \\ 1 & -q_1 & -q_2 \end{bmatrix} \tag{4.4}$$

or in vector notation

$$\begin{bmatrix} q_m & Q_p \\ -\lambda_m & -\lambda_p' \end{bmatrix} = \begin{bmatrix} U & p \\ p' & 0 \end{bmatrix}^{-1} \begin{bmatrix} 0 & \lambda_I \\ 1 & -q' \end{bmatrix} \tag{4.5}$$

where q_m is a 2×1 column vector for the *income slopes of demand*, Q_p is a 2×2 matrix for *Cournot price slopes of demand*, λ_m is the *income slope of the marginal utility of money* (λ), λ_p' is a 1×2 row vector for the *price slopes of the marginal utility of money*, U is a 2×2 Hessian matrix, p is a 2×1 column vector of prices 1 and 2, p' is a 1×2 row vector of prices 1 and 2, 0 is a 2×1 null vector, λ_I is a 2×2 diagonal matrix of λ, and q' is a 1×2 row vector of goods 1 and 2.[2]

Equation (4.4) can be written as

$$\begin{bmatrix} \dfrac{\partial q_1}{\partial m} & \dfrac{\partial q_1}{\partial p_1} & \dfrac{\partial q_1}{\partial p_2} \\[2ex] \dfrac{\partial q_2}{\partial m} & \dfrac{\partial q_2}{\partial p_1} & \dfrac{\partial q_2}{\partial p_2} \\[2ex] -\dfrac{\partial \lambda}{\partial m} & -\dfrac{\partial \lambda}{\partial p_1} & -\dfrac{\partial \lambda}{\partial p_2} \end{bmatrix} = \frac{1}{\Delta} \begin{bmatrix} a_{31} & \lambda a_{11} - a_{31}q_1 & -\lambda a_{21} - a_{31}q_2 \\[1ex] -a_{32} & -\lambda a_{12} + a_{32}q_1 & \lambda a_{22} + a_{32}q_2 \\[1ex] a_{33} & \lambda a_{13} - a_{33}q_1 & -\lambda a_{23} - a_{33}q_2 \end{bmatrix}$$

$$\tag{4.6}$$

where Δ is the determinant of the bordered Hessian matrix of the utility function, and a_{ij} is the element of the ith row and jth column in the cofactor matrix of the bordered Hessian, i.e.

$$a_{11} = -p_2^2 = \frac{\Delta}{\lambda} \left[\lambda u^{11} - \frac{\lambda}{\partial \lambda / \partial m} \left(\frac{\partial q_1}{\partial m} \right)^2 \right]$$

$$a_{12} = a_{21} = -p_1 p_2 = -\frac{\Delta}{\lambda} \left(\lambda u^{21} - \frac{\lambda}{\partial \lambda / \partial m} \frac{\partial q_2}{\partial m} \frac{\partial q_1}{\partial m} \right)$$

$$a_{22} = -p_1^2 = \frac{\Delta}{\lambda} \left[\lambda u^{22} - \frac{\lambda}{\partial \lambda / \partial m} \left(\frac{\partial q_2}{\partial m} \right)^2 \right]$$

$$a_{13} = a_{31} = p_2 f_{12} - p_1 f_{22} = \frac{\partial q_1}{\partial m} \Delta$$

$$a_{23} = a_{32} = p_2 f_{11} - p_1 f_{21} = \frac{\partial q_2}{\partial m} \Delta$$

$$a_{33} = f_{11}f_{22} - f_{12}f_{22} = -\frac{\partial \lambda}{\partial m}\Delta.$$

The Cournot price slopes are particularly noteworthy. They are elements of the block matrix Q_p in equation (4.6):

$$\frac{\partial q_1}{\partial p_1} = \left(\lambda u^{11} - \rho \frac{\partial q_1}{\partial m}\frac{\partial q_1}{\partial m}\right) - q_1 \frac{\partial q_1}{\partial m} \tag{4.7}$$

$$\frac{\partial q_1}{\partial p_2} = \left(\lambda u^{12} - \rho \frac{\partial q_1}{\partial m}\frac{\partial q_2}{\partial m}\right) - q_2 \frac{\partial q_1}{\partial m} \tag{4.8}$$

$$\frac{\partial q_2}{\partial p_1} = \left(\lambda u^{21} - \rho \frac{\partial q_2}{\partial m}\frac{\partial q_1}{\partial m}\right) - q_1 \frac{\partial q_2}{\partial m} \tag{4.9}$$

$$\frac{\partial q_2}{\partial p_2} = \left(\lambda u^{22} - \rho \frac{\partial q_2}{\partial m}\frac{\partial q_2}{\partial m}\right) - q_2 \frac{\partial q_2}{\partial m} \tag{4.10}$$

where u^{ij} is the element of the ith row and the jth column in U^{-1} (see equation (4.3)), and $\rho = \lambda/(\partial\lambda/\partial m)$.

Note that equations (4.7)–(4.10) are the set of Slutsky equations. Let us focus on equation (4.8) or (4.9). The term in parentheses on the right-hand side corresponds to the net substitution effect. The second term in the parentheses means that both goods 1 and 2 compete for the consumer's income. In accordance with Houthakker, this term is called the *general* substitution effect. The first term in the parentheses is, however, associated with the specific off-diagonal element (the element in the first row and second column) of the inverse matrix of the Hessian matrix of the utility function. It represents a *specific* interaction in the substitution effect. It may be either the substitution or complementary relationship between two goods 1 and 2. Therefore, this term is called the specific substitution effect. The general substitution effect and the specific substitution effect add up to the *total* substitution effect, which is the same as the net substitution effect in the ordinary Slutsky equation. It is important to note that the specific substitution effect vanishes when the utility function is additive. Readers may want to confirm that the specific substitution effect is absent from equation (3.34) or (3.35) in the previous chapter.

Given the utility function of three goods 1, 2, and 3, in which goods 1 and 2 form a block preference set and good 3 forms independently another set, the Hessian matrix can take the form

$$U = \begin{bmatrix} f_{11} & f_{12} & 0 \\ f_{21} & f_{22} & 0 \\ 0 & 0 & f_{33} \end{bmatrix}. \tag{4.11}$$

It is helpful to exemplify the Hessian matrix and the Cournot price slopes by the following utility function, which is not completely additive within the set but is somewhat interactive:

$$u = f(q_1, q_2, q_3)$$

$$= 20q_1 + 10q_2 + 20q_3 - \frac{1}{2}\left(q_1^2 + q_2^2 + q_3^2 + q_3^2 + 2\theta q_1 q_2\right) \tag{4.12}$$

where $-1 < \theta < 1$.[3] The corresponding Hessian matrix is

$$U = -\begin{bmatrix} 1 & \theta & 0 \\ \theta & 1 & 0 \\ 0 & 0 & 1 \end{bmatrix}. \tag{4.13}$$

Its inverse matrix is

$$U^{-1} = -\begin{bmatrix} \dfrac{1}{1-\theta^2} & -\dfrac{\theta}{1-\theta^2} & 0 \\ -\dfrac{\theta}{1-\theta^2} & \dfrac{1}{1-\theta^2} & 0 \\ 0 & 0 & 1 \end{bmatrix}. \tag{4.14}$$

Barten defines a consumer's preference to be almost additive if

$$U^{-1} \approx -\begin{bmatrix} f_{11} & 0 & 0 \\ 0 & f_{22} & 0 \\ 0 & 0 & f_{33} \end{bmatrix}^{-1} \begin{bmatrix} 1 & -\theta & 0 \\ -\theta & 1 & 0 \\ 0 & 0 & 1 \end{bmatrix} \begin{bmatrix} f_{11} & 0 & 0 \\ 0 & f_{22} & 0 \\ 0 & 0 & f_{33} \end{bmatrix}^{-1}$$

$$= -\begin{bmatrix} \dfrac{1}{f_{11}^2} & -\dfrac{\theta}{f_{11}f_{22}} & 0 \\ -\dfrac{\theta}{f_{11}f_{22}} & \dfrac{1}{f_{22}^2} & 0 \\ 0 & 0 & \dfrac{1}{f_{33}^2} \end{bmatrix} = \begin{bmatrix} -1 & \theta & 0 \\ \theta & -1 & 0 \\ 0 & 0 & -1 \end{bmatrix}. \tag{4.15}$$

Note that each element in the inverse matrix in equation (4.15) is approximately the same as the corresponding element in U^{-1} in equation (4.14), if element θ is sufficiently close to zero.

The Cournot price slopes (equations (4.8) and (4.9), in particular) become

$$\frac{\partial q_1}{\partial p_2} = \left(\lambda \frac{\theta}{f_{11}f_{22}} - \rho \frac{\partial q_1}{\partial m}\frac{\partial q_2}{\partial m}\right) - q_2 \frac{\partial q_1}{\partial m} \qquad (4.16)$$

$$\frac{\partial q_2}{\partial p_1} = \left(\lambda \frac{\theta}{f_{11}f_{22}} - \rho \frac{\partial q_1}{\partial m}\frac{\partial q_2}{\partial m}\right) - q_1 \frac{\partial q_2}{\partial m}. \qquad (4.17)$$

The presence of θ in the above equations attests that some interactions are permitted between goods 1 and 2.

4.3   Demand Equations in Infinitesimal Changes

Given the traditional demand function and the expenditure share of good 1,

$$q_1 = q_1(m_1, p_1, p_2) \qquad (4.18)$$

and

$$S_1 = \frac{p_1 q_1}{m}. \qquad (4.19)$$

Their totally differentiated forms are

$$dq_1 = \frac{\partial q_1}{\partial m}dm + \frac{\partial q_1}{\partial p_1}dp_1 + \frac{\partial q_1}{\partial p_2}dp_2 \qquad (4.20)$$

and

$$S_1\, d(\ln q_1) = \frac{p_1}{m}dq_1. \qquad (4.21)$$

Substituting equations (4.7) and (4.8) into equation (4.20) and the resultant equation into equation (4.21) and rearranging its terms yields

$$S_1\, d(\ln q_1) = \mu_1 d(\ln m) + [\{\nu_{11} - \varphi\, \mu_1^2\} - \mu_1 S_1]\, d(\ln p_1)$$
$$+ [\{\nu_{12} - \varphi\, \mu_1\mu_2\} - \mu_1 S_1]\, d(\ln p_2) \qquad (4.22)$$

where $\mu_1 = \partial(p_1 q_1)/\partial m$ is the marginal value share of good 1,

$\nu_{11} = \lambda u^{11} p_1 p_1 / m$, $\nu_{12} = \lambda u^{12} p_1 p_2 / m$, and $\varphi = 1/[(\partial \lambda / \partial m)(m/\lambda)]$ is the income elasticity of the marginal utility of income.[4] Similarly, we have

$$S_2 \, d(\ln q_2) = \mu_2 \, d(\ln m) + [\{\nu_{21} - \varphi \mu_1 \mu_2\} - \mu_2 S_1] \, d(\ln p_1)$$

$$+ [\{\nu_{22} - \varphi \mu_2^2\} - \mu_2 S_2] \, d(\ln p_2) \qquad (4.23)$$

where $\mu_2 = \partial(p_2 q_2)/\partial m$ is the marginal value share of good 2, $\nu_{21} = \nu_{12}$, and $\nu_{22} = \lambda u^{22} p_2 p_2 / m$.

It is important to note that the specific substitution effects $\lambda \mu^{11}$, $\lambda \mu^{22}$, and $\lambda \mu^{12}$ are involved with ν_{11}, ν_{12}, ν_{21}, and ν_{22} in equations (4.22) and (4.23). Empirical validity of the almost additivity assumption depends on whether or not $\nu_{12} \, (= \nu_{21}) = 0$. Parameters μ_1 and μ_2 in equations (4.22) and (4.23) are the income elasticities weighted by the expenditure shares, i.e. $S_1(\partial \ln q_1 / \partial \ln m)$ and $S_2(\partial \ln q_2 / \partial \ln m)$. The two parameters in the brackets in those equations are compensated price elasticities weighted by the expenditure shares, i.e. $S_1(\partial \ln q_1 / \partial \ln p_1)$, $S_1(\partial \ln q_1 / \partial \ln p_2)$, $S_2(\partial \ln q_2 / \partial \ln p_1)$, and $S_2(\partial \ln q_2 / \partial \ln p_2)$, respectively.

Equations (4.22) and (4.23) are linear in the first differences of natural logarithms. They are called the *demand equations in infinitesimal changes*. The classical properties (see appendix E) hold under the restrictions imposed on some of the parameters. Homogeneity requires the sum of the two terms in the braces in equation (4.22) and the sum of those in equation (4.23) to be unity. The Slutsky symmetry requires the second term in the braces in equation (4.22) and the first term in the braces in (4.23) to be identical.

Note that we have

$$\nu_{11} + \nu_{12} = \varphi \mu_1. \qquad (4.24)$$

Post-multiplication of equation (4.3) by a column vector of prices $(p_1 p_2)'$ yields

$$\frac{1}{D} \begin{bmatrix} f_{22} & -f_{12} \\ -f_{21} & f_{11} \end{bmatrix} \begin{bmatrix} p_1 \\ p_2 \end{bmatrix} = \frac{1}{D} \begin{bmatrix} p_1 f_{22} & -p_2 f_{12} \\ -p_1 f_{21} & -p_2 f_{11} \end{bmatrix}. \qquad (4.25)$$

Scalar multiplication of equation (4.25) by $-D/\Delta$ gives

$$-\frac{1}{\Delta} \begin{bmatrix} p_1 f_{22} & -p_2 f_{12} \\ -p_1 f_{21} & -p_2 f_{11} \end{bmatrix} = \begin{bmatrix} \dfrac{a_{31}}{\Delta} \\ -\dfrac{a_{32}}{\Delta} \end{bmatrix} = \begin{bmatrix} \dfrac{\partial q_1}{\partial m} \\ \dfrac{\partial q_2}{\partial m} \end{bmatrix}. \qquad (4.26)$$

Since we have $a_{33}/\Delta = -\partial\lambda/\partial m$ and $a_{33} = D$ (see equations (4.3) and (4.6)) and hence $-D/\Delta = \partial\lambda/\partial m$, equation (4.26) becomes

$$
\begin{bmatrix} \dfrac{\partial q_1}{\partial m} \\[2ex] \dfrac{\partial q_2}{\partial m} \end{bmatrix} = \frac{\partial\lambda}{\partial m} \begin{bmatrix} \dfrac{p_1 f_{22} - p_2 f_{12}}{D} \\[2ex] \dfrac{-p_1 f_{21} + p_2 f_{11}}{D} \end{bmatrix} = \frac{\partial\lambda}{\partial m} \begin{bmatrix} p_1 u^{11} + p_2 u^{12} \\[1ex] p_1 u^{21} + p_2 u^{22} \end{bmatrix}. \qquad (4.27)
$$

Thus equation (4.24) is

$$
v_{11} + v_{12} = \frac{p_1^2}{m}\lambda u^{11} + \frac{p_1 p_2}{m}\lambda u^{12} = \frac{p_1\lambda}{m}(p_1 u^{11} + p_2 u^{12})
$$

$$
= p_1 \frac{\lambda}{m} \frac{1}{\partial\lambda/\partial m} \frac{\partial q_1}{\partial m} = \varphi\mu_1. \qquad (4.28)
$$

Similarly, we can get

$$
v_{21} + v_{22} = \varphi\mu_2. \qquad (4.29)
$$

Equations (4.28) and (4.29) add up to

$$
v_{11} + v_{12} + v_{21} + v_{22} = \varphi(\mu_1 + \mu_2) = \varphi < 0 \qquad (4.30)
$$

where $\varphi < 0$ because of the negative definite matrix of vs.

The adding-up property requires

$$
\mu_1 + \mu_2 = 1. \qquad (4.31)
$$

This property holds because the totally differentiated budget constraint is

$$
p_1 \frac{dq_1}{dm} + p_2 \frac{dq_2}{dm} = 1. \qquad (4.32)
$$

From an empirical standpoint, it is important to note that all vs and φ are directly related to the income elasticities.

4.4 Empirical Remarks

Barten (1964) estimates equations (4.22) and (4.23) by means of Zellner's iterative efficient method and Theil's method of the use of prior information.[5] He uses time-series data of household expenditure in the Netherlands for fourteen commodities and services during the periods 1921–39 and 1948–58.

The sample estimates of the direct (own) price elasticities are all negative with only one exception; the *posterior* estimates are all negative. The sample estimates of interaction (cross) price elasticities show that most of the goods are substitutes to each other and that the *posterior* estimates are consistent with the sample estimates. Both the sample and *posterior* estimates of the income elasticities suggest that food items are income-inelastic, whereas household durables are income-elastic. It is interesting to note that bread is the only one of nine food items that obeys Engel's law.

The interaction elasticities hold the key to determining the almost-additivity, the main point Barten addresses in the paper. The sample estimates of interaction elasticities of the eleven pairs of commodity groups range from -0.484 to 0.567 and the *posterior* estimates range from -0.093 to 0.334. None of them are zero. Barten suggests that these results are convincing evidence for the almost-additivity embodied in his demand analysis.

Later, Parks (1969) compared empirical results of three demand models: Houthakker's indirect addilog system, the Stone–Geary linear expenditure system, and the Rotterdam differential logarithmic system. He uses the concept of average information inaccuracy to evaluate the overall fit of the model to the data for the entire budget. He used time-series data of consumption expenditure by households in Sweden. He reports that the Rotterdam model shows the best performance.

4.5 Summary

The Rotterdam system of demand equations is a system of double-logarithmic demand functions in infinitesimal changes. To derive the demand function, it employs the general form of utility function, the utility-maximizing demand function, and the definition of the expenditure share. The utility function is assumed to be *almost* additive. Barten and Theil break down the Hicks–Allen net substitution effect of the Cournot price slope into the specific substitution effect and the general substitution effect. The specific substitution effect vanishes if the utility function is *not* almost additive.

Using time-series data of household expenditure in the Netherlands, Barten estimates the demand functions and presents evidence for near-additivity. He relates components in the Cournot price slopes to the income elasticities. Parks suggests that the Rotterdam system is the best-performing model in his empirical comparison of alternative functional forms.

Notes

1   Later, Barnett (1979) investigates theoretical foundations of the Rotterdam model.
2   Equation (4.5) is the Barten–Theil *fundamental matrix equation*. Also, see Goldberger (1967, p. 7).
3   This is the function used by Theil (1967, p. 183).
4   It is called the *money flexibility* by Frisch (1932, 1959) or the *income flexibility* by Houthakker (1960). See note 3 in chapter 3. Note that there is a conceptual difference between Houthakker and Barten and Theil. Readers may want to compare equations (4.22) and (3.26) to see the difference.
5   It is the method of using the available prior information of a stochastic nature with respect to the elasticities to be estimated.

Recommended Reading

Barnett, W.A. 1979: The theoretical foundations for the Rotterdam model. *Review of Economic Studies*, XLVI, January, 109–30.
Barten, A.P. 1964: Consumer demand functions under conditions of almost additive preferences. *Econometrica*, 32, 1–38.
Frisch, R. 1932: *New Methods of Measuring Marginal Utility*. Tübingen: Mohr.
—— 1959: A complete scheme for computing all direct and cross demand elasticities in a model with many sectors. *Econometrica*, 27, 177–96.
Goldberger, A.S. 1967: Functional form and utility: a review of consumer demand theory. Social Systems Research Institute, University of Wisconsin, Workshop Paper SFMP 6703, October, 1–122.
Houthakker, H.S. 1960: Additive preferences. *Econometrica*, 28, April, 244–57.
Parks, R.W. 1969: Systems of demand equations: an empirical comparison of alternative functional forms. *Econometrica*, 37, 611–29.
Theil, H. 1965: The information approach to demand analysis. *Econometrica*, 33, January, 67–87.
—— 1967: *Economics and Information Theory*. Amsterdam: North-Holland.

5 The Constant-Elasticity-of-Substitution Utility Function and its Generalization

In chapter 1, we learned that the linear logarithmic utility function is highly restrictive. In chapters 2 and 3, we also learned that attempts to generalize the linear logarithmic utility function were only partially successful.

This chapter examines two further generalizations of the earlier utility functions. One is the constant-elasticity-of-substitution (CES) utility function, the other is the S-branch utility function. As far as its functional form is concerned, the S-branch function belongs to the CES family. There is a symmetry between the CES utility function and the CES production function (chapter 9) and the S-branch utility function and the two-level CES production function (chapter 11). The CES utility function, as a well-behaved function, embraces a set of demand equations that are less restrictive than those of the linear logarithmic utility function and the Stone–Geary utility function. Although the expenditure system is linear in terms of income, it need not be linear in terms of prices. Unlike the Stone–Geary utility function, the CES demand function does not necessarily restrict goods to being Hicks–Allen substitutes only. However, the scope of the CES function is not wide enough to include inferior goods. Further, the function limits the elasticity of substitution to a constant.

The S-branch utility system relaxes some of the restrictive features that the CES utility function and the Stone–Geary utility function have. The S-branch model allows for complementary, independent, and substitutable relationships. In addition, it does not limit the own-price elasticity. Its expenditure system is nonlinear in terms of income and prices.

There are numerous studies on the CES utility function. They are Chetty (1969), Wales (1971), Heien (1972), Lee (1972), Sato (1972), Christensen and Manser (1976), and Moroney and Wilbratte (1976). However, Brown and Heien (1972) is the only major reference for the S-branch utility function, presumably because it is a complex function and its applicability is limited.

Section 5.1 examines the CES utility function and its properties. Section 5.2 examines the S-branch utility function and its properties. Section 5.3 discusses empirical results obtained by Wales and by Brown and Heien. Several other references are briefly discussed. Section 5.4 summarizes the chapter.

5.1   The Constant-Elasticity-of-Substitution Utility Function and its Properties

The CES function is

$$u = \left(\sum_{i=1}^{n} \beta_i q_i^{-\rho} \right)^{-1/\rho} \tag{5.1}$$

where u is utility, q_i is commodity, $\beta_i > 0$, and $\rho = (1 - \sigma)/\sigma < 1$.[1]
Its marginal utility is positive:

$$\frac{\partial u}{\partial q_i} = \beta_i u^{1+\rho} q_i^{-(1+\rho)} > 0. \tag{5.2}$$

The law of diminishing marginal utility prevails locally because

$$\frac{\partial^2 u}{\partial q_i^2} = \left(\frac{1+\rho}{u} \right) \mathrm{MU}_i \frac{\mathrm{MU}_i q_i - u}{q_i} < 0. \tag{5.3}$$

Given the symmetry between the CES utility function and the CES production function, the strict quasi-concavity of the utility function will be left until chapter 9.

The function is homogeneous. Scalar multiplication yields

$$\left[\sum_{i=1}^{n} \beta_i (\theta q_i)^{-\rho} \right]^{-1/\rho} = \theta u. \tag{5.4}$$

However, the function is not additive ($\partial^2 u / \partial q_i \partial q_j \neq 0$) but separable, i.e.

$$\frac{\partial(\mathrm{MU}_i/\mathrm{MU}_j)}{\partial q_k} = 0 \qquad (i \neq j \neq k). \tag{5.5}$$

Given the augmented objective function

$$\mathscr{L}(q, \lambda) = \left(\sum_i \beta_i q_i^{-\rho} \right)^{-1/\rho} + \lambda \left(m - \sum_i p_i q_i \right) \qquad (5.6)$$

the standard procedure for finding the constrained maximum of the utility function gives the demand function

$$q_i = \frac{\beta_i^\sigma p_i^{1-\sigma}}{\sum_{j=1}^n \beta_j^\sigma p_j^{1-\sigma}} \frac{m}{p_i} \qquad (i \in j). \qquad (5.7)$$

The Engel expenditure $(p_i q_i)$ function is then

$$p_i q_i = \frac{\beta_i^\sigma p_i^{1-\sigma}}{\sum_j \beta_j^\sigma p_j^{1-\sigma}} m. \qquad (5.8)$$

Note that the Engel expenditure function is linear in terms of income and thus the budget share is independent of income. This result was to be expected, because the given utility function is homothetic. Dividing the numerator and the denominator of equation (5.8) by $m^{1-\sigma}$ yields the corresponding budget share $(p_i q_i/m)$ equation:

$$S_i = \frac{\beta_i^\sigma (p_i/m)^{1-\sigma}}{\sum_j \beta_j^\sigma (p_j/m)^{1-\sigma}}. \qquad (5.9)$$

The elasticities are:

$$\epsilon_{ii} = -1 + (1 - \sigma) S_j \qquad (i \neq j) \qquad (5.10)$$

$$\epsilon_{ij} = -(1 - \sigma) S_j \qquad (i \neq j) \qquad (5.11)$$

$$\epsilon_{im} = 1. \qquad (5.12)$$

The own-price elasticity can be a negative constant, given that the budget share S_j is a positive constant. The cross-price elasticity is negative if $\sigma < 1$. The two goods are gross complements in this case. It is positive if $\sigma > 1$. The goods are then gross substitutes.[2] The unitary income elasticity implies that the CES utility function includes only normal goods and that the corresponding Engel curve is linear and passes through the origin.

The dual approach to the CES utility function enables us to get the expenditure share equations and the Allen–Uzawa partial elasticities of substitution. Since the expenditure share equations were already obtained by the primal approach, we get only the Allen–Uzawa elasticities of substitution.

The indirect utility function corresponding to the direct CES utility function (equation (5.1)) is

$$v = \left[\sum_{i=j} \beta_i^{\sigma} \left(\frac{p_i}{m} \right)^{1-\sigma} \right]^{1/(\sigma-1)} \tag{5.13}$$

First-order and second-order partial derivatives of v with respect to p_i are as follows.

$$\frac{\partial v}{\partial p_i} = - \beta_i^{\sigma} (1 - \sigma) p_i^{-\sigma} m^{\sigma-1} v^{\sigma} \tag{5.14}$$

$$\frac{\partial^2 v}{\partial p_i^2} = - \beta_i^{\sigma} \sigma (1 - \sigma) p_i^{-\sigma} m^{\sigma-1} [- (1 - \sigma) \beta_i^{\sigma} p_i^{-\sigma} m^{\sigma-1} v^{\sigma-1} - p_i^{-1}] v^{\sigma} \tag{5.15}$$

$$\frac{\partial^2 v}{\partial p_i \, \partial p_j} = - \beta_i^{\sigma} \beta_j^{\sigma} \sigma (1 - \sigma)^2 p_i^{-\sigma} p_j^{-\sigma} m^{2(\sigma-1)} v^{2\sigma-1} \quad (i \neq j). \tag{5.16}$$

The Allen–Uzawa partial elasticities of substitution are then

$$\sigma_{ii} = \frac{v(\partial^2 v/\partial p_i^2)}{(\partial v/\partial p_i)^2} = \sigma \left\{ 1 - \frac{S_i}{(1 - \sigma)[\beta_i^{\sigma} (p_i/m)^{1-\sigma}]^2} \right\} \tag{5.17}$$

$$\sigma_{ij} = \frac{v(\partial^2 v/\partial p_i \, \partial p_2)}{(\partial v/\partial p_i) \, (\partial v/\partial p_j)} = \sigma. \tag{5.18}$$

Note that the Allen–Uzawa cross-partial elasticity of substitution is a constant.

5.2 The S-Branch Utility Function and its Properties

Using the S-branch utility function, Brown and Heien widen the range for variations of price and income elasticities and obtain a nonlinear expenditure system.

Assuming that commodities are partitioned into S sets and each set is, in turn, decomposed into n subsets, the utility function for both levels in the general form is

$$u = f[q^{(1)} (q_1^{(1)}, q_2^{(1)}, \ldots), q^{(2)} (q_1^{(2)}, q_2^{(2)}, \ldots), \ldots, q^{(S)} (q_1^{(S)}, q_2^{(S)}, \ldots)] \tag{5.19}$$

where commodity $q_i^{(S)}$ is commodity i that belongs to group S. The form Brown and Heien suggest is

$$u = \left[\sum_{s=1}^{S} a^{(S)} \left\{ \sum_{i \in s}^{n^{(s)}} \beta_i^{(s)} (q_i^{(s)} - \gamma_i^{(s)})^{\rho^{(s)}} \right\}^{\rho/\rho(s)} \right]^{1/\rho} \tag{5.20}$$

where $\beta_i^{(s)} > 0$, $\gamma_i^{(s)} \geq 0$, $q_i^{(s)} - \gamma_i^{(s)} > 0$, $a^{(s)} > 0$, $\rho^{(s)} = (\sigma^{(s)} - 1)/\sigma^{(s)}$, and $\rho = (\sigma - 1)/\sigma$. In particular, note that the parameter γ_i is the same as the parameter for the *subsistence* level introduced in chapter 2. We know that the sub-function $\{\cdot\}$ is basically the ordinary CES function. In the presence of parameter γ, however, it is not homogeneous and hence the function $[\{\cdot\}]$ is not homothetic. The S-branch utility function is not additive. It is, however, weakly separable, because the marginal rate of substitution for any pair of goods within branch s is independent of a good outside of branch s, i.e.

$$\frac{\partial[(\partial u/\partial q_i^{(s)})/(\partial u/\partial q_j^{(s)})]}{\partial q_i^{(r)}} = 0 \qquad (r \neq s).^3 \tag{5.21}$$

Equation (5.20) can be viewed as the generalized CES utility function on the one hand or as the generalized Stone–Geary utility function on the other hand.

Given the utility function, the corresponding budget constraint is

$$m = \sum_{s=1}^{S} \left\{ \sum_{i=1}^{n^{(s)}} p_i^{(s)} q_i^{(s)} \right\}. \tag{5.22}$$

We first maximize each sub-utility function subject to the corresponding sub-budget constraint $\{\cdot\}$ to get the preliminary demand function for that particular sub-group. Then we substitute the preliminary demand functions for all sub-groups into the utility function (equation (5.20)), and maximize again the resulted utility function subject to the budget constraint. The final demand function that we obtain through this two-stage optimization is[4]

$$q_i^{(s)} = \gamma_i^{(s)} + \left(\frac{\beta_i^{(s)}}{p_i^{(s)}} \right)^{\sigma^{(s)}} \frac{a^{(s)\sigma} Q^{(s)(\sigma - \sigma^{(s)})/(\sigma^{(s)} - 1)}}{\sum_{r=1}^{S} a^{(r)\sigma} Q^{(r)(\sigma - 1)/\sigma^{(r)} - 1)}} \left(m - \sum_{r=1}^{S} \sum_{j \in r}^{n^{(r)}} p_j^{(r)} \gamma_j^{(r)} \right) \tag{5.23}$$

where $Q^{(s)} = \sum_{j \in s}^{n^{(s)}} (\beta_j^{(s)}/p_j^{(s)})^{\sigma^{(s)}} p_j^{(s)}$.

If $S = 1$, the demand function reduces to

$$q_i = \gamma_i + \left(\frac{\beta_i}{p_i} \right)^{\sigma} \left[\sum_{j=1}^{n} \left(\frac{\beta_j}{p_j} \right)^{\sigma} p_j \right]^{-1} \left(m - \sum_{j=1}^{n} p_j \gamma_j \right). \tag{5.24}$$

Since the case of $S = 1$ suffices understanding the properties of the S-branch utility function, we focus on equation (5.24). The corresponding budget share equation is

$$S_i = \frac{p_i q_i}{m} = \frac{p_i \gamma_i}{m} + \left[\frac{\beta_i^\sigma (p_i/m)^{1-\sigma}}{\sum_{j=1}^n \beta_j^\sigma (p_j/m)^{1-\sigma}} \right] \left(1 - \sum_{j=1}^n \frac{p_j \gamma_j}{m} \right). \quad (5.25)$$

Note that, in contrast to the cases of the linear logarithmic utility function and the Stone–Geary utility function, the budget share equation of the S-branch utility function is nonlinear. If $\sigma = 1$, equations (5.24) and (5.25) reduce to the Stone–Geary functions (2.12) and (2.22) in chapter 2.

The elasticities are as follows.

$$\epsilon_{ii} = \frac{\partial q_i}{\partial p_i} \frac{p_i}{q_i} = \left[(\sigma - 1) m - \frac{\sigma(m - p_j \gamma_j)}{S_i} \right] \left(S_i - \frac{p_i \gamma_i}{m} \right) \quad (i \ne j)(5.26)$$

$$\epsilon_{ij} = \frac{\partial q_i}{\partial p_j} \frac{p_j}{q_i} = (\sigma - 1) \frac{[S_i - (p_i/m) \gamma_i]}{[1 - \Sigma_k (p_k/m) \gamma_k]} \frac{S_j}{S_i} \quad (i \ne j; i, j \in k) \quad (5.27)$$

$$\epsilon_{im} = \frac{\partial q_i}{\partial m} \frac{m}{q_i} = \frac{\beta_i^\sigma (p_i/m)^{1-\sigma}}{[\Sigma_j \beta_j^\sigma (p_j/m)^{1-\sigma}] S_i} \quad (i \in j). \quad (5.28)$$

The above results imply that:

1 the S-branch demand function results in the own-price elasticity ranging anywhere between 0 and ∞ (as opposed to -1 permitted by the linear logarithmic utility function and a number less than 0 by the Stone–Geary utility function and the CES);
2 the S-branch model allows for complementary, independent, *and* substitutable relationships in the Hicks–Allen net sense (as opposed to the substitutable relationship only permitted by the linear logarithmic utility function, the Stone–Geary system, and the CES);
3 the S-branch utility function allows for normal goods as well as inferior goods (as opposed to normal goods only for the linear logarithmic system, the Stone–Geary system, and the CES).

Brown and Heien derive the Allen–Uzawa partial elasticities of substitution between any two supernumerary quantities within a branch ($S = 1$) and in different branches ($S > 1$). Although the intra-branch elasticity is not a constant, the inter-branch elasticity of substitution is still a constant. The two elasticities are

$$\sigma_{i\ j}^{(s)(r)} = \begin{cases} \dfrac{1}{\Omega}\,\sigma^{(s)} + \left(1 - \dfrac{1}{\Omega}\right) & (s = r) \qquad (5.29) \\[3mm] \sigma & (s \neq r) \qquad (5.30) \end{cases}$$

where

$$\Omega = \frac{\sum_{j\in s}^{n} p_j^{(s)} \left(q_j^{(s)} - \gamma_j^{(s)}\right)}{m - \sum_{r=1}^{S} \sum_{i\in r}^{n} p_i^{(r)} \gamma_i^{(r)}}.$$

5.3   Empirical Remarks

This section summarizes two empirical results: one for the CES utility function and the other for the S-branch utility function.

Wales (1971) estimates the expenditure system derived from the CES utility function augmented by Stone and Geary's subsistence-level parameter γ_i (see equation (2.1)). If parameter γ_i is zero, the system reduces to equation (5.8). The expenditure system reduces to the Cobb–Douglas linear expenditure system if $\rho = 0$, i.e. $\sigma = 1$. Wales develops the generalized system into a dynamic model and a stochastic model. The dynamic model is a theoretical specification that permits parameters γ_i to form a specific habit for consumption.[5] It has proven useful to treat the γ_i as functions of quantities in the recent past, i.e. lagged quantities. The stochastic model is an econometric specification that assumes residuals to be a singular covariance matrix. Using Canadian data for broadly aggregated categories of per capita consumption of nondurable goods (food, clothing, shelter, and miscellaneous), Wales estimates price and income elasticities and elasticities of substitution between goods. Most important, the estimated values of the elasticities of substitution between all supernumerary quantities $q_i - \gamma_i$ is 0.25 for the stochastic model and 0.18 for the dynamic model. Those numbers are statistically significant and considerably different from 1.0. Wales believes that the linear expenditure system, in which $\sigma = 1$, is an unsatisfactory description of preferences.

Additional applications suggested to interested readers are Chetty (1969), an estimation of the elasticity of substitution between money and commercial bank time deposits using time series data (1945–66) for the United States; Lee (1972), comments on measuring the nearness of near-money; Heien (1972), an analysis of multiperiod consumption with the CES utility function augmented by the Stone–Geary subsistence parameter using annual data from 1948 to 1956; Sato (1972), a study showing the constancy of income and own-price elasticities when the utility function is a generalized CES form and to comparing the results with those for the linear expenditure system.

Brown and Heien (1972) estimate the derived demand equations in expenditure form to show the usefulness and practicability of the S-branch utility tree, which is a generalization of the linear expenditure system. They employ Bard's nonlinear Gauss–Newton maximum likelihood estimation method. Their data are time series on per capita basis food in the United States from 1947 to 1968. They group twenty-eight food products into five categories: meat, vegetables, fruits, dairy products, and other breakfast foods. The relative sizes of the partial elasticities of substitution between items within a branch indicate that substitution among fruits (0.706) is easier than among vegetables (0.025). In addition, the overall elasticity of substitution, which differs significantly from unity (0.493), implies that substitution between branches is difficult. Brown and Heien conclude that the S-branch utility tree permits a wide range for the own-price elasticity and the cross-price elasticities, allows for a better assessment of elasticities of substitution, and is thus superior to the Stone–Geary utility function.

5.4 Summary

The CES utility function and the S-branch utility function generalize earlier utility functions. As a well-behaved function, the CES utility function does not necessarily restrict goods to being Hicks–Allen substitutes only. However, the scope of the CES function is not broad enough to accommodate inferior goods. The expenditure system is linear in terms of income. The utility function also limits the elasticity of substitution to a constant.

The S-branch utility function expands the range for variations of various elasticities associated with the Stone–Geary and CES utility functions. The expenditure system is not linear in terms of income. The Allen–Uzawa partial elasticity of substitution between any two goods within a branch is not a constant but it still a constant between two goods in different branches. The S-branch expenditure share function reduces to the Stone–Geary expenditure share function if the elasticity of substitution is unity.

Wales estimates the elasticities of substitution between supernumerary quantities of consumption of nondurable goods in Canada for the stochastic and dynamic versions of the CES function. He finds that elasticities are considerably different from 1.0 and hence that the linear expenditure system, in which $\sigma = 1$, is an unsatisfactory description of preferences. Brown and Heien estimate elasticities of substitution between food items within a branch of food and the overall elasticity of substitution between branches of food in the United States. The overall elasticity of substitution is significantly different from unity and the values for the Stone–Geary utility function and the CES utility function. Brown and Heien suggest that the S-branch utility function is superior to the Stone–Geary utility function, in particular.

Notes

1 The homogeneous CES utility function was suggested initially by Bergson (1936). Expanding log u around $\rho = 0$ by means of a Taylor's series formula and dropping the terms involving powers of ρ higher than one, the CES function becomes a quadratic form in logarithms. (See Kmenta (1967) who expanded the CES production function.) Some economists employ a quadratic utility function. However, Deaton and Muellbauer (1980a, p. 400) show that a quadratic utility function is inappropriate for modeling normal behavior of consumers. Readers should not construe the CES function to be inappropriate as a functional form because the Taylor-expanded CES function includes quadratic terms and cross-product terms. If, however, any higher-order terms are zero, the CES becomes a quadratic function.
2 Using the Slutsky equation, it is possible to show that the two goods can be net complements and net substitutes, respectively.
3 See Berndt and Christensen (1973a).
4 See Strotz (1959) and Gorman (1959) for the two-stage optimization.
5 For role of habit and dynamic adjustment, see Stone and Rowe (1957), Pollak and Wales (1969), Houthakker and Taylor (1970), and Heien (1972).

Recommended Reading

Bergson, A. 1936: Real income, expenditure proportionality, and Frisch's "new method". *Review of Economic Studies*, 4, 33–52.
Brown, M. and Heien, D. 1972: The S-branch utility tree: a generalization of the linear expenditure system. *Econometrica*, 40, July, 737–47.
Chetty, V.K. 1969: On measuring the nearness of near-moneys. *American Economic Review*, LIX, June, 270–81.

Christensen, L.R. and Manser, M.E. 1976: Cost-of-living indexes for U.S. meat and produce, 1947–1971. In N.E. Terleckjy (ed.), *Household and Production*. New York: Columbia University Press.

Gorman, W.M. 1959: Separable utility and aggregation. *Econometrica*, 27, 469–81.

Heien, D.M. 1972: Demographic effects and the multiperiod consumption function. *Journal of Political Economy*, 80, January/February, 125–38.

Houthakker, H.S. and Taylor, L.D. 1970: *Consumer Demand in the United States 1929–70*, second edition. Cambridge, MA: Harvard University Press.

Moroney, J.R. and Wilbratte, B.J. 1976: Money and money substitutes: a time series analysis of household portfolios. *Journal of Money, Credit and Banking*, VIII, May, 181–98.

Pollak, R.A. and Wales, T.J. 1969: Estimation of the linear expenditure system. *Econometrica*, 37, October, 611–28.

Sato, K. 1972: Additive utility functions with double-log consumer demand functions. *Journal of Political Economy*, 80, January/February, 102–24.

Stone, R. and Rowe, D.A. 1957: The market demand for durable goods. *Econometrica*, 25, 423–43.

Strotz, R.H. 1959: The utility tree–a correction and future appraisal. *Econometrica*, 27, 482–8.

Wales, T.J. 1971: A generalized linear expenditure model of the demand for non-durable goods in Canada. *Canadian Journal of Economics*, 4, November, 471–84.

6 The Transcendental Logarithmic Utility Function

The utility functions examined in chapters 1–5 assume either additivity or homotheticity or both. We have seen that these assumptions are highly restrictive and that hence additive and homothetic utility functions are inadequate for an analysis of consumer preferences.

In this chapter, we are going to examine a function free of the above assumptions, although they can be imposed *a posteriori* as testable parameter restrictions. The function is the transcendental logarithmic utility function (the translog utility function, for short). The utility function is quadratic in the logarithms of the quantities consumed. Its expenditure shares can vary with total expenditure and the range of substitution possibilities is broad. It was developed by Christensen et al. (1975).[1]

They exploit the duality between quantities in the direct utility function and price and income in the indirect utility function. Later, Christensen and Manser (1976, 1977) apply the translog utility function to test the data for consumption of meat in the United States.

Section 6.1 presents the direct and indirect forms of the translog utility function, and the expenditure share functions corresponding to these two forms. For convenience, in section 6.2, we shall discuss properties and assumptions associated with the translog function. In section 6.3, we examine various elasticities. Section 6.4 deals with the almost ideal demand system suggested by Deaton and Muellbauer (1980b), viewed as a specific case of the translog function. Section 6.5 discusses the empirical results obtained by Christensen and Manser and by Deaton and Muellbauer. Section 6.6 summarizes the chapter.

Detailed procedures for deriving the expenditure share functions and elasticities are found in the appendix at the end of the chapter.

6.1   Direct and Indirect Utility Functions and Expenditure Shares

As discussed in earlier chapters, there are two optimization problems in utility theory when the utility function is monotonic and convex: one in connection with the direct utility function for given prices and income, and the other in connection with the indirect utility function for given quantities. Both the direct and indirect utility functions are represented by the translog second-order approximation. The direct utility function is

$$- \ln u = \ln a_0 + \sum_{i=1}^{n} a_i \ln q_i + \frac{1}{2} \sum_{i=1}^{n} \sum_{j=1}^{n} \beta_{ij} \ln q_i \ln q_j \qquad (6.1)$$

and the indirect utility function is

$$\ln v = \ln a_0 + \sum_{i=1}^{n} a_i \ln\left(\frac{p_i}{m}\right) + \frac{1}{2} \sum_{i=1}^{n} \sum_{j=1}^{n} \beta_{ij} \ln\left(\frac{p_i}{m}\right) \ln\left(\frac{p_j}{m}\right)$$

$$(i \neq j; i, j = 1, ..., n) \qquad (6.2)$$

where u is the index of direct utility, v is the index of indirect utility, q_i is commodity i, m is the consumer's income, p_i is the price of commodity i, and $\beta_{ij} = \beta_{ji}$. As noted by Christensen et al. and shown in earlier chapters, the direct utility function is negative in the logarithm to maintain a symmetry with the indirect utility function.

The expenditure share function is obtained by the usual procedure for optimizing the direct utility function or by the procedure for optimizing the indirect utility function incorporated with Roy's identity. In the case of the direct utility function, the required procedure is standard constrained maximization. Given the translog function and the budget constraint $\Sigma p_i q_i = m$, the maximum utility is achieved at

$$\frac{\partial \ln u}{\partial \ln q_i}\left[= \frac{\partial u}{\partial q_i}\frac{q_i}{u} = \mathrm{MU}_i \frac{q_i}{u} = -\left(a_i + \sum_j \beta_{ij} \ln q_j\right)\right] = \lambda \frac{p_i q_i}{u}. \qquad (6.3)$$

Note that equation (6.3) implies $\mathrm{MU}_i = \lambda p_i$, which is the well-known first-order condition for a maximum utility. Add the first-order conditions together for all i and use the budget constraint to obtain

$$\frac{\lambda}{u} = \frac{1}{m} \sum_k \frac{\partial \ln u}{\partial \ln q_k} = -\frac{1}{m} \left[\left(a_i + \sum_j \beta_{ij} \ln q_j \right) + \left(a_j + \sum_i \beta_{ij} \ln q_i \right) \right]$$

$$(k = i, j). \tag{6.4}$$

Now divide equation (6.3) by equation (6.4) to get the following expenditure share functions:

$$S_i = \frac{p_i q_i}{m} = \frac{a_i + \Sigma_j \beta_{ij} \ln q_j}{(a_i + \Sigma_j \beta_{ij} \ln q_j) + (a_j + \Sigma_i \beta_{ij} \ln q_i)}. \tag{6.5}$$

As noted in earlier chapters, the procedure to derive the share function from the indirect utility function is different from the procedure to derive the share function from the direct utility function. First, differentiate the logarithmic indirect utility function with respect to the logarithmic p_j and m. Second, substitute the results into the logarithmic form of Roy's identity stated in appendix H. The result is the share function

$$S_i = \frac{a_i + \Sigma_j \beta_{ij} \ln(p_j/m)}{[a_i + \Sigma_j \beta_{ij} \ln(p_j/m)] + [a_j + \Sigma_i \beta_{ij} \ln(p_i/m)]} \tag{6.6}$$

The functional forms of equations (6.5) and (6.6) are identical, but their arguments are not. Recall that prices and income were treated as given when we optimized the direct utility function, whereas quantities were given when we optimized the indirect utility function. Note that the expenditure share in equation (6.6) is not linear and not independent of the total expenditure for all i.

6.2 Properties of the Indirect Utility Function

Given the symmetry between the direct and indirect utility functions (and thus between their share functions), it is redundant to examine properties and assumptions for both functions. In general, one implies the other. We shall discuss the features associated with the indirect utility function only.

The indirect translog utility function must meet the regularity conditions – monotonicity and convexity. Monotonicity holds as long as

$$v_i = \frac{\partial v}{\partial (p_i/m)} = \frac{v}{p_i/m} \left[a_i + \sum_j \beta_{ij} \ln\left(\frac{p_j}{m}\right) \right] > 0. \tag{6.7}$$

The positivity of equation (6.7) should be confirmed *a posteriori* on the basis of the estimated coefficients at each data point.

The function should be convex. Given two goods i and j, the second-order partial derivatives are

$$v_{ii} = \frac{\partial^2 v}{\partial(p_i/m)^2} = \frac{v}{(p_i/m)^2}(\beta_{ii} - N_i + N_i^2) \tag{6.8}$$

$$v_{ij} = \frac{\partial^2 v}{\partial(p_i/m)\,\partial(p_j/m)} = \frac{v}{(p_i/m)(p_j/m)}(\beta_{ij} + N_i N_j) \qquad (i \neq j) \tag{6.9}$$

where $N_i = a_i + \Sigma_j\, \beta_{ij}\, \ln(p_j/m)$.

Equations (6.7), (6.8), and (6.9) are substituted into equation (B.4) in appendix B. The bordered Hessian ($|\bar{H}_2|$) must be positive for convexity. This result should also be confirmed by researchers on the basis of the estimated coefficients.

The translog utility function does not require *a priori* additivity and homotheticity.[2] In connection with these assumptions, there are some complexities involved with the relationship between the direct utility function and the indirect utility function. In general, however, if the direct utility function is additive and homothetic, the indirect utility function is also additive and homothetic.[3]

The indirect translog function is strongly additive if

$$\frac{\partial^2 \ln v}{\partial \ln(p_i/m)\,\partial \ln(p_j/m)} = \beta_{ij} = 0 \qquad (i \neq j). \tag{6.10}$$

The function is strongly separable if

$$\frac{\partial(v_i/v_j)}{\partial(p_k/m)} = v_j v_{ik} - v_i v_{jk} = 0 \qquad (i \neq j \neq k). \tag{6.11}$$

Given the symmetry between direct and indirect utility functions, the condition for functional separability (equation (6.11)) implies that the marginal rate of substitution of good i for good j is independent of good k. Substitute equations (6.7) and (6.9) into equation (6.11) in order to obtain

$$\frac{v^2 D}{\Pi_h\,(p_h/m)}(\beta_{ik} S_j - \beta_{jk} S_i) = 0 \qquad (i \neq j \neq k; i, j, k \in h) \tag{6.12}$$

where D is the denominator of equation (6.6). This result suggests that the indirect function is strongly separable under the condition of

$$\beta_{ij} = \beta_{jk} = 0. \tag{6.13}$$

Christensen et al. refer to this condition as the *explicit additivity restrictions*. If the above $\beta \neq 0$, we substitute share functions (6.6) into equation (6.12) to obtain

$$(a_j \beta_{ik} - a_i \beta_{jk}) + (\beta_{ik} \beta_{ij} - \beta_{jk} \beta_{ii}) \ln\left(\frac{p_i}{m}\right) + (\beta_{ik} \beta_{jj} - \beta_{jk} \beta_{ij}) \ln\left(\frac{p_j}{m}\right)$$

$$+ (\beta_{ik} \beta_{jk} - \beta_{jk} \beta_{ik}) \ln\left(\frac{p_k}{m}\right) = 0. \tag{6.14}$$

From equation (6.14), it is possible to get

$$\frac{a_i}{a_j} = \frac{\beta_{ii}}{\beta_{ji}} = \frac{\beta_{ij}}{\beta_{jj}} = \frac{\beta_{ik}}{\beta_{jk}} \tag{6.15}$$

by which equation (6.12) becomes zero; therefore, the utility function is separable. Equation (6.15) is referred to as simply the *additive restrictions*.[4] With the separability assumption, it is important to note that the translog function is decomposed into a Cobb–Douglas function of translog subaggregates and a translog function of Cobb–Douglas subaggregates. The process for decomposition will be shown in chapter 13.

The indirect utility function is linearly homogeneous if the function, after having its arguments p_i/m and p_j/m multiplied by scalar θ, yields the following result:

$$\ln \theta \sum_i a_i + \ln \theta \sum_i \sum_j \beta_{ij} \ln\left(\frac{p_j}{m}\right) + \frac{1}{2} (\ln \theta)^2 \sum_i \sum_j \beta_{ij} + \ln \nu$$

$$= \ln \theta + \ln \nu \qquad (i \neq j). \tag{6.16}$$

Obviously, the above relationship holds under the conditions:

$$\sum_i a_i = 1 \tag{6.17}$$

$$\sum_j \beta_{ij} = 0 \tag{6.18}$$

$$\sum_i \beta_{ji} = 0 \tag{6.19}$$

$$\sum_i \sum_j \beta_{ij} = 0. \tag{6.20}$$

6.3   Elasticities

The own-price elasticity, cross-price elasticities, and the income elasticity are, respectively, as follows:

$$\epsilon_{ii} = \frac{\partial q_i}{\partial p_i}\frac{p_i}{q_i} = 1 + \frac{\partial S_i}{\partial p_i}\frac{p_i}{S_i} = -1 + \frac{1}{D}\left(\frac{\beta_{ii}}{S_i} - \sum_j \beta_{ij}\right) \qquad (6.21)$$

$$\epsilon_{ij} = \frac{\partial q_i}{\partial p_j}\frac{p_j}{q_i} = \frac{\partial S_i}{\partial p_j}\frac{p_j}{S_i} = \frac{1}{D}\left(\frac{\beta_{ij}}{S_i} - \sum_j \beta_{ij}\right) \qquad (i \neq j) \qquad (6.22)$$

$$\epsilon_{im} = \frac{\partial q_i}{\partial m}\frac{m}{q_i} = 1 + \frac{\partial S_i}{\partial m}\frac{m}{S_i} = 1 + \frac{1}{D}\left(-\frac{\Sigma_j \beta_{ij}}{S_i} + \sum_i \sum_j \beta_{ij}\right). \qquad (6.23)$$

Note that the price and income elasticities of the demand for good i are concerned with terms $\partial q_i/\partial p_i$ and $\partial q_i/\partial m$ instead of terms $\partial S_i/\partial p_i$ and $\partial S_i/\partial m$ and that the definition of expenditure share is $S_i \equiv p_i q_i/m$.

We now turn our attention to the Allen–Uzawa partial elasticities of substitution. They require to have

$$\frac{\partial v}{\partial p_i} = \frac{v}{p_i}\left[a_i + \sum_j \beta_{ij}\ln\left(\frac{p_j}{m}\right)\right] \qquad (6.24)$$

$$\frac{\partial^2 v}{\partial p_i^2} = \frac{v}{p_i^2}\left\{-1 + \beta_{ii} + \left[a_i + \sum_j \beta_{ij}\ln\left(\frac{p_j}{m}\right)\right]^2\right\} \qquad (6.25)$$

$$\frac{\partial^2 v}{\partial p_i\,\partial p_j}\left(=\frac{\partial^2 v}{\partial p_j\,\partial p_i}\right) = \frac{v}{p_i p_j}\left\{\beta_{ij} + \left[a_i + \sum_j \beta_{ij}\ln\left(\frac{p_j}{m}\right)\right]\right.$$
$$\left.\times\left[a_j + \sum_i \beta_{ij}\ln\left(\frac{p_i}{m}\right)\right]\right\} \qquad (i \neq j). \qquad (6.26)$$

The own- and cross-elasticities of substitution are then

$$\sigma_{ii} = \frac{v(\partial^2 v/\partial p_i^2)}{(\partial v/\partial p_i)\,(\partial v/\partial p_i)} = 1 + \frac{\beta_{ii} - a_i - \Sigma_j \beta_{ij}\ln(p_j/m)}{D^2 S_i^2} \qquad (6.27)$$

$$\sigma_{ij} = \frac{v(\partial^2 v/\partial p_i\,\partial p_j)}{(\partial v/\partial p_i)\,(\partial v/\partial p_j)} = 1 + \frac{\beta_{ij}}{D^2 S_i S_j} \qquad (i \neq j). \qquad (6.28)$$

Note that the cross-partial elasticity of substitution σ_{ij}, in particular, is not constant and equal for all pairs of commodities. However, it becomes unity if $\beta_{ij} = 0$, i.e. if the utility function is additive.

6.4 The Almost Ideal Demand System

Deaton and Muellbauer (1980b) proposed a demand system that they call an *almost ideal demand system*. Their model is similar to the Rotterdam model, in that it is an arbitrary first-order linear approximation to a demand system. It is also similar to the translog model because the system is based on translog functions and methods. Therefore, the almost ideal demand model is as general as the Rotterdam model and the translog model and permits more empirical flexibility than either. Deaton and Muellbauer fitted the model to postwar British data. They reject the homogeneity and symmetry restrictions as earlier studies did. They do not discuss elasticities of substitution. I classify and deal with the almost ideal demand model as a specific case of the translog function. I shall briefly discuss here how to derive the almost ideal demand system.

Deaton and Muellbauer begin with a cost (or expenditure) function that is linearly homogeneous in cost of subsistence and cost of bliss.[5] The function is

$$\ln[C(u, p)] = (1 - \mu) \ln[a(p)] + u \ln[b(p)] \qquad (6.29)$$

where C is cost; u is the utility index, $0 < u < 1$; p is the price vector; $a(p)$ is the cost of subsistence; and $b(p)$ is the cost of bliss. They specify the cost of subsistence in translog form and the cost of bliss in Cobb–Douglas translog form and combine them to get

$$\ln C = a_0 + \sum_k a_k \ln p_k + \frac{1}{2} \sum_k \sum_j \beta_{jk} \ln p_k \ln p_j + u\gamma_0 \prod_k p_k^{\gamma_k}$$
$$(6.30)$$

The above equation is called the almost ideal demand system cost function. It is linearly homogeneous in p if

$$\sum_i a_i = 1 \qquad (6.31)$$

$$\sum_j \beta_{kj} = \sum_k \beta_{kj} = 0 \qquad (6.32)$$

$$\sum_j \gamma_j = 0. \qquad (6.33)$$

Note that we have a cost function in the place where the indirect utility function is traditionally introduced.[6]

The demand function can be found by taking the following derivative:

$$\frac{\partial \ln C}{\partial \ln p_i} = \frac{p_i q_i}{C} = S_i \qquad (6.34)$$

where S_i is the cost share of good q_i. The above procedure corresponds to Shephard's lemma (see appendix K) applied to the cost function representing a production technology. Since total cost = total expenditure = total income for a utility maximizing consumer, equation (6.30) and the equation resulting from equation (6.34) are combined together to get the expenditure share function

$$S_i = a_i + \sum_j \beta_{ij} \ln p_j + \beta_i \ln\left(\frac{m}{P}\right) \qquad (6.35)$$

where P is the translog form of the aggregate price index.

6.5 Empirical Remarks

This section summarizes empirical results obtained by Christensen and Manser (1977) and Deaton and Muellbauer (1980b).

Christensen and Manser use the direct and indirect translog utility functions to study US consumption of meat disaggregated into four categories: fish, beef, poultry, and pork. Using annual time series for 1947 to 1971, they estimate two budget share equations (equations (6.5) and (6.6)) by means of the iterative Zellner efficient estimation procedure (IZEF). They test first a number of hypotheses about the additivity of meat demand. Test results show that the additivity hypothesis does not hold for both the direct and the indirect translog utility functions. Christensen and Manser then divide the commodities seven ways into two additive sub-groups. They found group-wise additivity between beef as a sub-group and the remaining three types of meat as another sub-group. With reference to the hypothesis on the explicit additivity (equivalent to the linear additivity) of beef and the additivity (nonlinear additivity) of beef, their results suggest that the indirect utility function is beef-additive and that the direct utility function is explicitly beef-additive. Christensen and Manser calculated price elasticities, expenditure (or income) elasticities, and Allen–Uzawa partial elasticities of substitution. Their results from direct and indirect models indicate that the demand for beef is expenditure elastic and that the demands for poultry and pork are expenditure inelastic. For own-price elasticities, the results of the two models differ. The direct translog model indicates that demand for all four commodities is price responsive, while the indirect translog model indicates that only demand for beef and poultry are price responsive and demand for pork and fish are not. The results for Allen–Uzawa partial elasticities of substitution are quite diverse. In general, the Allen–Uzawa elasticities of substitution for the direct model exceed those for the indirect model for every pair of commodities except for beef and poultry. The largest difference is the degree of substitution of fish for beef, poultry, and pork. In summary, Christensen and Manser conclude that the two models show different results but the overall explanatory power is similar. Although neither set is implausible, their implications for consumer behavior are different. Further research is necessary to reconcile the models.

Deaton and Muellbauer have estimated the almost ideal demand system using postwar British annual data for eight nondurable goods and services from 1954 to 1974, to test homogeneity and symmetry through linear restrictions on fixed parameters. They compare estimated values of R^2 and the Durbin–Watson statistic for the model unrestricted with homogeneity and the model restricted with homogeneity, and conduct an F-test for the validity of imposing homogeneity. They reject homogeneity for food, clothing, housing, and transport. Deaton and Muellbauer also find that the imposition of homogeneity generates positive serial correlation. Testing for symmetry, Deaton and Muellbauer cautiously reject it.

6.6 Summary

The translog utility function is a recent innovation. The function is a translog second-order approximation. It does not require *a priori* homotheticity and additivity assumptions. From the indirect utility function, we derive the expenditure share functions. Roy's identity is used to derive the functions. The expenditure share functions are not linear and are dependent on income. The Allen–Uzawa partial elasticities of substitution are not constant.

The translog function's flexibility is an attractive feature but no longer prevails under additive and explicit-additive conditions. The function is decomposed into a Cobb–Douglas function of translog subaggregates or a translog function of Cobb–Douglas subaggregates under these conditions. As an arbitrary first-order linear approximation to a demand system and a translog-specific case, the almost ideal demand system is as general as the Rotterdam system and translog models and more empirically flexible.

Empirical results of the translog share functions applied to disaggregated meat items by Christensen and Manser do not support the hypothesis of pair-wise additivities between items. Instead, they suggest that there is group-wise additivity between beef and remaining items. The results for own-price elasticities, income elasticities, and Allen–Uzawa partial elasticities of substitution of the direct and indirect translog models are diverse. In general, demand for all four meat items is price responsive. The Allen–Uzawa partial elasticities of substitution suggest that meat items are substitutes for each other.

Empirical results of the almost ideal demand system suggest that demand functions fitted to aggregate time-series data are not homogeneous and probably not symmetric. Although estimating various elasticities is not the primary concern of Deaton and Muellbauer in their study, they report estimated values of own-price elasticities for the restricted model and unrestricted model. However, there is no discussion of the Allen–Uzawa partial elasticities of substitution.

Appendix

A6.1   *Expenditure Share Functions*

Given two goods 1 and 2, the indirect utility function is

$$\ln v = \ln a_0 + a_1 \ln\left(\frac{p_2}{m}\right) + a_2 \ln\left(\frac{p_2}{m}\right) + \frac{1}{2}\beta_{11}\left[\ln\left(\frac{p_1}{m}\right)\right]^2 \tag{1}$$
$$+ \beta_{12} \ln\left(\frac{p_1}{m}\right) \ln\left(\frac{p_2}{m}\right) + \frac{1}{2}\beta_{22}\left[\ln\left(\frac{p_2}{m}\right)\right]^2.$$

Differentiating equation (1) partially with respect to p_1, p_2, and m yields

$$\frac{\partial \ln v}{\partial \ln p_1} = \frac{\partial v}{\partial p_1}\frac{p_1}{v} = a_1 + \beta_{11}\ln\left(\frac{p_1}{m}\right) + \beta_{12}\ln\left(\frac{p_2}{m}\right) \tag{2}$$

$$\frac{\partial \ln v}{\partial \ln p_2} = \frac{\partial v}{\partial p_2}\frac{p_2}{v} = a_2 + \beta_{21}\ln\left(\frac{p_1}{m}\right) + \beta_{22}\ln\left(\frac{p_2}{m}\right) \tag{3}$$

$$\frac{\partial \ln v}{\partial \ln m} = \frac{\partial v}{\partial m}\frac{m}{v} = -\left[a_1 + \beta_{11}\ln\left(\frac{p_1}{m}\right) + \beta_{12}\ln\left(\frac{p_2}{m}\right)\right] -$$

$$- \left[a_2 + \beta_{21} \ln\left(\frac{p_1}{m}\right) + \beta_{22} \ln\left(\frac{p_2}{m}\right) \right]. \tag{4}$$

In accordance with Roy's identity, we have

$$S_1 = \frac{p_1 q_1}{m}$$

$$= - \frac{\partial \ln v/\partial \ln p_1}{\partial \ln v/\partial \ln m}$$

$$= \frac{a_1 + \beta_{11} \ln(p_1/m) + \beta_{12} \ln(p_2/m)}{1 + [\beta_{11} \ln(p_1/m) + \beta_{12} \ln(p_2/m)] + [\beta_{21} \ln(p_1/m) + \beta_{22} \ln(p_2/m)]} \tag{5}$$

$$S_2 = \frac{p_2 q_2}{m}$$

$$= - \frac{\partial \ln v/\partial \ln p_2}{\partial \ln v/\partial \ln m}$$

$$= \frac{a_2 + \beta_{21} \ln(p_1/m) + \beta_{22} \ln(p_2/m)}{1 + [\beta_{11} \ln(p_1/m) + \beta_{12} \ln(p_2/m)] + [\beta_{21} \ln(p_1/m) + \beta_{22} \ln(p_2/m)]}. \tag{6}$$

A6.2 Price and Income Elasticities

The elasticities are as follows.

Own-Price Elasticity

$$\epsilon_{11} = \frac{\partial q_1}{\partial p_1} \frac{p_1}{q_1} = -1 + \frac{\partial S_1}{\partial p_1} \frac{p_1}{S_1} = -1 + \frac{\beta_{12}/S_1 - (\beta_{11} + \beta_{12})}{D} \tag{7}$$

$$\epsilon_{22} = \frac{\partial q_2}{\partial p_2} \frac{p_2}{q_2} = -1 + \frac{\partial S_2}{\partial p_2} \frac{p_2}{S_2} = -1 + \frac{\beta_{22}/S_2 - (\beta_{21} + \beta_{22})}{D} \tag{8}$$

Cross-Price Elasticity

$$\epsilon_{12} = \frac{\partial q_1}{\partial p_2} \frac{p_2}{q_1} = \frac{\partial S_1}{\partial p_2} \frac{p_2}{S_1} = \frac{\beta_{12}/S_1 - (\beta_{12} + \beta_{22})}{D} \tag{9}$$

$$\epsilon_{21} = \frac{\partial q_2}{\partial p_1} \frac{p_1}{q_2} = \frac{\partial S_2}{\partial p_1} \frac{p_1}{S_2} = \frac{\beta_{21}/S_2 - (\beta_{11} + \beta_{21})}{D} \tag{10}$$

Income Elasticity

$$\epsilon_{1m} = \frac{\partial q_1}{\partial m}\frac{m}{q_1} = 1 + \frac{\partial S_1}{\partial m}\frac{m}{S_1}$$

$$= 1 + \frac{(\beta_{11} + 2\beta_{12} + \beta_{22}) - (\beta_{11} + \beta_{12})/S_1}{D} \tag{11}$$

$$\epsilon_{2m} = \frac{\partial q_2}{\partial m}\frac{m}{q_2} = 1 + \frac{\partial S_2}{\partial m}\frac{m}{S_2}$$

$$= 1 + \frac{(\beta_{11} 2\beta_{12} + \beta_{22}) - (\beta_{21} + \beta_{22})/S_2}{D}. \tag{12}$$

where D is the denominator of equation (5).

A6.3   The Allen–Uzawa Partial Elasticities of Substitution (AES)

The own- and cross-Allen–Uzawa partial elasticities of substitution (AES) are as follows.

Own-AES

$$\sigma_{11} = \frac{v\,(\partial^2 v/\partial p_1^2)}{(\partial v/\partial p_1)\,(\partial v/\partial p_1)} = 1 - \frac{1 - \beta_{11}}{D^2 S_1^2} \tag{13}$$

$$\sigma_{22} = \frac{v\,(\partial^2 v/\partial p_2^2)}{(\partial v/\partial p_2)\,(\partial v/\partial p_2)} = 1 - \frac{1 - \beta_{22}}{D^2 S_2^2} \tag{14}$$

Cross-AES

$$\sigma_{12}\,(= \sigma_{21}) = \frac{v\,(\partial^2 v/\partial p_1\,\partial p_2)}{(\partial v/\partial p_1)\,(\partial v/\partial p_2)} = 1 + \frac{\beta_{12}}{D^2 S_1\,S_2}. \tag{15}$$

Notes

1   Barnett (1985) argues that the flexible functional forms behave poorly in general. He introduces the *minflex-Laurent translog function* derived by

the analogous expansion in the logarithm. Also see Diewert and Wales (1987).

2   Shafer and Sonnenschein (1982) have shown that a market demand function has the properties commonly attributed to an individual demand curve when preferences are homothetic and the distribution of income is independent of prices. This is Eisenberg's theorem. However, they admit that, with a fixed distribution of income, homotheticity of individual preferences is sufficient, though not necessary, for a market demand function to be consistent with a consumer demand function. The necessary and sufficient condition for the consistency is subject to further research. Although their arguments are important, they are not directly relevant to us.

3   The direct utility function is homothetic and hence additive as long as the indirect utility function is homothetic. If the direct utility function is, in turn, additive and homothetic, the indirect utility function is additive and homothetic. Since a detailed discussion of the relationships goes beyond the boundaries of this book, interested readers should consult Houthakker (1960), Samuelson (1965a), and Lau (1969).

4   The *explicit additive restrictions* and the *additive restrictions* are often called the *linear additivity* and the *nonlinear additivity*, respectively. For the steps taken to derive equations (6.13) and (6.15), see Berndt and Christensen (1973a, b).

5   Deaton and Muellbauer investigate consumer demand systems on the basis of a cost function (a representation of the corresponding production technology curvature) rather than on the basis of an indirect utility function (a representation of the corresponding direct utility contour). They implicitly assume that an optimizing agent *produces* his utility by combining subsistence and bliss as inputs. This view is similar to that of Becker (1971, pp. 45–7). His *revised* approach to consumer choice suggests that the theory of consumer behavior could use production functions rather than utility functions.

6   See note 7 in chapter 1 and appendix J.

Recommended Reading

Berndt, E.R. and Christensen, L.R. 1973: The internal structure of functional relationships: separability, substitution, and aggregation. *Review of Economic Studies*, July, 403–10.

—— 1973: The translog function and the substitution of equipment, structures, and labor in U.S. manufacturing 1929–68. *Journal of Econometrics*, 1, March, 81–113.

Christensen, L.R., Jorgenson, D.W. and Lau, L.J. 1975: Transcendental logarithmic utility functions. *American Economic Review*, LXV, June, 367–83.

—— and Manser, M.E. 1976: Cost-of-living indexes for U.S. meat and produce, 1947–1971. In N.E. Terleckjy (ed.), *Household and Production*. New York: Columbia University Press.

—— and —— 1977: Estimating U.S. consumer preferences for meat with a flexible utility function. *Journal of Econometrics*, 5, January, 37–53.

Deaton, A. and Muellbauer, J. 1980: *Economics and Consumer Behavior*. Cambridge: Cambridge University Press, 75–80.

—— and —— 1980: An almost ideal demand system. *American Economic Review*, 70, June, 312–26.

Houthakker, H.S. 1960: Additive preferences. *Econometrica*, 28, April, 244–57.

Lau, L.J. 1969: Duality and the structure of utility functions. *Journal of Economic Theory*, 1, 374–96.

Samuelson, P.A. 1965: Using full duality to show that simultaneously additive direct and indirect utilities implies unitary price elasticity of demand. *Econometrica*, 33, 781–96.

7 The Constant-Elasticity-of-Substitution–Translog Utility Function

So far, we have examined the linear logarithmic (Cobb–Douglas) utility function, the Stone–Geary utility function, the Houthakker addilog utility function, the Rotterdam system of demand, the CES and the S-branch utility functions, and the Christensen–Jorgensen–Lau translog utility function. These functions have developed one after the other as the result of economists' continuous search for a more flexible form of utility function. The linear logarithmic function is additive and homothetic, whereas the Stone–Geary function and the Houthakker function are additive and nonhomothetic. The Rotterdam system rests on an *almost* additive utility function. The CES class is homothetic and nonadditive (but separable). The translog utility function does not require us to assume additivity and homotheticity *a priori* as part of the maintained hypothesis. However, the function is vulnerable to additivity conditions. Its separable form collapses to either a Cobb–Douglas function of translog subaggregates or a translog function of Cobb–Douglas subaggregates.[1] The translog function's fragility has motivated economists to search for even more flexible functions.

This chapter introduces the CES–translog utility function and examines its properties. Despite growing concern over functions beyond the translog among economists, Chung (1988) is the only reference on the CES–translog utility function at present. The function is the CES–translog second-order approximation and constitutes a symmetry with the CES–translog production function. Diewert (1971) and Pollak et al. (1984) should be credited for their innovative works on the latter. However, the CES–translog is by no means perfect. It is also broken down to the CES or the translog specifications under certain conditions.

Considering recent trends in production theory, research in consumer behavior should progress toward an advanced form of function beyond even the CES–translog utility function.[2]

Section 7.1 discusses the function and its properties. In section 7.2, we derive and examine the system of expenditures. Section 7.3 deals with empirical results. Section 7.4 summarizes the chapter. The appendix to this chapter gives details for the derivation of the expenditure share functions and elasticities.

7.1 The Function and its Properties

The direct and indirect utility functions are, respectively,

$$-\ln u = a_0 + \frac{1}{1-\sigma}\ln\left[\sum_i a_i q_i^{1-\sigma}\right] + \frac{1}{2}\sum_i\sum_j \beta_{ij}\ln q_i \ln q_j \quad (7.1)$$

and

$$\ln v = a_0 + \frac{1}{1-\sigma}\ln\left[\sum_i a_i \left(\frac{p_i}{m}\right)^{1-\sigma}\right] + \frac{1}{2}\sum_i\sum_j \beta_{ij}\ln\left(\frac{p_i}{m}\right)\ln\left(\frac{p_j}{m}\right)$$
$$(7.2)$$

where q_i is commodity i, p_i is the price of commodity i, m is the income or total expenditure for consumption, $\Sigma a_i = 1$, and $\beta_{ij} = \beta_{ji}$. Note that only the conditions of identifiability ($\Sigma a_i = 1$) and symmetry ($\beta_{ij} = \beta_{ji}$) have been imposed on this function. Also note that the CES–translog utility function reduces to the CES utility function when all of the βs are zero. The first-order derivatives of the utility function, either direct or indirect with respect to q_i or p_i/m (*not* with respect to p_i), should be positive.

Given the indirect utility function, the first-order partial derivatives are

$$\frac{\partial v}{\partial(p_i/m)} = \frac{v}{p_i/m}\left[\frac{a_i (p_i/m)^{1-\sigma}}{\Sigma_k a_k (p_k/m)^{1-\sigma}} + \sum_j \beta_{ij}\ln\left(\frac{p_j}{m}\right)\right] \quad (i,j \in k). \quad (7.3)$$

Since v and p_i/m are positive, positive monotonicity requires only the bracketed term to be positive. Given the estimated parameters obtained from the fitted share functions, the bracketed term must be positive at each data point.

The function is convex if the bordered Hessian is negative semidefinite. Given two goods i and j, we need to get second-order partial derivatives: $\partial^2 v/\partial(p_i/m)^2$ and $\partial^2 v/\partial(p_i/m)\partial(p_j/m)$. The first-order and the second-order partial derivatives are substituted into equation (B.4) in appendix B. The determinant should be positive for convexity.

The CES–translog utility function is not additive but can be separable only under certain conditions. Given the separability condition (6.11) in chapter 6, it is possible to get

$$S_j \frac{\partial S_i}{\partial (p_k/m)} - S_i \frac{\partial S_j}{\partial (p_k/m)} = 0 \qquad (i \neq j \neq k) \qquad (7.4)$$

yielding

$$a_k = 0 \qquad (7.5)$$

$$\beta_{ik} = \beta_{jk} = \beta_{kk} = 0 \qquad (7.6)$$

for separability. The utility function is not homothetic. However, it can be homothetic under the conditions stated below. For scalar θ, we get

$$a_0 + \frac{1}{1-\sigma} \ln\left\{ \sum_i a_i \left[\theta \left(\frac{p_i}{m}\right)^{1-\sigma} \right] \right\} + \frac{1}{2}\left\{ \sum_i \sum_j \beta_{ij} \ln\left[\theta \left(\frac{p_i}{m}\right) \right] \ln\left[\theta \left(\frac{p_j}{m}\right) \right] \right\}$$

$$= \ln \theta + \ln v \qquad (7.7)$$

if $\Sigma_i \beta_{ij} = \Sigma_j \beta_{ij} = 0$ and $\Sigma_i \Sigma_j \beta_{ij} = 0$. Note that the above conditions are similar to the homotheticity conditions for the translog utility function. We would intuitively expect the CES–translog to be homothetic under similar conditions as those for the translog because the CES component included in the CES–translog utility function is the only difference between the translog and the CES–translog. The CES component itself is homogeneous, and therefore should not require additional conditions for homotheticity to those required by the translog function.

It is interesting to know that the utility function, either direct or indirect, is monotonically transformed into a form that is linearly homogeneous in the term p/m if $\Sigma \beta_{ij} = 0$ for all j. More specifically, the CES–translog reduces to the CES form just as the translog reduces to the Cobb–Douglas form. The resulting function should then yield expenditure shares that are independent of total expenditure, as shown in chapter 5. In addition, the CES–translog utility function reduces to the translog form if $\sigma \to 1$, and its share functions reduce to the share functions corresponding to the translog utility function if $\sigma = 1$.

7.2   Expenditure Share Functions and Elasticities

The expenditure share functions in this section are derived from the indirect utility function. The procedures for deriving them are the same as the procedures taken in the previous chapters. We first differentiate the indirect utility function with respect to prices and income and then substitute the differentiated results into Roy's identity. The expenditure share function is

$$S_i = \frac{p_i \, q_i}{m} = \frac{a_i \, (p_i/m)/\Sigma_k \, a_k \, (p_k/m)^{1-\sigma} + \Sigma_j \, \beta_{ij} \, (p_j/m)}{1 + \Sigma_k \Sigma_j \, \beta_{kj} \ln(p_j/m)} \qquad (i, j \in k).$$

$$(7.8)$$

Given the share functions for goods i and j, the own-price elasticity ϵ_{ii} and the cross-price elasticity ϵ_{ij} are

$$\epsilon_{ii} = -1 + \frac{\partial S_i}{\partial p_i} \frac{p_i}{S_i} = -1 + \frac{1}{D} \left[\frac{\beta_{ii} + (1 - \sigma) \, \Omega}{S_i} - \sum_j \beta_{ij} \right] \qquad (7.9)$$

$$\epsilon_{ij} = \frac{\partial S_i}{\partial p_j} \frac{p_j}{S_i} = \frac{1}{D} \left[\frac{\beta_{ij} - (1 - \sigma) \, \Omega}{S_i} - \sum_i \beta_{ij} \right] \qquad (i \neq j) \qquad (7.10)$$

where

$$\Omega = \frac{\Pi_k \, a_k \, (p_k/m)^{1-\sigma}}{[\Sigma_k \, a_k \, (p_k/m)^{1-\sigma}]^2}.$$

It is interesting to observe the systematic differences between equations (6.21) and (7.9) and between equations (6.22) and (7.10).[3]

The income elasticity ϵ_{im} is

$$\epsilon_{im} = 1 + \frac{\partial S_i}{\partial m} \frac{m}{S_i} = 1 + \frac{1}{D} \left[\frac{-\Sigma_j \beta_{ij}}{S_i} + \sum_i \sum_j \beta_{ij} \right]. \qquad (7.11)$$

Finally, the Allen–Uzawa elasticities of substitution are[4]

$$\sigma_{ii} = \frac{\nu \, (\partial^2 \nu/\partial p_i^2)}{(\partial \nu/\partial p_i) \, (\partial \nu/\partial p_i)}$$

$$= 1 + \frac{\beta_{ii} - [\sigma + (a_i/a_j) \, (p_i/p_j)^{1-\sigma}] \, \Omega - \Sigma_j \, \beta_{ij} \ln(p_j/m)}{D^2 \, S_i^2} \qquad (7.12)$$

$$\sigma_{ij} = \frac{\nu\,(\partial^2\nu/\partial p_i\,\partial p_j)}{(\partial\nu/\partial p_i)\,(\partial\nu/\partial p_j)}$$

$$= 1 + \frac{\beta_{ij} - (1 - \sigma)\,\Omega}{D^2 S_i S_j}. \tag{7.13}$$

All of the elasticities above require the estimated values of parameters included in the expenditure share functions to be known.

Detailed procedures for deriving the share functions and various elasticities are presented in the appendix to this chapter.

7.3 Empirical Remarks

I have estimated the expenditure share equation (7.8) by means of Zellner's iterative efficient method.[5] The main objective of the estimation was to compare the results to equation (7.8) and equation (6.6). For this reason, the same data were used as those used by Christensen and Manser (1977).

The primary results are as follows.

1 The estimated value of σ is 1.388, which is highly significant (t value = 25.646). As noted earlier, the CES–translog share function does not collapse to the translog share function unless $\sigma = 1$. Therefore, the specification of the CES–translog expenditure share function is valid.

2 None of the estimated values of β_{ij} and $\Sigma\,\beta_{ij}$ are zero, suggesting that it is improper to assume additivity and homotheticity. These results reject the CES specification.

3 Estimated values of the cross-price elasticities and the Allen–Uzawa partial elasticities of substitution suggest that all meats are *net* substitutes for each other ($\sigma_{ij} > 0$). However, fish and beef, fish and poultry, pork and beef are gross substitutes ($\epsilon_{ij} > 0$) only in the case of a change in beef price, and pork and poultry only in the case of a change in poultry price.

4 Estimated values of the income elasticities suggest that the demand for fish, poultry, and pork is income-elastic, whereas the demand for beef is not. Contrary to the results obtained by Christensen and Manser, beef, as a necessity and the major meat consumption item in the United States, is the only meat item that behaves according to Engel's law.

7.4   Summary

This chapter has examined a CES–translog utility function, the innovation regarded as the last word in the 1980s. Its expenditure share equations are certainly more flexible than the translog specifications, permitting a wider range of substitution possibilities than in the case of the translog function. The CES–translog utility function is, however, by no means perfect. The function reduces to either the CES form or the translog form under certain conditions.

The estimated value of the elasticity of substitution (σ) is not unity, implying that the CES–translog specification is valid for the meat items under consideration. The results also suggest that it is wrong to assume additivity and homotheticity. The Allen–Uzawa partial elasticities of substitution suggest that all meat items are net substitutes for each other. Contrary to Christensen and Manser's results, beef is not income-elastic.

Appendix

A7.1   Derivation of the Expenditure Share Equations

Given two goods 1 and 2, the indirect CES–translog utility function is

$$\ln v = a_0 + \frac{1}{1-\sigma} \ln\left[a_1 \left(\frac{p_1}{m}\right)^{1-\sigma} + a_2 \left(\frac{p_2}{m}\right)^{1-\sigma} \right] + \frac{1}{2}\left\{ \beta_{11}\left[\ln\left(\frac{p_1}{m}\right)\right]^2 \right.$$

$$\left. + \beta_{22}\left[\ln\left(\frac{p_2}{m}\right)\right]^2 + 2\beta_{12}\ln\left(\frac{p_1}{m}\right)\ln\left(\frac{p_2}{m}\right)\right\}. \tag{1}$$

Differentiating the above function with respect to p_1, p_2, and m, and then rearranging terms, we get

$$\frac{\partial v}{\partial p_1}\frac{p_1}{v} = \frac{a_1\,(p_1/m)^{1-\sigma}}{a_1\,(p_1/m)^{1-\sigma} + a_2\,(p_2/m)^{1-\sigma}} + \beta_{11}\ln\left(\frac{p_1}{m}\right) + \beta_{12}\ln\left(\frac{p_2}{m}\right) \tag{2}$$

$$\frac{\partial v}{\partial p_2}\frac{p_2}{v} = \frac{a_2\,(p_2/m)^{1-\sigma}}{a_1\,(p_1/m)^{1-\sigma} + a_2\,(p_2/m)^{1-\sigma}} + \beta_{12}\ln\left(\frac{p_1}{m}\right) + \beta_{22}\ln\left(\frac{p_2}{m}\right) \tag{3}$$

$$\frac{\partial v}{\partial m}\frac{m}{v} = -1 - \left[\beta_{11}\ln\left(\frac{p_1}{m}\right) + \beta_{12}\ln\left(\frac{p_1}{m}\right)\right] - \left[\beta_{12}\ln\left(\frac{p_1}{m}\right) + \beta_{22}\ln\left(\frac{p_2}{m}\right)\right].$$

$$\tag{4}$$

If we substitute equations (2), (3), and (4) into Roy's identity (presented in appendix H), we get

$$S_1 = \left\{ a_1\left(\frac{p_1}{m}\right)^{1-\sigma} \left[a_1\left(\frac{p_1}{m}\right)^{1-\sigma} + a_2\left(\frac{p_2}{m}\right)^{1-\sigma} \right]^{-1} + \beta_{11}\ln\left(\frac{p_1}{m}\right) + \beta_{12}\ln\left(\frac{p_2}{m}\right) \right\}$$

$$\times \left\{ 1 + \left[\beta_{11}\ln\left(\frac{p_1}{m}\right) + \beta_{12}\ln\left(\frac{p_2}{m}\right) \right] + \left[\beta_{12}\ln\left(\frac{p_1}{m}\right) + \beta_{22}\ln\left(\frac{p_2}{m}\right) \right] \right\}^{-1}$$

$$(5)$$

$$S_2 = \left\{ a_2\left(\frac{p_1}{m}\right)^{1-\sigma} \left[a_1\left(\frac{p_1}{m}\right)^{1-\sigma} + a_2\left(\frac{p_2}{m}\right)^{1-\sigma} \right]^{-1} + \beta_{12}\ln\left(\frac{p_1}{m}\right) + \beta_{22}\ln\left(\frac{p_2}{m}\right) \right\}$$

$$\times 1 + \left[\beta_{11}\ln\left(\frac{p_1}{m}\right) + \beta_{12}\ln\left(\frac{p_2}{m}\right) \right] + \left[\beta_{12}\ln\left(\frac{p_1}{m}\right) + \beta_{22}\ln\left(\frac{p_2}{m}\right) \right] \right\}^{-1}.$$

$$(6)$$

A7.2 The Own-Price Elasticities, the Cross-Price Elasticities, and the Income Elasticities

The elasticities for good 1 are as follows.

Own-Price Elasticity

$$\epsilon_{11} = -1 + \frac{\partial S_1}{\partial p_1}\frac{p_1}{S_1} = -1 + \frac{D\,(\partial N/\partial p_1) - N\,(\partial D/\partial p_1)}{D^2}\frac{p_1}{S_1}$$

$$= -1 + \frac{(1-\sigma)\,\Omega + \beta_{11} - (\beta_{11} + \beta_{12})\,S_1}{DS_1} \tag{7}$$

Cross-Price Elasticity

$$\epsilon_{12} = \frac{\partial S_1}{\partial p_2}\frac{p_2}{S_1} = \frac{D\,(\partial N/\partial p_2) - N\,(\partial D/\partial p_2)}{D^2}\frac{p_2}{S_1}$$

$$= \frac{-(1-\sigma)\,\Omega + \beta_{12} - (\beta_{21} + \beta_{22})\,S_1}{DS_1} \tag{8}$$

Income Elasticity

$$\epsilon_{1m} = 1 + \frac{\partial S_1}{\partial m}\frac{m}{S_1} = 1 + \frac{D\,\partial N/\partial m - N\,\partial D/\partial m}{D^2}\frac{m}{S_1}$$

$$= 1 + \frac{-(\beta_{11} + \beta_{12}) + (\beta_{11} + 2\beta_{12} + \beta_{22})\,S_1}{DS_1} \tag{9}$$

where N is the numerator of equation (5), D is the denominator of equation (5), and

$$\Omega = \frac{a_1\,(p_1/m)^{1-\sigma}\,a_2\,(p_2/m)^{1-\sigma}}{[a_1\,(p_1/m)^{1-\sigma} + a_2\,(p_2/m)^{1-\sigma}]^2}.$$

The elasticities for good 2 can be derived through the same procedure as for good 1.

A7.3   The Allen–Uzawa Partial Elasticity of Substitution

We need to take the second-order partial derivatives of equation (1) with respect to p_1 and p_2 to get

$$\frac{\partial^2 v}{\partial p_1^2} = \frac{v}{p_1^2}S_1^2\,D^2 + \frac{v}{p_1^2}\left\{-\left[\frac{a_1\,(p_1/m)^{1-\sigma}}{a_2\,(p_2/m)^{1-\sigma}} + \sigma\right]\Omega\right.$$

$$\left. + \beta_{11}\left[1 - \ln\!\left(\frac{p_1}{m}\right)\right] - \beta_{12}\ln\!\left(\frac{p_2}{m}\right)\right\} \tag{10}$$

$$\frac{\partial^2 v}{\partial p_1\,\partial p_2} = v\left[-(1-\sigma)\frac{1}{p_1}\frac{1}{p_2}\,\Omega + \beta_{12}\frac{1}{p_1}\frac{1}{p_2}\right]$$

$$+ \frac{\partial v}{\partial p_2}\left[\frac{\Omega}{a_2\,(p_2/m)^{1-\sigma}}\frac{1}{p_1} + \beta_{11}\ln\!\left(\frac{p_1}{m}\right)\frac{1}{p_1} + \beta_{12}\ln\!\left(\frac{p_2}{m}\right)\frac{1}{p_1}\right]. \tag{11}$$

Substituting equations (2) and (10) and equations (2), (3) and (11) into the respective formula for the own- and cross-Allen–Uzawa partial elasticities of substitution (AES) yields the following.

Own-AES

$$\sigma_{11} = \frac{v\,(\partial^2 v/\partial p_1^2)}{(\partial v/\partial p_1)\,(\partial v/\partial p_1)}$$

$$= 1 + \left\{ \beta_{11} - \left[\sigma + \frac{a_1\,(p_1/m)^{1-\sigma}}{a_2\,(p_2/m)^{1-\sigma}} \right] \Omega \right.$$

$$\left. - \left[\beta_{11} \ln\!\left(\frac{p_1}{m}\right) + \beta_{12} \ln\!\left(\frac{p_2}{m}\right) \right] \right\} (D^2 S_1^2)^{-1} \qquad (12)$$

Cross-AES

$$\sigma_{12}\,(=\sigma_{21}) = \frac{v\,(\partial^2 v/\partial p_1\,\partial p_2)}{(\partial v/\partial p_1)\,(\partial v/\partial p_2)} = 1 + \frac{\beta_{12} - (1-\sigma)\,\Omega}{D^2 S_1 S_2}. \qquad (13)$$

Notes

1 See chapter 13.
2 See Diewert (1971) for the generalized Leontief production function, Pollak et al. (1984) for the CES–translog production function, and Behrman et al. (1992) for the CET–CES-generalized Leontief production function.
3 Equations (7.9) and (7.10) include additional terms $(1-\sigma)\Omega/S_i$ and $-(1-\sigma)\Omega/S_i$, respectively. Note that equation (7.9) reduces to equation (6.21) and equation (7.10) to equation (6.22) if the elasticity of substitution σ equals one.
4 Note that equations (7.12) and (7.13) reduce to equations (6.27) and (6.28), respectively, if $\sigma = 1$.
5 Chung (1988) is the only reference at present.

Recommended Reading

Berndt, E.R. 1973: The translog function and the substitution of equipment, structures, and labor in U.S. manufacturing 1929–68. *Journal of Econometrics*, 1, March, 81–113.
—— and Christensen, L.R. 1973: The internal structure of functional relationships: separability, substitution, and aggregation. *Review of Economic Studies*, July, 403–10.

Blackorby, C., Primont, D. and Russell, R.R. 1977: On testing separability restrictions with flexible functional forms. *Journal of Econometrics*, 5, January, 195–209.

Christensen, L.R., Jorgenson, D.W. and Lau, L.J. 1975: Transcendental logarithmic utility functions. *American Economic Review*, LXV, June, 367–83.

—— and Manser, M.E. 1976: Cost-of-living indexes for U.S. meat and produce, 1947–1971. In N.E. Terleckjy (ed.), *Household and Production*, New York: Columbia University Press.

—— and —— 1977: Estimating U.S. consumer preferences for meat with a flexible utility function. *Journal of Econometrics*, 5, January, 37–53.

Chung, J.W. 1988: The CES–translog utility function and consumer expenditure system: theory and application. Presented at 1988 North American Winter Meetings of the Econometric Society, New York, December.

Denny, M. and Fuss, M. The use of approximation analysis to test for separability and the existence of consistent aggregates. *American Economic Review*, 67, June, 404–18.

Diewert, W.E. 1971: An application of the Shepard duality theorem: a generalized Leontief production function. *Journal of Political Economy*, 79, 481–507.

Pollak, R.A., Sickles, R.C. and Wales, T.J. 1984: The CES–translog: specification and estimation of a new cost function. *Review of Economics and Statistics*, 66, November, 602–7.

Part II

Production Functions

8 The Cobb–Douglas Production Function

It has been over half a century since Charles W. Cobb and Paul H. Douglas (1928) introduced and tested the so-called Cobb–Douglas production function. The origin of the production function, as recalled by Douglas himself, is interesting.[1] In the spring of 1927, when he was temporarily lecturing at Amherst College, he charted three curves for labor, capital, and output in US manufacturing from 1899 to 1922 on logarithmic paper and observed correlations among the three series. The output curve lay from one-third to one-quarter of the distance between the labor curve and the capital curve. Douglas was not a mathematician. To formalize the relationship, he visited Cobb, who was on the mathematics faculty of Amherst. Almost immediately, they devised a mathematical function which has since been known as the Cobb–Douglas production function. In their seminal paper, they suggested that there are laws of production that govern the proportions of productive factors. The actual distribution of output into capital and labor was consistent with the estimated values of the respective parameters and hence the productive factors received their marginal products. This is the theoretical basis for the *value-added specification* of an aggregate production function relating aggregate output to aggregate input of capital and labor services. As the first neoclassical production function stated in an explicit form, the Cobb–Douglas function has been widely employed by later economists, particularly in the 1960s, for empirical analyses of production and factor markets. Among countless studies confirming the usefulness of the Cobb–Douglas production function, the following are frequently cited as major references: Douglas (1948), Walters (1963), Intriligator (1965), Nerlove (1965,

1967), Moroney (1967), Griliches and Ringstad (1971), Lau and Yoto-poulos (1971), and Griliches (1980).

The Cobb–Douglas function is monotonic and convex. It assumes additivity and homotheticity. Among the many limitations of the Cobb–Douglas production function are that the Allen–Uzawa partial elasticity of substitution is restricted to unity and the factor share of output is constant. These results stem from the additivity and homotheticity assumptions imposed on the production function.

Section 8.1 presents the production function and examines its properties. Section 8.2 deals with the issues on the factor-intensity. Section 8.3 derives the demand for factors. In section 8.4, we discuss the duality between output and cost and derive the factor shares of output and the Allen–Uzawa partial elasticities of substitution. Section 8.5 derives the price equation corresponding to the Cobb–Douglas production function. Section 8.6 presents empirical results. Section 8.7 summarizes the chapter.

8.1 The Function and its Properties

The function is written as

$$y = f(x_1, \ldots, x_n) = A \prod_{i=1}^{n} x_i^{a_i} \tag{8.1}$$

where y is output, x_i is input i, $A > 0$, $0 < a_i < 1$, and $\Sigma_i a_i = 1$.

The Cobb–Douglas production function is a monotonically increasing function. As shown below, its marginal product (MP) is always positive:

$$MP_i = \frac{\partial y}{\partial x_i} = a_i \frac{y}{x_i} > 0 . \tag{8.2}$$

The theory of marginal productivity suggests that, at the optimum, we have

$$MP_i = \frac{w_i}{p} \tag{8.3}$$

where w_i is the price of input i and p is the price of output. The ratio of two marginal products is referred to as the marginal rate of technical substitution (MRTS). Given equation (8.3), it is possible to have

$$\frac{MP_i}{MP_j} = \frac{a_i x_j}{a_j x_i} = \frac{w_i}{w_j} \qquad (i \neq j) . \tag{8.4}$$

Equation (8.4) represents the expansion path. For the constant input prices, the expansion path is linear in the input space. We will discuss the implications of the linear expansion path in section 8.3.

The Cobb–Douglas function is convex to the origin. For convexity, the bordered Hessian must be negative definite. The second-order bordered Hessian requires us to obtain second-order partial derivatives of the production function. The differentiated results are

$$\frac{\partial y^2}{\partial x_i^2} = -\frac{a_i (1 - a_i) y}{x_i^2} < 0 \tag{8.5}$$

$$\frac{\partial^2 y}{\partial x_i \partial x_j} = a_i (1 - a_i) \frac{y}{x_i x_j} > 0 \qquad (i \neq j) . \tag{8.6}$$

In particular, a negative feature of equation (8.5) implies that the Cobb–Douglas production function satisfies the law of diminishing marginal product. We substitute equations (8.2), (8.5), and (8.6) into equation (B.4) in appendix B to obtain

$$|\overline{H}_2| = [a_i^2 (1 - a_i) + a_i (1 - a_i)^2] \frac{y^3}{x_i^2 x_j^2} > 0 \qquad (i \neq j) . \tag{8.7}$$

Note that the bordered Hessian is positive and that therefore the production function is strictly quasi-concave.[2] Figure 1.1 presented in chapter 1 is directly applicable to the Cobb–Douglas production function. The two regularity conditions – monotonicity and convexity – suffice for the Cobb–Douglas to be *well behaved*. If the isoquant is concave, the firm hires only one factor of production. Therefore the concave isoquant cannot be standard.

By assumption (see equation (8.1)), the Cobb–Douglas function is known as homogeneous of degree one or linearly homogeneous. Algebraically, we have the following relationship:

$$A \prod_i (\theta x_i)^{a_i} = \theta y \tag{8.8}$$

where θ is a scalar. This result implies that if all factors of production are increased in a given proportion ($\theta = 1, 2, \ldots$), output increases in exactly the same proportion. This characteristic of production technology is called constant returns to scale. Figure 8.1 shows constant returns to scale of two inputs. A typical phenomenon observed under linear homogeneity is Euler's theorem. The theorem suggests that, if each input is paid its marginal product, the total product is exhausted. Each parameter directly indicates the share of output paid to the respective input. From equations (8.2) and (8.3), we obtain

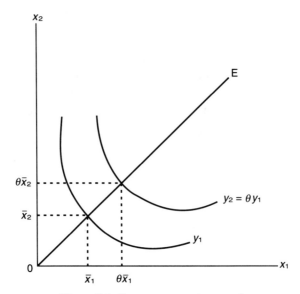

Figure 8.1 Constant returns to scale.

$$a_i = \frac{w_i\, x_i}{p\ y}\ . \tag{8.9}$$

Note that the Cobb–Douglas function yields a constant factor share. Equation (8.9) implies that each input receives its marginal product because it can be rewritten as

$$a_i\, y = MP_i x_i\ . \tag{8.10}$$

Adding up the above receipt for all inputs then exhausts total product, i.e.

$$\sum_i a_i\, y = y = \sum_i MP_i x_i = y \sum_i \left(\frac{a_i}{x_i}\right) x_i\ . \tag{8.11}$$

The above equation is called Euler's theorem and has played the central role in the marginal product theory of income distribution. However, it implies that the long-run profit is zero at any price and therefore that the conventional profit-maximization procedure is broken down.

If the value of parameter a_i is greater than the value of parameter a_j, the output share of input i is greater than the share of input j. It also follows that the ratio of the parameters a_i/a_j indicates relative factor shares, i.e.

$$\frac{a_i}{a_j} = \frac{w_i x_i/p\ y}{w_j x_j/p\ y} = \frac{w_i x_i}{w_j x_j} \qquad (i \neq j) \ . \tag{8.12}$$

This ratio implies that equi-proportional changes in both relative factor prices (an increase) and relative inputs (a decrease) keep the relative shares of inputs constant. The total differential of logarithmic version of equation (8.9) also implies the wage-price guideposts given by the Council of Economic Advisors in the 1960s: an increase in the money wage rate and labor productivity by the same percentage amount leaves the price level unchanged. Note that the relationship between the money wage rate and productivity is rigid.

The Cobb–Douglas function is not additive, as the function is stated (see equation (8.6)). However, its logarithmic transformation ensures additivity because

$$\frac{\partial^2 \ln y}{\partial \ln x_i\, \partial \ln x_j} = 0 \qquad (i \neq j) \ . \tag{8.13}$$

The elasticity of substitution between factors i and j is unity *a priori* for all i and j.[3] Substituting equation (8.4) into

$$\sigma \equiv \frac{\text{Percentage change in } x_i/x_j}{\text{Percentage change in } w_j/w_i}$$

gives

$$\sigma = \frac{\mathrm{d}(x_i/x_j)}{\mathrm{d}(w_j/w_i)} \frac{w_j/w_i}{x_i/x_j} = \frac{a_i\, a_j}{a_j\, a_i} = 1 \qquad (i \neq j) \ . \tag{8.14}$$

Note that the elasticity of substitution can be unitary even if $a_i + a_j \neq 1$. The result implies that the input ratio x_i/x_j increases by 1 percent as the input–price ratio w_j/w_i increases by 1 percent. This particular degree of substitution of x_i for x_j is extremely restrictive. It is helpful to illustrate graphically the elasticity of substitution. Let us call two inputs x_i and x_j capital and labor, respectively, for our convenience. In figure 8.2 below, angles κ_1 and κ_2 represent the capital–labor ratios and angles ω_1 and ω_2 represent the wage–rental ratios. Assuming that point E_1 is the initial equilibrium point, the elasticity of substitution equals the ratio of the decrease in the gradient to the decrease in the tangent gradient, i.e. $[(\kappa_2 - \kappa_1)/\kappa_1]/[(\omega_2 - \omega_1)/\omega_1]$. In the case of Cobb–Douglas, values of the numerator and the denominator are the same, yielding $\sigma = 1$.

The elasticity of substitution has important policy implications. It determines the relative factor shares of output. Given the definition

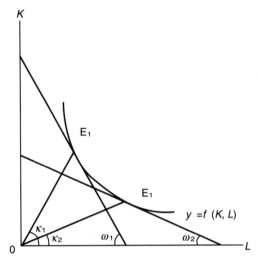

Figure 8.2 Capital–labor ratios and wage–rental ratios.

of σ (equation (8.14)), the capital–labor ratio will vary when the wage–rental ratio changes. Then the relative factor shares will also vary. If $\sigma = 1$, however, the capital–labor ratio and the wage–rental ratio rise by the same proportion; thus capital's share rises exactly the same as labor's share. The relative factor shares of output will remain constant, i.e. a_i/a_j stays the same.[4]

8.2   Factor Intensity

The Cobb–Douglas production function provides a convenient tool for understanding the factor intensity which is a crucial concept for the modern theory of international trade, often referred to as the Heckscher–Ohlin theory. The theory suggests that a capital-abundant country exports capital-intensive commodities and imports labor-intensive commodities. If the capital–labor ratio ($k = K/L$) of output y_1 (κ_1) is greater than that of output y_2 (κ_2) for the given wage–rental ratio ($\omega = w/r$), output y_1 is called the capital-intensive good whereas output y_2 is called the labor-intensive good. Figure 8.3 shows the case of Cobb–Douglas production technology, where constant returns to scale prevails. We can also check the factor intensity with equation (8.4), which can be rewritten as

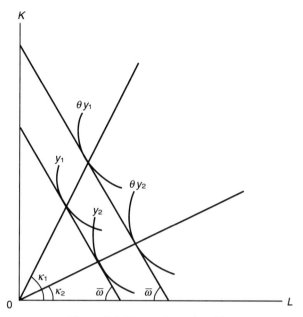

Figure 8.3 Factor intensity (1).

$$\frac{x_i}{x_j} = \frac{a_i \, w_j}{a_j \, w_i} \quad (i \neq j) \,. \tag{8.15}$$

Equation (8.15) establishes a well-defined space for mappings. Given two different slopes and the zero intercept for two different industries as shown in equation (8.15), the two schedules do not intersect each other, implying that, for the given wage–rental ratio, industries are uniquely characterized in terms of the factor intensity. For example, industry h is labor intensive, whereas industry k is capital intensive. In the logarithmic space, shown in figure 8.4, we have MW > NW for OW. In other words, factor-intensity reversal never occurs. However, the factor intensity of an industry may be correlated with that of another industry. Assuming perfect competition, under which each of the factor prices is the same across industries, the relative factor intensity is

$$\frac{x_{ih}/x_{jh}}{x_{ik}/x_{jk}} = \frac{a_{ih}/a_{jh}}{a_{ik}/a_{jk}} \quad (i \neq j; h \neq k) \,. \tag{8.16}$$

It is important to know whether or not the factor intensities of a

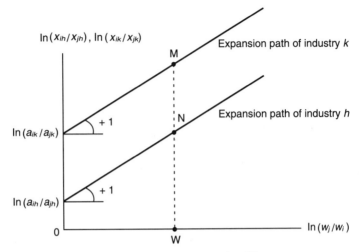

Figure 8.4 Factor intensity (2).

particular output are variable. If the capital–output and labor–output ratios are constant, there is no substitution between capital and labor. The relative factor intensity is independent of the relative factor price, implying that the factor intensity of industry i and the factor intensity of industry j are proportional. Unless the term on the right-hand side of equation (8.16) is zero, the factor intensities of industries h and k are correlated.

Let us now investigate the relationship between the factor–price ratio and the commodity–price ratio. This relationship is particularly important in international economics. It is assumed that each industry employs factors in the lowest-cost proportion under full employment of fixed total quantities of capital and labor. The competitive condition for equilibrium allocations of inputs is equation (8.4). As shown in figure 8.5, it is assumed that good y_1 is capital intensive whereas y_2 is labor intensive. It is also assumed that the factor-intensity reversal will never occur. Note that the capital–labor ratio of good y_1 (κ_1) is always higher than the capital–labor ratio of good y_2 (κ_2) for the given wage–rental ratio (ω_1).

As the wage rate decreases relatively more than the rental cost (or the wage rate decreases whereas the rental cost increases or the wage rate decreases when the rental cost remains the same) and thus the wage–rental ratio decreases from ω_1 to ω_2, the capital–labor ratios decrease in both industries from κ_1 to κ_1' and from κ_2 to κ_2', respectively.

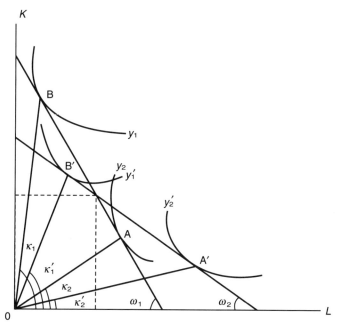

Figure 8.5 Factor–price ratios and factor intensities.

The capital-intensive industry contracts output from y_1 to y_1' or remains the same and the labor-intensive industry expands from y_2 to y_2'. Thus the price of the labor-intensive good y_2 (p_2) decreases and the relative price of the labor-intensive good, *ceteris paribus*, decreases.[5] The marginal product of labor decreases, whereas the marginal product of capital increases as the result of smaller capital–labor ratios in both industries. Therefore, the marginal rate of technical substitution (MRTS = MP_L/MP_K) decreases and thus the wage–rental ratio decreases. Under full employment of capital and labor, the relative output share of labor decreases. In contrast, a higher relative price of the labor-intensive commodity (with a protective trade policy – tariffs or nontariff barriers) will result in a higher wage–rental ratio, and hence a higher relative output share of labor (wL/rK).[6] The positive relationship between the factor–price ratio and the commodity–price ratio is shown in figure 8.6. The one-to-one correspondence (or the univalence of mapping) shown in the figure is the analytical foundation for the modern theory of international trade. The positive correlation between a protective trade policy and the larger output share of the scarcer factor in the protective country is the basis of the

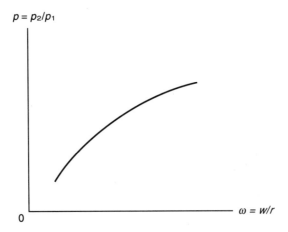

Figure 8.6 Relationship between commodity–price ratio and factor–price ratio.

Stolper–Samuelson theorem, the only theorem that addresses income distribution in the context of international trade.

8.3   Derived Demand for Productive Factors

Traditionally, economists derive demand for factors from two different principles: profit maximization and cost minimization.

The profit-maximization method involves unconstrained maximization of profit. The objective function to be maximized is

$$\pi = R - C \tag{8.17}$$

where π is total profit, R is total revenue, and C is total cost. Given production function (8.1), the total revenue is

$$R = p\,y = p\,A \prod_i x_i^{a_i}. \tag{8.18}$$

The cost equation is

$$C = \sum_i w_i\,x_i + b \tag{8.19}$$

where b is total fixed cost. Equation (8.17) is specified as

$$\pi = p\,A \prod_i x^{a_i} - \sum_i w_i\,x_i - b. \tag{8.20}$$

The first-order condition is

$$\frac{\partial \pi}{\partial x_i} = p \, a_i \frac{y}{x_i} - w_i = 0 \, . \tag{8.21}$$

Note that the first term on the right-hand side is the marginal revenue product ($p\mathrm{MP}_i$), which is equal to the money wage at the optimum. This relationship itself is the demand for a factor, as standard micro-economics textbooks show. Of course, we assume that the second-order condition for profit maximization holds. The demand function for factor i obtained from equation (8.21) is

$$x_i = a_i \left(\frac{w_i}{p} \right)^{-1} y \, . \tag{8.22}$$

The cost-minimization method of deriving factor demands begins with the augmented objective function.

$$\mathscr{L}(x; \lambda) = \sum_i w_i x_i + b + \lambda \left(y - A \prod_i x^{a_i} \right) \, . \tag{8.23}$$

The function minimizes the total cost subject to the production function. The first-order conditions for a minimum of the Lagrangian function are

$$\frac{\partial \mathscr{L}}{\partial x_i} = w_i - \lambda \, a_i \frac{y}{x_i} = 0 \tag{8.24}$$

$$\frac{\partial \mathscr{L}}{\partial \lambda} = y - A \prod_i x_i^{a_i} = 0 \, . \tag{8.25}$$

Equation (8.24) yields equation (8.4), the equation representing the expansion path along which the firm achieves the least-cost factor combination. It is important to keep in mind that a homogeneous production function gives a linear expansion path. The linear feature implies that the optimal input ratio remains the same for constant factor prices. In other words, it is independent of output. Rewriting equation (8.24), we can obtain the demand function for factor i:

$$x_i = \frac{a_i \, w_j}{a_j \, w_i} x_j \, . \tag{8.26}$$

It is interesting to note that the two different principles yield two different specifications of the function. However, none of the specifi-cations is satisfactory, because values of the parameters associated with the real wages in equation (8.22) and the relative wages in equation (8.26) are restricted to −1 and 1, respectively, in the logarithmic form of both equations.

8.4   Output–Cost Duality and Allen–Uzawa Partial Elasticities of Substitution

In this section we discuss Shephard's duality existing between the Cobb–Douglas production function and the corresponding cost function. The rationale for this modern approach to the theory of production is that a production technology is identically represented by either the production function or the corresponding cost function.

We combine the Cobb–Douglas production function (equation (8.1)), its MRTS equation (equation (8.4)) and the cost equation (equation (8.19)) in accordance with the procedures taken in appendix J to obtain the cost function corresponding to the Cobb–Douglas production function. The cost function transformed into logarithmic form is written as

$$\ln C = \ln \zeta + \sum_i a_i \ln w_i + \ln y \qquad (8.27)$$

where $\zeta = (A\Pi_i a_i^{a_i})^{-1}$. Note that the cost function is of the Cobb–Douglas form. Parameter a_i appears orderly in accordance with the production function. Clearly, a production technology is identically represented by either the production function or the corresponding cost function.

The new approach to the cost-minimizing factor shares (thus demand for factors) is based upon the cost function (equation (8.27)).

Differentiate the total cost function with respect to each of the factor prices, i.e.

$$\frac{\partial \ln C}{\partial \ln w_i} = \frac{\partial C}{\partial w_i}\frac{w_i}{C} = \frac{x_i w_i}{C} = S_i = a_i \qquad (8.28)$$

where $\partial \ln C/\partial \ln w_i = x_i$ by Shephard's lemma[7] and S_i is the cost share of input x_i. Equality $S_i = a_i$ shown in equation (8.28) proves that the cost share and output share of input x_i are the same and constant. Note that equations (8.9) and (8.28) are identical. As shown in appendix J, Shephard's duality holds for any production function. Shephard's lemma helps avoid the tedious algebra involved in finding a constrained cost minimum, which can be especially hard when the production function is complex.

We now turn our attention to the Allen–Uzawa partial elasticities of substitution.[8] R.G.D. Allen (1938) first derived the formula (see appendix L) and Hirofumi Uzawa (1962) elaborated it. The so-called Allen–Uzawa partial elasticity of substitution is

$$\sigma_{ij} = \frac{C(\partial^2 C/\partial w_i \partial w_j)}{(\partial C/\partial w_i)(\partial C/\partial w_j)} \quad (i \neq j) . \tag{8.29}$$

If $i = j$, the Allen–Uzawa partial elasticity of substitution becomes

$$\sigma_{ii} = \frac{C(\partial^2 C/\partial w_i^2)}{(\partial C/\partial w_i)(\partial C/\partial w_i)} . \tag{8.30}$$

It is therefore necessary to differentiate equation (8.27) successively. The results are

$$\frac{\partial C}{\partial w_i} = a_i \frac{C}{w_i} \tag{8.31}$$

$$\frac{\partial^2 C}{\partial w_i^2} = a_i \frac{(a_i - 1)C}{w_i^2} \tag{8.32}$$

$$\frac{\partial^2 C}{\partial w_i \partial w_j} = a_i a_j \frac{C}{w_i w_j} . \tag{8.33}$$

Substituting equations (8.31) and (8.32) into equation (8.30) yields the Allen–Uzawa own elasticity of substitution:

$$\sigma_{ii} = -\frac{1 - a_i}{a_i} . \tag{8.34}$$

Substituting equations (8.31) and (8.33) into equation (8.29) above gives the Allen–Uzawa cross-partial elasticity of substitution:

$$\sigma_{ij} = 1 . \tag{8.35}$$

Observe that the value of the Allen–Uzawa cross-partial elasticity of substitution is the same as that of the elasticity of substitution obtained in section 8.1 (see equation (8.14)).

As an additive and homogeneous production function, the Cobb–Douglas function does indeed yield restrictive results: the Allen–Uzawa partial elasticity of substitution is 1 (constant and identical) for all pairs of inputs. This result is not attractive.

8.5   The Price Equation

For an analysis of price behavior (inflation), the price equation should be properly grounded in theory. The price equation corresponding to the Cobb–Douglas production function is obtained from the processes required to minimize the cost.

Equation (8.24) raised to power a_i yields

$$\lambda^{a_i} a_i^{a_i} y^{a_i} x^{-a_i} = w_i^{a_i} . \tag{8.36}$$

For all inputs multiplied together, it is possible to obtain

$$\lambda = \phi \prod_i w_i^{a_i} \tag{8.37}$$

where $\phi = \Pi_i \, a_i^{a_i}$. The Shephard–Samuelson theorem suggests that the Lagrange multiplier λ is the same as the marginal cost (MC) and average cost (AC), which is the same as the price of output, under perfect competition in the long run.[9] Therefore, equation (8.37) is a price function that provides a theoretical basis for an empirical analysis of the cost-push inflation. It also becomes the unit cost function, which we will use to derive the factor-share functions in chapter 10.

8.6   Empirical Remarks

Cobb and Douglas (1928) tried to develop and measure a formula, the Cobb–Douglas production function, to show that there are laws of production. Their empirical results suggest that there are definite and observable laws of production that govern the factors of production.

Douglas (1948) gathered additional data that supported the validity of the Cobb–Douglas production function. Using both the time-series and the cross-sectional data, he estimated the values of parameters a_i in equation (8.1) for the United States, Australia, Canada, and South Africa. Overall, he found that the values of output elasticity of labor (a_L) and output elasticity of capital (a_K) summed approximately to unity. Average values of the parameters for these countries are (0.63, 0.34), (0.60, 0.37), (0.47, 0.52), and (0.66, 0.32), respectively.

Later, Walters (1963), Griliches (1967, 1980), Moroney (1967), and many others carried out econometric studies of the Cobb–Douglas production function. Although industries, countries, data, and number of inputs under their consideration are all different to each other, the sums of parameter values are not far from unity. In the case of Walters, he reports evidence on the marginal productivity law at the micro-level, including evidence for economies of scale. He uses cross-sectional data for various countries. But Walters gives no convincing evidence for the marginal productivity at the macro-level with time-series data. Griliches attempts to identify the major sources of productivity growth in US manufacturing since the Second World War. Using cross-sectional data, he suggests that the assumption of unitary elasticity of substitution is reasonable, labor quality emerges as a significant explanatory variable, and modest degrees of increasing returns to scale exist. Moroney also uses cross-sectional data for sixteen US manufacturing industries in 1957. Although he suggested that the production technology is subject to increasing returns to scale in twelve cases, constant returns to scale in one case, and decreasing returns to scale in the remaining three cases, the sums of two parameter values are close enough to one. What Moroney suggests is that Euler's theorem is valid. In other words, the factor shares are largely constant. Additional works on the subject are Lau and Yotopoulos (1971), an application of the Cobb–Douglas production function to Indian agriculture; and Griliches (1980), a study on returns to scale to research and development expenditure.

8.7 Summary

Cobb and Douglas believed that there are observable laws of production that govern the proportions of productive factors. To identify the laws, they proposed a production function which has become known as the Cobb–Douglas production function. There is no other production function known more widely to economists than the Cobb–Douglas function. It is a well-behaved production function in terms of monotonicity and convexity. The function explains neatly the marginal productivity theory. As the simplest form of the neoclassical production functions, the Cobb–Douglas function helps readers understand each step of the derivations of various basic relationships as clearly as possible. Those relationships are the demand for factors, the cost function, and the price equation.

However, the additivity and homotheticity assumptions associated with the function yield highly restrictive results, because they imply that the factor shares are constant and that the elasticity of substitution and the Allen–Uzawa cross-partial elasticity of substitution are limited to unity.

In general, empirical results confirm the theoretical validity of the Cobb–Douglas production function. Output elasticities of productive factors add up approximately to unity.

Notes

1 See Douglas (1967).
2 If the configuration of production technology is concave in the three-dimensional space, it implies that the technology contour is convex to the origin in the two-dimensional input space. See appendix B for details.
3 For the definition of the elasticity of substitution, see Hicks (1932, pp. 117, 245), Lerner (1933), Robinson (1933, pp. 256–7), and Allen (1964, pp. 340–3, 503–9). For problems of its unitary feature in many branches of economic theory, see Arrow et al. (1961, p. 225).
4 It is possible to convert equation (8.12) into

$$\widehat{\left(\frac{a_i}{a_j}\right)} = \widehat{\left(\frac{x_i}{x_j}\right)} - \widehat{\left(\frac{w_i}{w_j}\right)}$$

where a circumflex represents percentage change. If $\widehat{(x_i/x_j)}$ equals $\widehat{(w_i/w_j)}$ and thus $\sigma = 1$, then $\widehat{(a_i/a_j)}$ is zero, implying that (a_i/a_j) stays the same.
5 The case of when output y_2 remains the same is not shown in the figure.
6 See Caves (1960, pp. 68–76).
7 See appendix K.
8 For the definition of the Allen–Uzawa elasticity of substitution, see Allen (1964, p. 508) and Uzawa (1962).
9 See appendix I.

Recommended Reading

Cobb, C.W. and Douglas, P.H. 1928: A theory of production. *American Economic Review*, 18, March, 139–65.
Douglas, P.H. 1948: Are there laws of production? *American Economic Review*, 38, 1–41.
Griliches, Z. 1967: Production functions in manufacturing: some preliminary results. In M. Brown (ed.), *The Theory and Empirical Analysis of Production*, New York: Columbia University Press, 275–322.
—— 1980: Returns to research and development expenditures in the private

sector. In J. Kendrick and B. Vaccara (eds), *New Developments in Productivity Measurement and Analysis*, Chicago, IL: NBER.

—— and Ringstad, V. 1971: *Economies of Scale and the Form of the Production Function*. Amsterdam: North-Holland.

Intriligator, M.D. 1965: Embodied technical change and productivity in the United Kingdom, 1929–1958. *Review of Economics and Statistics*, XLVII, February, 65–70.

Lau, L.J. and Yotopoulos, P.A. 1971: A test for relative efficiency and an application to Indian agriculture. *American Economic Review*, 61, 94–109.

Moroney, J. 1967: Cobb–Douglas production functions and returns to scale in U.S. manufacturing industry. *Western Economic Journal*, VI, December, 39–51.

Nerlove, M. 1965: *Estimation and Identification of Cobb–Douglas Production Function*. Chicago, IL: Rand McNally.

—— 1967: Recent empirical studies of the CES and related production function. In M. Brown (ed.), *The Theory and Empirical Analysis of Production*, New York: Columbia University Press.

Walters, A.A. 1963: Production and cost function: an econometric survey. *Econometrica*, 31 (1–2), 1–66.

9 The Constant-Elasticity-of-Substitution Production Function

As discussed in the previous chapter, the major weakness of the Cobb–Douglas production function is that the elasticity of substitution is restricted to one and the factor shares of output are constant. It is highly unlikely that the rate of substitution and the factor shares are uniform across industries. Recall that the limitations reflect the assumptions underlying the function.

Thirty years ago, Arrow et al. (1961) derived a production function that has been referred to as the constant-elasticity-of-substitution (CES) production function. The function has three key parameters: the efficiency parameter, the distribution parameter (often called the capital-intensity parameter), and the substitution parameter. The elasticity of substitution is a constant for each industry, but may be different for different industries. The factor shares of output may also vary across industries. Among many studies on the theory and empirical analysis of the CES are McKinnon (1962), Brown and de Cani (1963), Ferguson (1963, 1965, 1969), Fuchs (1963), Kendrick and Sato (1963), Kurz and Manne (1963), Minhas (1963), Walters (1963), Dhrymes and Kurz (1964), Dhrymes (1965), Brown and Conrad (1967), Griliches (1967), Kmenta (1967), Nerlove (1967), McFadden (1978b), and Chung (1980).

Despite being a significant improvement in flexibility over the Cobb–Douglas form, the CES function of Arrow et al. (often referred to as ACMS) has several major restrictions. Since the CES function is homogeneous and quasi-additive,[1] its factor shares are independent of total output and its elasticity of substitution is the same for all input pairs. Although the constant value of the elasticity of substitution can take on a wide range of values, it is not as flexible as a variable. We introduce the CES production function and examine its underlying properties, including its elasticity of substitution, in section 9.1. Section 9.2 discusses factor shares of output, relative factor shares, and relative factor intensity. In section 9.3, we employ two different principles to derive two different demand functions for a productive factor and compare differences in their specifications. Section 9.4 deals with the duality existing between output and cost. Section 9.5 discusses ACMS's empirical results, followed by empirical remarks for several others. Section 9.6 summarizes the chapter.

9.1 The Function and its Properties

The CES production function is written as follows:

$$y = \gamma \left[\sum_i \delta_i x_i^{-\rho} \right]^{-1/\rho} \tag{9.1}$$

where y is output, x_i is input i ($i = 1, 2$),[2] γ is the efficiency parameter ($\gamma > 0$), δ_i is the distribution parameter[3] ($0 < \delta_i < 1$), and ρ is the substitution parameter ($-1 < \rho < \infty$).

The first-order derivative of the CES function with respect to the factor i is the marginal product of i (MP_i) that is equal to the real factor price at the optimum by the theory of marginal productivity:

$$\mathrm{MP}_i: \quad \frac{\partial y}{\partial x_i} = \frac{\delta_i}{\gamma^\rho} y^{1+\rho} x_i^{-(1+\rho)} = \frac{w_i}{p} \tag{9.2}$$

where w is the price of input i, and p is the price of output. Given factors i and j, the ratio of marginal products of the two factors is referred to as the marginal rate of technical substitution (MRTS) of factor i for factor j. The ratio is

$$\mathrm{MRTS}: \quad \frac{\partial y/\partial x_i}{\partial y/\partial x_j} = \frac{\delta_i}{\delta_j} \left(\frac{x_j}{x_i} \right)^{1+\rho} = \frac{w_i}{w_j} \quad (i \neq j) . \tag{9.3}$$

The second-order derivatives are as follows:

$$\frac{\partial^2 y}{\partial x_i^2} = \frac{1+\rho}{y} \mathrm{MP}_i \frac{\mathrm{MP}_i x_i - y}{x_i} \tag{9.4}$$

$$\frac{\partial^2 y}{\partial x_i \, \partial x_j} = \frac{1+\rho}{y} \, \mathrm{MP}_i \, \mathrm{MP}_j \qquad (i \neq j) \,. \tag{9.5}$$

Given the parameter restrictions imposed on equation (9.1), equation (9.2) is positive, implying that the CES is a monotonically increasing function. Next, equations (9.4) and (9.5) are negative and positive, respectively. The negativity of equation (9.4) is based upon Euler's theorem explained below. We substitute equations (9.2), (9.4) and (9.5) into equation (B.4) in appendix B to get

$$|\overline{H}_2| = \frac{1+\rho}{y} \, \mathrm{MP}_i \, \mathrm{MP}_j \, (\mathrm{MP}_i \mathrm{AP}_j + \mathrm{MP}_j \mathrm{AP}_i) \qquad (i \neq j) \,. \tag{9.6}$$

The result is positive, implying that the curvature of CES production technology is strictly quasi-concave.[4]

The CES function is linearly homogeneous because the following relationship holds:

$$\theta \, y = \gamma \left[\sum_i \delta_i \, (\theta \, x_i)^{-\rho} \right]^{-1/\rho} \tag{9.7}$$

where θ is a scalar.[5]

Because the CES function is homogeneous of degree one, Euler's theorem holds, i.e.

$$\sum_i \mathrm{MP}_i x_i = \sum_i \left(\frac{\delta_i}{\gamma^\rho} y^{(1+\rho)} x_i^{-(1+\rho)} \right) x_i = y \,. \tag{9.8}$$

It suggests that the total output and total cost of the factors are the same if each of the factors is paid its marginal product. The CES function is not additive because equation (9.5) is not equal to zero. However, it is important to stress that its monotonic transformation is additive.[6] I refer to this nature as *quasi-additive*.

Assuming that the factor prices (w) are constant, equation (9.3) yields an equation for the expansion path:

$$\frac{x_i}{x_j} = \left(\frac{\delta_i}{\delta_j} \right)^{1/(1+\rho)} \left(\frac{w_j}{w_i} \right)^{1/(1+\rho)} \tag{9.9}$$

Note that, given the factor–price ratio, this function has a logarithmic linear expansion path, which is usually the case for any linearly homogeneous production function.

The elasticity of substitution is defined as

$$\sigma \equiv \frac{d(x_i/x_j)}{d(w_j/w_i)} \frac{w_j/w_i}{x_i/x_j} \qquad (i \neq j) \, . \tag{9.10}$$

It is obtained by differentiating equation (9.9). The result is

$$\sigma = \frac{1}{1 + \rho} \, . \tag{9.11}$$

Note that the elasticity is a constant. As discussed in chapter 8, it turns out to be a constant because the function is homothetic and quasi-additive. Also note that the elasticity of substitution is different from unity as long as the substitution parameter $\rho \neq 0$. Given the admissible values of the substitution parameter ρ ($-1 < \rho < \infty$), the elasticity of substitution can vary within a broad range: $0 < \sigma < \infty$. The larger is the value of σ, the flatter is the isoquant, and the greater is the substitutability. If, however, the parameter ρ equals zero, the value of elasticity of substitution σ is exactly one, and the CES function reduces to the Cobb–Douglas form. In other words, the Cobb–Douglas function is a special case of the CES function.

9.2   Productivity, Factor Shares of Output, and Factor Intensity

As discussed in the previous chapter, the relationship between labor productivity and wages is rigid in the Cobb–Douglas context. Arrow et al. observed that there was a significant correlation between productivity and wages in all industries and that the correlation varied considerably from industry to industry and from country to country. The primary objective in their work was to introduce a production function that permits the possibility of different elasticities of substitution for different industries. In logarithmic terms equation (9.2) is

$$\ln\left(\frac{y}{x_i}\right) = -\sigma \ln\left(\frac{\delta_i}{\gamma^\rho}\right) + \sigma(\ln w_i - \ln p) \, . \tag{9.12}$$

Note that the elasticity of substitution plays an important role in this productivity equation. If the values of the elasticity of substitution are different from industry to industry, there is a possibility of different correlations between labor productivity and wages for different industries.

The elasticity of substitution also plays an important role in the factor-share equations. The share function derived from equation (9.2) and the relative share function derived from equation (9.9) are

$$\frac{w_i x_i}{p\,y} = \left(\frac{\delta_i}{\gamma^\rho}\right)^\sigma \left(\frac{w_i}{p}\right)^{1-\sigma} \tag{9.13}$$

$$\frac{w_i x_i}{w_j x_j} = \left(\frac{\delta_i}{\delta_j}\right)^\sigma \left(\frac{w_j}{w_i}\right)^{\sigma-1} \quad (i \neq j)\ . \tag{9.14}$$

Note that the share of output is independent of total output. Recall that this is a fundamental trait of a homothetic production function.

At this point, it is useful to compare equations (9.13) and (9.14) with equations (8.9) and (8.12), respectively. We can clearly see the importance of the elasticity of substitution in equations (9.13) and (9.14). Note that the factor-share function is not independent of factor prices, unless the elasticity of substitution is one (or $\rho = 0$). In other words, the factor-share function is determined not only by the constant terms (δ, γ and σ) but also by the factor prices and is therefore not constant across industries. Under perfect competition in the factor market, each factor price is the same across industries. Even if factor prices are the same across industries, the relative share of an input is different from industry to industry and thus the estimated values of σ ($\neq 1$) are different from industry to industry. Equation (9.14) verifies the relationship between the elasticity of substitution and the relative output share. If $\sigma > 1$, the capital–labor ratio (x_i/x_j) rises more than the wage–rental ratio (w_j/w_i). It follows that labor's share of output decreases, whereas capital's share of output increases. If $\sigma < 1$, the capital–labor ratio rises less than the wage–rental ratio; thus labor's share increases and capital's share decreases.

We can ask similar questions as those raised above on factor shares. They are concerned with the factor intensity (e.g. capital–labor ratio) of an industry. It is important to know whether or not an industry is capital intensive or labor intensive. Here, we examine the factor intensity of one industry relative to that of another. The elasticity of substitution again plays a crucial role. As mentioned earlier, equation (9.3) is the equation for the expansion path. It represents relative capital intensity in equilibrium. Given industries h and k, the relative factor-intensity ratio is

$$\frac{x_{ih}/x_{jh}}{x_{ik}/x_{jk}} = \frac{(\delta_{ih}/\delta_{jh})^{\sigma_h}}{(\delta_{ik}/\delta_{jk})^{\sigma_k}} \left(\frac{w_j}{w_i}\right)^{\sigma_h - \sigma_k} \quad (i \neq j; h \neq k)\ . \tag{9.15}$$

Suppose that $\sigma_h = \sigma_k$, as in the case of the Cobb–Douglas function (i.e. $\sigma_h = \sigma_k = 1$) and the Leontief function ($\sigma_h = \sigma_k = 0$; see chapter 14). The factor–price ratio then vanishes from the equation. The relative factor intensity is independent of the factor–price ratio, implying that one industry is always either more capital intensive or more labor intensive than the other industry. In other words, the factor-intensity reversal never occurs. If, however, $\sigma_h \neq \sigma_k$, as shown in figure 9.1, factor-intensity reversal may occur. This is one of the most serious cases in which the modern theory of international trade (the Heckscher–Ohlin theory) can be invalidated.

9.3   Demand for Inputs

The CES production function has been widely applied in empirical work for investigating the demand for productive factors. Economists employ either the profit-maximization principle or the cost-minimization principle for this purpose. The two principles yield different specifications of the factor demand functions.

As shown in the previous chapter, the marginal revenue product of factor i ($\mathrm{MRP}_i = p\mathrm{MP}_i$) is itself the demand for that particular factor under profit maximization because the MRP is derived from the first-order condition for maximum profit. The total profit to be maximized is written as

$$\max \pi = R - C$$

$$= p \, \gamma \left(\sum_i \delta_i x_i^{-\rho} \right)^{-1/\rho} - \sum_i w_i x_i \qquad (9.16)$$

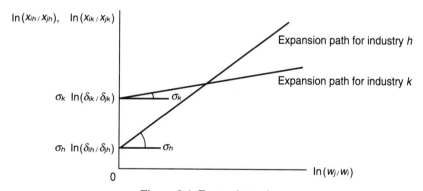

Figure 9.1 Factor intensity.

where π is the total profit, R is the total revenue, and C is the total cost. The first-order condition yields

$$\frac{\partial \pi}{\partial x_i} = p \, \frac{\delta_i}{\gamma^\rho} \, y^{1+\rho} x_i^{-(1+\rho)} - w_i = 0 \tag{9.17}$$

which can be transformed into a logarithmic linear function in real wages and output, i.e.

$$\ln x_i = \ln\left(\frac{\delta_i}{\gamma^\rho}\right)^\sigma - \sigma \ln\left(\frac{w_i}{p}\right) + \ln y \ . \tag{9.18}$$

Assuming that the second-order conditions for profit maximization hold, equation (9.18) is the derived demand function for factor i. Note that the elasticity of substitution again plays a significant role. The elasticity itself constitutes the slope associated with the factor prices.

The demand for factor i under cost minimization is derived from the MRTS condition, which is the necessary condition for the least-cost factor combination. The Lagrangian function for cost minimization is written as follows:

$$L(x; \gamma) = \sum_i w_i x_i + \lambda \left[y - \gamma \left(\sum_i \delta_i x_i^{-\rho} \right)^{-1/\rho} \right] . \tag{9.19}$$

The first-order conditions for cost minimization are

$$\frac{\partial L}{\partial x_i} = w_i - \lambda \, \frac{\delta_i}{\gamma^\rho} \, y^{1+\rho} x_i^{-(1+\rho)} = 0 \tag{9.20}$$

$$\frac{\partial L}{\partial \lambda} = y - \gamma \left(\sum_i \delta_i x_i^{-\rho} \right)^{-1/\rho} = 0 \ . \tag{9.21}$$

From equation (9.20) we obtain equation (9.3). Combining equations (9.1) and (9.3) yields

$$\ln x_i = \ln\left(\frac{1}{\gamma}\right) + \ln\left[\frac{\delta_j}{\gamma} + \frac{\delta_i}{\gamma}\left(\frac{\delta_j}{\delta_i}\right)^{1-\sigma}\left(\frac{w_i}{w_j}\right)^{1-\sigma}\right] + \ln y \qquad (i \neq j) \tag{9.22}$$

after logarithmic transformation.

For both equations (9.18) and (9.22), it is undesirable to restrict the coefficient of output to unity. Later economists have attempted to allow the coefficient associated with output to be flexible. The CES version suggested by Brown and de Cani (1963) permits a variable degree of homogeneity, obtained by raising the right-hand side of the original CES function to a power referred to as the homogeneity parameter (ν). If the homogeneity parameter is equal to one, the function exhibits constant returns to scale; if it is greater than one, increasing returns to scale; and if it is less than one, decreasing returns to scale. The output coefficient is no longer unity in the latter two cases. However, the elasticity of substitution remains constant.

9.4 Dual Approach to Production

The CES production function is useful for analyzing price dynamics. It is possible to derive a CES form of the price equation from the CES production function. This transformation illustrates the duality between output and its price.

We first raise equation (9.20) to the power $1 - \sigma$ and then multiply through the resulting equation by δ_i to obtain

$$\delta_i \lambda^{1-\sigma} (y^{1+\rho} x_i^{-(1+\rho)})^{1-\sigma} = \delta_i \left(\frac{\delta_j}{\gamma^\rho}\right)^{-(1-\sigma)} w_i^{1-\sigma} \qquad (i \neq j) . \quad (9.23)$$

Summing the equation for all i ($i = 1, 2$), we get

$$\lambda = \zeta \left(\sum_i \phi_i w_i^{1-\sigma}\right)^{1/(1-\sigma)} \quad (9.24)$$

where $\zeta = \gamma^{-1/\sigma}$ and $\phi_i = \delta_i (\delta_i/\gamma^\rho)^{\sigma-1}$. As shown in appendix I (the Shephard–Samuelson theorem), we have

$$\lambda = AC = MC = P \quad (9.25)$$

under perfect competition. Therefore equation (9.24) is the price equation, which may be linearized (or approximated) by the Taylor expansion method as Kmenta (1967) and Chung (1980) did for the CES production function. Note again that the crucial parameter in the equation is the elasticity of substitution.

The duality between output and cost facilitates us to derive the factor-share function and the Allen–Uzawa elasticities of substitution. We first convert equation (9.24) into the total cost function by multiplying both sides of the equation by y. The total cost function is

$$C = \zeta \left(\sum_i \phi_i w_i^{1-\sigma}\right)^{1/(1-\sigma)} y . \quad (9.26)$$

Its first-order and second-order partial derivatives are

$$\frac{\partial C}{\partial w_i} = \phi_i \, w_i^{-\sigma} \left(\sum_i \phi_i \, w_i^{1-\sigma} \right)^{-1} C \tag{9.27}$$

$$\frac{\partial^2 C}{\partial w_i \partial w_j} = \sigma \left(\sum_k \phi_k \, w_k^{1-\sigma} \right)^{-2} C \prod_k \phi_k \, w_k^{-\sigma} \qquad (i \neq j; i, j \in k) . \tag{9.28}$$

Multiply both sides of equation (9.27) by w_i/C to get the factor-share function:

$$\frac{\partial C}{\partial w_i} \frac{w_i}{C} = S_i = \frac{\phi_i \, w_i^{1-\sigma}}{\sum_j \phi_j \, w_j^{1-\sigma}} \qquad (i \in j) . \tag{9.29}$$

Given equation (9.24), equation (9.29) can be written as equation (9.13). Note that the factor shares are independent of output. Substitute equation (9.27) and (9.28) into equation (L.6) from appendix L to get

$$\sigma_{ij} = \sigma \qquad (i \neq j) . \tag{9.30}$$

Note that the Allen–Uzawa partial elasticity (σ_{ij}) is identical to the ordinary elasticity of substitution (σ). This result is due to the assumptions underlying the CES production function discussed in section 9.1.

9.5 Empirical Remarks

The primary empirical intent of Arrow et al. (1961) is to estimate the CES production function or its transforms to measure the three parameters associated with the CES production function: the efficiency parameter (γ), the distribution parameter (δ), and the substitution parameter (ρ) or the elasticity of substitution ($\sigma = 1/(1 + \rho)$). The authors assess and compare the results with earlier production studies as well as with theoretical assumptions. The range of topics presented by the authors is indeed vast, yet all revolve around the central question of the substitution between capital and labor.

Arrow et al. assumed that, of the parameters to be estimated, the substitution and distribution parameters remain constant while the efficiency parameter should vary from country to country. For a constant value of the substitution parameter, the elasticity of substitution should also be constant. Instead of being restricted to unity as assumed by the Cobb–Douglas production function, however, it is allowed to vary for individual industries. Constant returns to scale and Hicks-neutral technological change are the assumptions maintained throughout the paper.

The authors estimate parameters for cross-sectional and time-series data covering twenty-four three-digit SIC industries in nineteen different countries. The cross-sectional data seem to reflect that the elasticity of substitution between capital and labor is somewhat different from unity (0.93 for all manufacturing, 1.20 for agriculture, 1.17 for mining, and 0.82 for electric power in the United States and Japan). So, as wages increase relative to capital costs, industries with greater elasticities of substitution become more capital intensive. The vastly different elasticities of capital and labor in the various countries suggest the need for either specific production functions or even more general ones. The results of the distribution parameter suggest that industries with a high or low elasticity, such as electrical power (0.819) and apparel (0.055), do not see large shifts in their capital intensity. For most industries under consideration, however, wage variations between the United States and Japan cause the capital–labor ratio to change. Concerning the assumption of neutral production efficiency, the authors report that there are disparities among countries. They attribute the differences to comparative advantages and disadvantages in the global market. The relative median efficiency parameter levels for the United States and Japan are 0.43, 0.13, and 0.14 for manufacturing, agriculture, and coal mining, respectively.

Finally, time-series data for US non-farm production for 1949–55 yield an elasticity of substitution of 0.569. This value is significantly different from the Cobb–Douglas value of 1. Also, the study rejects the hypothesis that capital–output and labor–output ratios are constant at any point in time. This implies that capital and labor are substituted frequently to each other to produce output. Results obtained from time series are different from the results from the cross-sectional data probably because service industries were used in the time series and not in the cross-sectional data.

There are a large number of empirical studies in addition to Arrow et al. Readers should see McKinnon (1962), one of the earliest empirical studies of two-digit US manufacturing with time-series data for the postwar period to estimate elasticities of substitution; Brown and de Cani (1963), a time-series analysis under the assumption of technological change unrestricted to Hicks-neutrality; Ferguson (1963, 1965), cross-sectional and time-series studies of two-digit manufacturing industries to understand the nature of production technology; Fuchs (1963), an estimation of the elasticities of substitution in manufacturing industries with cross-sectional data; Kendrik and Sato (1963), a time-series study restricted to Hicks-neutral technology; Minhas (1963), an international comparison of production technology; Dhrymes and Kurz (1964), an investigation of technology and scale in the electricity industry; Dhrymes (1965), a cross-sectional analysis of production behavior in manufacturing and the service industries; Griliches (1967), cross-sectional estimates to show labor quality as a significant explanatory variable and the presence of a moderate degree of increasing returns to scale with respect to capital and labor; Lee (1970), a study to identify determinants of the changes in relative factor share in the factor-augmenting technology model for US manufacturing; and Chung (1980), an application of the CES function to the modern theory of international trade. For many other empirical studies done in this area, see Nerlove (1967), a comprehensive survey.

It is notable that most of the time-series results on the US aggregate production function conclude that the elasticity of substitution is less than one. These results imply that the assumption of unitary elasticity of substitution is not appropriate.

9.6 Summary

The CES production function is an attractive form that has been widely employed by many economists over the past three decades. The chief characteristic of the function is that the elasticity of substitution is constant. This is a significant improvement in flexibility over the unitary elasticity of the Cobb–Douglas function, but the range for variation in elasticity is still quite limited. As a homothetic and quasi-additive function, the CES form also treats the factor share of output in a highly rigid manner.

Empirical results reported by Arrow et al. and many others suggest that elasticities of substitution between capital and labor for various industries in various countries are different from the Cobb–Douglas value of 1.

Appendix

A9.1   Expansion Path

Given two inputs, capital (K) and labor (L), the CES production function is written as

$$y = \gamma [\delta K^{-\rho} + (1 - \delta) L^{-\rho}]^{-1/\rho} . \qquad (1)$$

The marginal product of capital (MP_K), labor (MP_L), and the marginal rate of technical substitution (MRTS) are, respectively, as follows:

$$\text{MP}_K : \quad \frac{\partial y}{\partial K} = \frac{\delta}{\gamma^{\rho}} y^{1+\rho} K^{-(1+\rho)} = \frac{r}{p} \qquad (2)$$

$$\text{MP}_L : \quad \frac{\partial y}{\partial L} = \frac{1 - \delta}{\gamma^{\rho}} y^{1+\rho} L^{-(1+\rho)} = \frac{w}{p} \qquad (3)$$

$$\text{MRTS} : \quad \frac{\text{MP}_K}{\text{MP}_L} = \frac{1 - \delta}{\delta} \left(\frac{K}{L} \right)^{1+\rho} = \frac{w}{r} \qquad (4)$$

where r is the rental cost and w are wages. Solving equation (4) with respect to (K/L), we obtain the equation for the expansion path:

$$\frac{K}{L} = \left(\frac{\delta}{1 - \delta} \right)^{\sigma} \left(\frac{w}{r} \right)^{\sigma} \qquad (5)$$

where $\sigma = 1/(1 + \rho)$.

A9.2   Elasticity of Substitution

Taking the first-order differential of equation (4) with respect to the wage–rental ratio (w/r) and substituting the resulting equation and equation (5) into the formula stated below, we get

$$\sigma = \frac{d(K/L)}{d(w/r)} \frac{w/r}{K/L}$$

$$= \left(\frac{\delta}{1-\delta} \right)^{1/(1+\rho)} \frac{1}{1 + \rho} \left(\frac{w}{r} \right)^{-\rho/(1+\rho)} \frac{w/r}{[\delta/(1 - \delta)]^{1/(1+\rho)} (w/r)^{1/(1+\rho)}}$$

$$= \frac{1}{1 + \rho} . \qquad (6)$$

A9.3 Derivation of the Demand for Labor

Under the profit-maximization principle, the objective function is

$$\pi = p\, \gamma [\delta K^{-\rho} + (1 - \delta) L^{-\rho}]^{-1/\rho} - (rK + wL) . \qquad (7)$$

The necessary condition for unconstrained maximization of profit is

$$\frac{\partial \pi}{\partial L} = p\, \frac{1 - \delta}{\gamma^\rho} y^{1+\rho} L^{-(1+\rho)} - w = 0 . \qquad (8)$$

Rearranging terms in equation (8) yields

$$L = \left(\frac{1 - \delta}{\gamma^\rho}\right)^{1/(1+\rho)} \left(\frac{w}{p}\right)^{-1/(1+\rho)} y . \qquad (9)$$

Under the cost-minimization principle, the objective function is

$$\mathscr{L} = wL + rK + \lambda \{ y - \gamma [\delta K^{-\rho} + (1 - \delta) L^{-\rho}]^{-1/\rho} \} . \qquad (10)$$

The necessary conditions for cost are

$$\frac{\partial \mathscr{L}}{\partial K} = r - \lambda \left[\frac{\delta}{\gamma^\rho} y^{1+\rho} K^{-(1+\rho)} \right] = 0 \qquad (11)$$

$$\frac{\partial \mathscr{L}}{\partial K} = w - \lambda \left[\frac{1 - \delta}{\gamma^\rho} y^{1+\rho} L^{-(1+\rho)} \right] = 0 \qquad (12)$$

$$\frac{\partial \mathscr{L}}{\partial \lambda} = y - \gamma [\delta K^{-\rho} + (1 - \delta) L^{-\rho}]^{-1/\rho} = 0 . \qquad (13)$$

From equations (11)–(13), we arrive at the demand function stated as follows.

$$L = \left[\frac{1 - \delta}{\gamma} + \frac{\delta}{\gamma} \left(\frac{1 - \delta}{\delta}\right)^{1-\sigma} \left(\frac{r}{w}\right)^{1-\sigma} \right]^{1/\gamma} y . \qquad (14)$$

Notes

1 For the definition of quasi-additivity, see section 9.1.
2 The original version of the CES production function deals with two inputs, capital and labor. For the CES function generalized by n factors, see chapter 10.

3 It is often called the capital intensity parameter.
4 See note 2 in chapter 8.
5 See Brown and de Cani (1963) for the CES production function of any degree of homogeneity.
6 Note that any monotonic transformation of a production technology surface will leave the isoquant unchanged.

Recommended Reading

Arrow, K.J., Chenery, H.B., Minhas, B.S. and Solow, R.M. 1961: Capital–labor substitution and economic efficiency. *Review of Economics and Statistics*, 63, August, 225–50.

Brown, M. and de Cani, J.S. 1963: Technological change and the distribution of income. *International Economic Review*, 4, September, 289–309.

—— and Conrad, A.H. 1967: The influence of research and education on CES production relations. In M. Brown (ed.), *The Theory and Empirical Analysis of Production*. New York: Columbia University Press.

Chung, J.W. 1980: Trade liberalization and factor prices: an application to the U.S. manufacturing sector. *Journal of Policy Modeling*, 2, January, 101–20.

Dhrymes, P.J. 1963: A comparison of productivity behavior in manufacturing and service industries. *Review of Economics and Statistics*, 45, 64–9.

—— and Kurz, M. 1964: Technology and scale in electricity generation. *Econometrica*, 32, 287–315.

Ferguson, C.E. 1963: Cross-section production functions and the elasticity of substitution in American manufacturing industry. *Review of Economics and Statistics*, 45, 305–13.

—— 1965: Time-series production functions and technological progress in American manufacturing industry. *Journal of Political Economy*, April, LXXIII, 135–47.

Fuchs, V.R. 1963: Capital labor substitution, a note. *Review of Economics and Statistics*, November, 45, 436–8.

Griliches, Z. 1967: Production functions in manufacturing: some preliminary results. In M. Brown (ed.), *The Theory and Empirical Analysis of Production*, New York: Columbia University Press.

Kendrick, J. and Sato, R. 1963: Factor prices, productivity, and economic growth. *American Economic Review*, 53, 974–1003.

Kmenta, J. 1967: On estimation of the CES production function. *International Economic Review*, 8, June, 180–9.

Kurz, M. and Manne, A.S. 1963: Engineering estimates of capital–labor substitution in metal industry. *American Economic Review*, 53, September, 662–81.

McFadden, D. 1978: Estimation techniques for the elasticity of substitution and other production parameters. In M. Fuss and D. McFadden (eds), *Production Economics: A Dual Approach to Theory and Applications, 2*, Amsterdam: North-Holland.

124   *Production Functions*

McKinnon, R.I. 1962: Wages, capital costs, and employment in manufacturing: a model applied to 1947–58 U.S. data. *Econometrica*, 30, July, 501–21.

Minhas, B. 1963: *An International Comparison of Factor Costs and Factor Use*. Amsterdam: North-Holland.

Nerlove, M. 1965: *Estimation and Identification of Cobb–Douglas Production Functions*. Chicago, IL: Rand McNally.

——1967: Recent empirical studies of the CES and related production function. In M. Brown (ed.), *The Theory and Empirical Analysis of Production*, New York: Columbia University Press.

Walters, A.A. 1963: Production and cost function: an econometric survey. *Econometrica*, 31 (1–2), 1–66.

10 The Generalized Constant-Elasticity-of-Substitution Production Function

Since the constant-elasticity-of-substitution (CES) production function was introduced by Arrow et al. (1961), econometric studies of production have concentrated largely on the relationship between capital and labor. In response to the need for an appropriate specification of the substitution possibilities among more factors of production, there have been several attempts to generalize it, notably by Uzawa (1962), McFadden (1963), and Mukerji (1963). This chapter deals with Uzawa's generalization.

In his paper, Uzawa discusses the properties of a generalized n-factor CES function whose partial elasticities of substitution between any pair of inputs are constant and independent of factor prices. Reversely, he suggests that if the partial elasticities of substitution are independent of factor prices and are identical for all pairs, the production function with n factors has the CES form. Recall that the original CES function introduced in the previous chapter is (quasi) additive and homothetic, and that an additive and homothetic production function restricts its Allen–Uzawa elasticities of substitution to a constant that is identical for all pairs of inputs. It was in this paper that Uzawa discussed the unit cost function corresponding to the n-factor CES production function and used it to present an alternative formula for the partial elasticity of substitution suggested by Allen (1964). For this reason, economists today refer to the partial elasticity of substitution as the Allen–Uzawa partial elasticity of substitution. It is notable that Uzawa's analytical procedure is basically the same as the dual approach that economists employ widely today.

The n-factor CES function is monotonic for the same reason as the two-factor CES function discussed in the previous chapter. Convexity prevails if the nth-order bordered Hessian determinant is negative definite, i.e. $(-1)^n |\overline{H}_n| > 0$. The n-factor CES production function is based upon the same assumptions as the two-factor CES production function already discussed. It is redundant to discuss the regularity conditions and the assumptions for the n-factor CES function, so they are not discussed in this chapter.

Uzawa begins with Allen's formula for the partial elasticity of substitution. Section 10.1 presents it. Section 10.2 shows how Uzawa derives the unit cost function and uses it to get a revised form of Allen's formula, called the Allen–Uzawa partial elasticity of substitution. Section 10.3 discusses the n-factor CES production function and its elasticities. We shall observe that the Allen–Uzawa partial elasticity of substitution is restricted to a constant for any pair of inputs. Section 10.4 makes empirical remarks. Section 10.5 summarizes the chapter.

10.1   The Partial Elasticity of Substitution

In a general form, an n-factor production function is

$$f(\boldsymbol{x}) = f(x_1, \ldots, x_n) \tag{10.1}$$

where x_i is input i. The function assumes that constant returns to scale and the law of diminishing marginal rate of technical substitution prevail.

The partial elasticity of substitution defined by Allen is

$$\sigma_{ij} = \frac{\sum_k x_k f_k}{x_i x_j} \frac{F_{ij}}{F} \qquad (i \neq j; i, j \in k) \tag{10.2}$$

where $f_i = \partial f/\partial x_i = \text{MP}_i$, F is the determinant of the bordered Hessian, i.e.

$$\begin{vmatrix} 0 & f_1 & \cdots & f_n \\ f_1 & f_{11} & \cdots & f_{1n} \\ \vdots & & & \\ f_n & f_{n1} & \cdots & f_{nn} \end{vmatrix}$$

and F_{ij} is the cofactor of the element $f_{ij} = \partial^2 f/\partial x_i \partial x_j$ in determinant F.[1] Note that $\sigma_{ij} = \sigma_{ji}$.

10.2 The Unit Cost Function and the Allen–Uzawa Partial Elasticity of Substitution

The total cost equation is written as

$$C = \sum_{i=1}^{n} w_i x_i \tag{10.3}$$

where C is total cost and w_i is the price of factor i. The unit (average) cost equation, then, is

$$\lambda = \frac{C}{y} = \frac{\Sigma_i w_i x_i}{y} \tag{10.4}$$

where λ is the unit cost function and y is the output. If output (which can be any amount) is restricted to unity, the average cost required to produce one unit of output is the total cost itself. Therefore the unit cost equation is the same as equation (10.3).

We minimize the unit cost

$$\sum_i w_i x_i \tag{10.5}$$

subject to the production function of one unit of output

$$1 = f(x_1, ..., x_n) . \tag{10.6}$$

We set the first-order derivatives equal to zero. The results are as follows:

$$\begin{aligned} x_1 &= x_1(w_1, ..., w_n) \\ &\vdots \\ x_n &= x_n(w_1, ..., w_n) . \end{aligned} \tag{10.7}$$

Equations (10.7) are the cost-minimizing input demand functions. They are simply an extended version of the case of two inputs, shown in the previous chapter (equation (9.22) or (14) in the appendix to chapter 9), given $y = 1$. Substituting equations (10.7) into equation (10.4), we have

$$\lambda = w_1 x_1(w_1, ..., w_n) + \cdots + w_n x_n(w_1, ..., w_n) . \tag{10.8}$$

The above equation is the unit cost function.[2] It is now possible to rewrite equation (10.2) as

$$\sigma_{ij} = \frac{\lambda(\partial x_i/\partial w_j)}{x_i x_j} \qquad (i \neq j) . \qquad (10.9)$$

Note that the term $\Sigma x_k f_k$ in equation (10.2) is the same as the unit cost equation (10.4), $\lambda = \Sigma w_i x_i$, and that the term F_{ij}/F is equivalent to the substitution effect $\partial x_i/\partial w_j$ in the Slutsky equation, as shown in appendix F. Paul Samuelson (1947, p. 68) and Shephard (1970) have shown that[3]

$$x_i = \frac{\partial \lambda}{\partial w_i} \qquad (10.10)$$

yielding

$$\frac{\partial x_i}{\partial w_j} = \frac{\partial(\partial \lambda/\partial w_i)}{\partial w_j} = \frac{\partial^2 \lambda}{\partial w_i \, \partial w_j} \qquad (i \neq j) . \qquad (10.11)$$

Substituting equations (10.10) and (10.11) into equation (10.9) gives

$$\sigma_{ij} = \frac{\lambda(\partial^2 \lambda/\partial w_i \partial w_j)}{(\partial \lambda/\partial w_i)(\partial \lambda/\partial w_j)} \qquad (i \neq j) . \qquad (10.12)$$

This is the formula known as the *Allen–Uzawa partial elasticity of substitution* in the modern literature of microeconomics.

10.3   The *n*-Factor Constant-Elasticity-of-Substitution Production Function, Elasticities of Substitution, and Factor Shares

Uzawa extends the two-factor CES to the *n*-factor case. The *n*-factor function is

$$y = \gamma \left(\sum_{i=1}^{n} \delta_i x_i^{-\rho} \right)^{-1/\rho} . \qquad (10.13)$$

The unit cost function corresponding to the above production function is obtained through the same procedure as that taken in the previous chapter (section 9.4). The result is

$$\lambda = \zeta \left(\sum_{i=1}^{n} \phi_i w^{(1-\sigma)} \right)^{1/(1-\sigma)} \qquad (10.14)$$

where $\zeta = \gamma^{-1/\sigma}$, $\sigma = 1/(1 + \rho)$, and $\phi_i = \delta_i(\delta_i/\gamma^\rho)^{-(1-\sigma)}$. Recall that parameter σ included in equation (10.14) is the elasticity of substitution discussed in the previous chapter. The first- and second-order derivatives required to compute the Allen–Uzawa partial elasticities of substitution are as follows:

$$\frac{\partial \lambda}{\partial w_i} = \phi_i\, w_i^{-\sigma}\, \Omega^{-1}\, \lambda \tag{10.15}$$

$$\frac{\partial^2 \lambda}{\partial w_i \partial w_j} = \sigma\, \phi_i\, w_i^{-\sigma}\, \phi_j\, w_j^{-\sigma}\, \Omega^{-2}\, \lambda \qquad (i \neq j) \tag{10.16}$$

where $\Omega = \sum_{i=1}^{n} \phi_i\, w_i^{1-\sigma}$. Substituting equations (10.14), (10.15), and (10.16) into equation (10.12) yields the Allen–Uzawa elasticities of substitution:

$$\sigma_{ij} = \sigma. \tag{10.17}$$

Note that, as Uzawa suggests, all Allen–Uzawa elasticities of substitution are constant, independent of factor prices, and identical for different pairs of factors.[4]

Rearranging terms in equation (10.15), we get the factor shares of the unit cost. They are

$$\frac{\partial \lambda}{\partial w_i} \frac{w_i}{\lambda} = \frac{\phi_i\, w_i^{1-\sigma}}{\Omega}. \tag{10.18}$$

Recall that $\partial \lambda/\partial w_i = x_i$.

The factor shares are independent of output. The results on the elasticity of substitution and the factor share suggest that the generalized CES function does not surpass the boundary of the original ACMS's CES function.

10.4   Empirical Remarks

Uzawa does not conduct an empirical study in his paper. The latest study on the multi-factor CES production function is the work done by Pollak et al. (1984) as a special case in their CES–translog context.[5] The inputs they consider are capital, labor, energy, and materials. Their CES results are only part of their work. They include the CES results mainly for comparing the multi-factor CES production function's econometric performance with those of the translog and the

CES–translog production functions. The results are summarized in chapter 13.

10.5   Summary

Uzawa characterizes an n-factor production function. For this purpose, he focuses on the partial elasticity of substitution formula proposed by Allen. Uzawa converts Allen's formula to a form on the basis of the unit cost function corresponding to the n-factor production function. The revised formula is today referred to as the *Allen–Uzawa partial elasticity of substitution*. Economists use it quite extensively.

An n-factor production function belongs to the class of CES functions if the function yields all Allen–Uzawa elasticities of substitution constant regardless of factor prices. Uzawa verifies the constancy of the Allen–Uzawa elasticities of substitution for the n-factor CES function. It is also possible to verify that the factor shares are independent of output. The n-factor CES is homothetic and quasi-additive and thus as inflexible as the two-factor CES function.

Notes

1 See appendix L.
2 This procedure is the same as that of appendix J.
3 Equation (10.10) is Shephard's lemma. See appendix K.
4 McFadden (1963) also proved the proposition suggesting that the generalized CES function restricts the range for substitution.
5 Dhrymes and Kurz (1964) consider three inputs: capital, labor, and fuel. However, they exclude fuel from the labor equation and labor from the fuel equation. Therefore, their case corresponds to the two-input CES.

Recommended Reading

Arrow, K.J., Chenery, H.B., Minhas, B.S. and Solow, R.M. 1961: Capital–labor substitution and economic efficiency. *Review of Economics and Statistics*, 63, August, 225–50.
Dhrymes, P.J. and Kurz, M. 1964: Technology and scale in electricity generation. *Econometrica*, 32, 287–315.
McFadden, D. 1963: Constant elasticity of substitution production function. *Review of Economic Studies*, 30, 73–83.

Mukerji, V. 1963: A generalized SMAC function with constant ratios of elasticities of substitution. *Review of Economic Studies*, 30, 233–6.
Uzawa, H. 1962: Production function with constant elasticities of substitution. *Review of Economic Studies*, 29, 291–9.

11 The Two-Level Constant-Elasticity-of-Substitution Production Function

The two-level CES production function was proposed by Sato (1967). It is another generalization of the original CES function. The production function has two levels of the CES form: the lower level and the upper level. Each input in the upper-level branch has a CES aggregate of input elements in its own lower level as subsets. An obvious intent of Sato is to improve earlier results of elasticities of substitution.

The function is additive over the branches, if it is monotonically transformed, and homothetic. The factor shares are independent of output due to the homotheticity assumption. The Allen–Uzawa partial elasticity of substitution between two inputs within an upper-level branch is referred to as the *intra-class elasticity of substitution* and the Allen–Uzawa partial elasticity of substitution between one input in one branch and another input in another branch is referred to as the *inter-class elasticity of substitution*. The inter-class elasticity of substitution is constant and identical for all input pairs in both branches because of additivity over the branches and homotheticity. However, the intra-class elasticity of substitution is not. For example, capital may be disaggregated into structure and equipment and labor may be broken down into skilled labor and unskilled labor. While the Allen–Uzawa partial elasticity of substitution between structure in the capital branch and skilled labor in the labor branch is constant, the Allen–Uzawa partial elasticity of substitution between structure and equipment or between skilled labor and unskilled labor is not. The intra-class elasticity of substitution is the main difference between the version of the two-level CES function by Sato and versions of generalized CES functions by Uzawa (1962) and McFadden (1963), and Mukerji (1963).[1] If the values of all the intra-class elasticities of substitution are equal to the constant value of the inter-class elasticities of substitution, the corresponding production function should be the n-factor CES production function which was discussed in the previous chapter. The two-level production function is a complex function to deal with and thus has limited empirical applicability. Sato (1967) and Bowles (1970) are the main references.

There are five sections in this chapter. In the first section, we present the two-level production function and examine its properties. Section 11.2 derives the intra-class and inter-class Allen–Uzawa partial elasticities of substitution. We shall see that the intra-class elasticities of substitution are not constant, whereas the inter-class elasticities of substitution are constant. Section 11.3 shows how Sato derives the factor share functions. Section 11.4 covers the empirical results obtained by Sato. Section 11.5 summarizes the chapter.

11.1 The Function and its Properties

The lower-level branch s is written as

$$x^{(s)} = \left[\sum_{i=1}^{n} k_i^{(s)} (x_i^{(s)})^{-a^{(s)}} \right]^{-1/a^{(s)}} \tag{11.1}$$

where $x^{(s)}$ is aggregate input of branch s; $x_i^{(s)}$ is disaggregated input i in branch s; $k_i^{(s)} > 0$; $-1 < a^{(s)} (= (1 - \sigma^{(s)})/\sigma^{(s)}) < \infty$. The upper level that comprises the lower-level branch s is stated as

$$y = \left[\sum_{s=1}^{n} \kappa^{(s)}(x^{(s)})^{-a} \right]^{-1/a} \tag{11.2}$$

where y is output; $\kappa^{(s)} > 0$; $-1 < a (= (1 - \sigma)/\sigma) < \infty$. For simplicity, the efficiency parameter γ is restricted to 1 for both levels. Note that both levels are written in the CES form. Substituting equation (11.1) into equation (11.2) yields Sato's two-level CES production function stated in a composite form as

$$y = \left(\sum_{s} \kappa^{(s)} \left\{ \left[\sum_{i} k_i^{(s)}(x_i^{(s)})^{-a^{(s)}} \right]^{-1/a^{(s)}} \right\}^{-a} \right)^{-1/a}. \tag{11.3}$$

Given the parameter restrictions imposed on equations (11.1) and (11.2), the two-level CES function is monotonic, i.e.

$$\frac{\partial y}{\partial x_i^{(s)}} = \frac{\partial y}{\partial x^{(s)}} \frac{\partial x^{(s)}}{\partial x_i^{(s)}} = \kappa^{(s)} \left(\frac{y}{x^{(s)}}\right)^{1+a} k_i^{(s)} \left(\frac{x^{(s)}}{x_i^{(s)}}\right)^{1+a^{(s)}} > 0 . \tag{11.4}$$

Each level is convex because the CES function (which is corresponding
to the upper level) is convex, as shown in equation (9.6) in chapter 9,
and an input in the upper level and inputs in the lower level maintain
a CES relationship. The two-level CES function is homothetic because
each level of the function is homothetic, i.e.

$$\theta y = \left(\sum_s \kappa^{(s)} \left\{ \left[\sum_i k_i^{(s)} (\theta x_i^{(s)})^{-a^{(s)}} \right]^{-1/a^{(s)}} \right\}^{-a} \right)^{-1/a} . \tag{11.5}$$

where θ is a scalar. The function is not additive (but quasi-additive)
within a branch but separable between two branches. It is easy to show
that

$$\frac{\partial y/\partial x_i^{(s)}}{\partial y/\partial x_j^{(s)}} = \frac{k_i^{(s)}}{k_j^{(s)}} \left(\frac{x_i^{(s)}}{x_j^{(s)}}\right)^{-1/\sigma^{(s)}} \neq 0 \qquad (i \neq j) \tag{11.6}$$

and hence

$$\frac{\partial[(\partial y/\partial x_i^{(s)})/(\partial y/\partial x_j^{(s)})]}{\partial x_i^{(r)}} = 0 \qquad (s \neq r) . \tag{11.7}$$

For the upper level, the additivity feature follows the case of the CES
discussed in chapter 9 (equation (9.5)).

11.2   Intra-class and Inter-class Elasticities of Substitution

We employ the Allen–Uzawa formula for the partial elasticity of substitution shown in the previous chapter. It is derived from the unit cost function. The unit cost functions corresponding to the lower-level and the upper-level production functions are written, respectively, as follows:

$$\lambda^{(s)} = \left[\sum_i (k_i^{(s)})^{\sigma^{(s)}} (w_i^{(s)})^{1-\sigma^{(s)}} \right]^{1/(1-\sigma^{(s)})} \tag{11.8}$$

$$\lambda = \left[\sum_s (\kappa^{(s)})^{\sigma} (w^{(s)})^{1-\sigma} \right]^{1/(1-\sigma)} . \tag{11.9}$$

Readers are referred to section 9.4 for detailed procedures for deriving equations (11.8) and (11.9). Also, note that

$$\lambda^{(s)} = w^{(s)} . \tag{11.10}$$

Term $\lambda^{(s)}$ is the minimum factor cost (either the minimum wages or the minimum imputed rental cost) if the factor market is competitive and hence adjusts instantaneously.[2] Differentiating equation (11.9) along with (11.8) and (11.10), we have

$$\frac{\partial \lambda}{\partial w_i^{(s)}} = (k_i^{(s)})^{\sigma^{(s)}}(w_i^{(s)})^{-\sigma^{(s)}}(\kappa^{(s)})^{\sigma}(w^{(s)})^{\sigma^{(s)}-\sigma}\lambda^{\sigma} \tag{11.11}$$

$$\frac{\partial^2 \lambda}{\partial w_i^{(s)} \partial w_j^{(s)}} = (\kappa^{(s)})^{\sigma}\left[\prod_i (k_i^{(s)})^{\sigma^{(s)}}(w_i^{(s)})^{-\sigma^{(s)}}\right](w^{(s)})^{(2\sigma^{(s)}-\sigma)}$$

$$\times [\sigma(\kappa^{(s)})^{\sigma}\lambda^{(\sigma^{(s)}-1)}(w^{(s)})^{-\sigma} + (\sigma^{(s)} - \sigma)(w^{(s)})^{-1}]\lambda^{\sigma}$$

$$(i \neq j; i, j \in s) \tag{11.12}$$

$$\frac{\partial^2 \lambda}{\partial w_i^{(s)} \partial w_j^{(r)}} = \sigma\left[\prod_s (k_i^{(s)})^{\sigma^{(s)}}(w_i^{(s)})^{-\sigma^{(s)}}\right]\left[\prod_s (k_i^{(s)})^{\sigma}(w^{(s)})^{(\sigma^{(s)}-\sigma)}\right]\lambda^{(2\sigma-1)}$$

$$(i \in s \text{ and } j \in r; s \neq r). \tag{11.13}$$

The intra-class Allen–Uzawa partial elasticity of substitution between x_i and x_j within class s is

$$\sigma_{i^{(s)}j^{(s)}} = \frac{\lambda(\partial^2\lambda/\partial w_i^{(s)} \partial w_j^{(s)})}{(\partial\lambda/\partial w_i^{(s)})(\partial\lambda/\partial w_j^{(s)})} \qquad (i \neq j; i, j \in s) . \tag{11.14}$$

We substitute equations (11.11) and (11.12) into equation (11.14) to obtain

$$\sigma_{i^{(s)}j^{(s)}} = \frac{1}{\Omega}\sigma^{(s)} + \left(1 - \frac{1}{\Omega}\right)\sigma \tag{11.15}$$

where $\Omega = (\kappa^{(s)})^{\sigma}(w^{(s)})^{1-\sigma}/\Sigma_q(\kappa^{(q)})^{\sigma}(w^{(q)})^{1-\sigma}$. Note that $\sigma \neq \sigma^{(s)} \neq \sigma_{i^{(s)}j^{(s)}}$. They are the inter-class *direct* elasticity of substitution, the intra-class *direct* elasticity, and the intra-class Allen–Uzawa partial elasticity of substitution, respectively.[3]

The inter-class elasticity of substitution between x_i in branch s and x_j in branch r is

$$\sigma_{i^{(s)}j^{(r)}} = \frac{\lambda(\partial^2\lambda/\partial w_i^{(s)}\partial w_j^{(r)})}{(\partial\lambda/\partial w_i^{(s)})(\partial\lambda/\partial w_j^{(r)})} \qquad (i \in s \text{ and } j \in r; s \neq r). \tag{11.16}$$

Substituting equation (11.11) and (11.13) into equation (11.16) yields

$$\sigma_i^{(s)}{}_j^{(r)} = \sigma .\tag{11.17}$$

Note that the inter-class elasticities of substitution at the lower level are limited to a constant that is identical for all pairs of inputs in both branches. Also note that they are identical to the elasticity of substitution for the upper-level function, which itself is that of the CES function discussed in chapter 9. This result is attributed to the assumptions for the two-level production function.

11.3   Factor-Share Functions

We derive the factor-share functions in this section. The two-level CES production function yields the share functions for both levels. They are the functions representing the optimal factor combinations. It is expected that the two functions are independent of output because the production function is homothetic.

As shown in the previous section, the upper-level production function itself is the same as the single-level CES production function. Therefore, the share function corresponding to the upper level should be exactly the same as the function shown in chapter 9. For convenience, the share of an input (equation (9.29)) is restated here:

$$S^{(s)} = \frac{\partial C}{\partial w^{(s)}} \frac{w^{(s)}}{C} = \frac{\phi^{(s)}(w^{(s)})^{1-\sigma}}{\sum_q \phi^{(q)}(w^{(q)})^{1-\sigma}}\tag{11.18}$$

Concerning the share functions for the lower level, we first derive the equations:

$$\frac{\partial y}{\partial x_i^{(s)}} = \frac{\partial y}{\partial x^{(s)}} \frac{\partial x^{(s)}}{\partial x_i^{(s)}} = \frac{w_i^{(s)}}{p}\tag{11.19}$$

$$\frac{\partial x^{(s)}}{\partial x_i^{(s)}} = k_i^{(s)} \left(\frac{x^{(s)}}{x_i^{(s)}}\right)^{1+a^{(s)}} = \frac{w_i^{(s)}}{w^{(s)}}\tag{11.20}$$

which yield, respectively,

$$\frac{w_i^{(s)} x_i^{(s)}}{py} = S_i^{(s)} = \frac{\partial x^{(s)}}{\partial x_i^{(s)}} \frac{x_i^{(s)}}{x^{(s)}} S^{(s)}\tag{11.21}$$

$$\frac{\partial x^{(s)}}{\partial x_i^{(s)}} \frac{x_i^{(s)}}{x^{(s)}} = (k_i^{(s)})^{\sigma^{(s)}} \left(\frac{w_i^{(s)}}{w^{(s)}}\right)^{1-\sigma^{(s)}} .\tag{11.22}$$

Combining equations (11.21) and (11.22) gives

$$S_i^{(s)} = (k_i^{(s)})^{\sigma^{(s)}} \left(\frac{w_i^{(s)}}{w^{(s)}} \right)^{1-\sigma^{(s)}} S^{(s)} . \tag{11.23}$$

Note that both the upper-level and the lower-level share functions are independent of output.

11.4 Empirical Remarks

Sato (1967) is the primary reference. He estimates the parameters for both the upper- and lower-level equations. He uses plant and equipment data from US national income statistics for privately owned manufacturing establishments from 1929 to 1963. Sato chooses plant and equipment on the ground that they are highly substitutable. Technological change comes into play as the primary reason for substitutability. In addition, relative changes in prices and in efficiency make plant and equipment substitutable for each other.

Using the resultant parameters, Sato compares estimated and actual relative stocks of equipment (E) and plant structures (S), investment in structures, and an aggregate index of capital. Finally, he finds that the estimated value of the Allen–Uzawa partial elasticity of substitution between plant and equipment (the intra-class elasticity of substitution) is $\sigma_{ES} = 1.6340$, which is somewhat higher than the Cobb–Douglas value (= 1). This result suggests strong substitutability between the two factors. In reality, however, this is not the case, because technological innovation for equipment has a greater overall effect. It is therefore concluded that technological change should have been assumed to be neutral with respect to equipment and plant structure to avoid this discrepancy.

11.5 Summary

The two-level production function introduced by Sato consists of the lower-level CES and the upper-level CES functions. The intra-class elasticities of substitution at the lower level are not constant and therefore the function should be regarded as an improvement from Uzawa's generalization. As a function of homotheticity and inter-class additivity, however, its share functions are independent of output and the inter-class elasticities of substitution remain constant. The estimated value of the intra-class elasticity of substitution between two components of capital stock – plant and equipment – for the US manufacturing sector is larger than one but much less than infinity, confirming the neoclassical theory of investment.

Notes

1 Mukerji attempted to generalize the n-factor CES production function beyond Uzawa but her production function still yields a constant Allen–Uzawa partial elasticity of substitution.
2 The minimum factor cost $\lambda^{(s)}$ is a kind of aggregate factor price index corresponding to the Fisher–Törnqvist index, a discrete approximation of the Divisia aggregate price index. See Hulten (1973) and Fuss (1977a).
3 Sato also shows the results for the *direct* partial elasticity of substitution. The definition of the direct partial elasticity of substitution is

$$-\frac{\partial \ln(q_i/q_j)}{\partial \ln(p_i/p_j)} \; .$$

Recommended Reading

Diewert, W.E. 1976: Exact and superlative index numbers. *Journal of Econometrics*, 4, 116–45.
Fuss, M.A. 1977: The demand for energy in Canadian manufacturing. *Journal of Econometrics*, 5, January, 89–116.
Hulten, C.R. 1973: Divisia index numbers. *Econometrica*, 41, November, 1017–26.
McFadden, D. 1963: Constant elasticity of substitution production function. *Review of Economic Studies*, 30, 73–83.
Mukerji, V. 1963: A generalized SMAC function with constant ratios of elasticities of substitution. *Review of Economic Studies*, 30, 233–6.
Sato, K. 1967: A two-level constant-elasticity of substitution production function. *Review of Economic Studies*, 34, 201–18.
Uzawa, H. 1962: Production function with constant elasticities of substitution. *Review of Economic Studies*, 29, 291–9.

12 The Transcendental Logarithmic Production Function

We have observed in chapters 8–11 that homotheticity and additivity have played a significant role in simplifying the analytical procedure for tests of production technology. Most previous studies of factor market behavior have assumed homotheticity or separability or both. We know, of course, that the assumptions are restrictive. The factor shares of output are independent of total output if the production function is homothetic, and the elasticities of substitution are constant and equal for any pair of inputs if the function is homothetic and additive (or separable – see appendices C and D).

The value-added specification (the national income account) is the typical form of a neoclassical production function. It requires aggregate indices of capital and labor. There have been two major conditions for aggregation that justify the value-added specification: the Leontief aggregation condition and the Hicksian aggregation condition.[1] Separability of capital and labor from other inputs provides another ground for generating aggregate indices of capital and labor and hence for imputing account for addition in value to the national income.[2] However, the validity of the value-added specification is subject to a test.

In response to the restrictions of homotheticity and separability, Christensen et al. (1973) proposed a production frontier and a corresponding price frontier that do not assume homotheticity and separability. Each frontier is a translog second-order approximation of the quantities or prices of any number of inputs. The frontiers are quadratic in the logarithms. These newly proposed frontiers are called transcendental logarithmic production frontiers or cost frontiers, or simply translog production or cost functions. Although it is possible to impose homotheticity and separability on the translog function as testable parameter restrictions, they are not required to be part of the maintained hypothesis. Christensen et al. show that the translog frontier provides a greater variety of substitution of transformation patterns than those restricted by constant elasticities of substitution. The function does not place *a priori* restrictions on the Allen–Uzawa partial elasticity of substitution. They utilize the duality between the production and cost frontiers by showing that the form of the functions determining output shares of inputs and the Allen–Uzawa partial elasticities of substitution for the two frontiers are identical. The validity of the value-added specification is tested *a posteriori* with parameters as restricted for separability.

The flexible nature of the translog production function has proven highly useful in bridging the gap between theoretical and empirical research. The translog is superior to all other production functions examined so far. It is being widely used today by economists investigating production technology and factor markets. Selected studies are: Berndt and Christensen (1973b), Hudson and Jorgenson (1974), Berndt and Wood (1975), Burgess (1975), Humphrey and Moroney (1975), Griffen and Gregory (1976), Fuss (1977a), Halvorsen (1977), Halvorsen and Ford (1979), Pindyck (1979), Field and Grebenstein (1980), Hazilla and Kopp (1984), Pollak et al. (1984), Chung (1987), and Westbrook and Buckley (1990).

The usual procedure for employing the translog function can be summarized as follows:

1   justify use of the translog cost function corresponding to production technology on the basis of Shephard's duality theory;
2   derive a set of factor-share (or input demand) functions by means of Shephard's lemma;
3   estimate the factor-share functions to compute various elasticities including the Allen–Uzawa partial elasticities of substitution;
4   test for the regularity condition.

Section 12.1 discusses the various properties of the translog function. We first focus on its monotonicity and convexity and then turn our attention to the conditions for homotheticity and separability. In section 12.2, we derive the factor-share functions (the demand for productive inputs) on the basis of cost minimization. For this purpose, we show the crucial roles played by Shephard's duality theory and Shephard's lemma. We also derive various elasticities of substitution, including Allen–Uzawa partial elasticities of substitution, and note the superiority of the translog specification to most of the other specifications discussed in this book. Section 12.3 examines empirical results. The estimated Allen–Uzawa partial elasticities of substitution are our primary concern. Section 12.4 summarizes the chapter. The appendix to the chapter shows the procedures for deriving factor-share functions for capital and labor, and formulas for elasticities.

12.1   The Function and its Properties

We begin with the translog production function of n inputs. Given the n-input production function $y = f(x_1, \ldots, x_n)$, the translog function is written as

$$\ln y = \ln a_0 + \sum_{i=1}^{n} a_i \ln x_i + \frac{1}{2} \sum_{i=1}^{n} \sum_{j=1}^{n} \beta_{ij} \ln x_i \ln x_j$$

$$(i \neq j; i, j = 1, \ldots, n) \qquad (12.1)$$

where y is the output and x_i is input i.

The quadratic nature of the translog production function ensures regularity to be held at least locally. In other words, the translog function is monotonic and convex, and thus well behaved in these regions.

Monotonicity requires the marginal products of inputs to be positive, i.e. $MP_i = \partial y / \partial x_i > 0$ for each input. This condition holds for the translog if the following equation is positive, i.e. if

$$\frac{\partial y}{\partial x_i} = \frac{y}{x_i} \left(a_i + \sum_j \beta_{ij} \ln x_j \right) > 0 \ . \qquad (12.2)$$

Since $y < 0$ and $x_i > 0$, monotonicity depends on the qualitative nature of the parenthesized term. The term as a whole is the same as the input i's share of total output S_i:

$$S_i \left(= a_i + \sum_j \beta_{ij} \ln x_j \right) = f_i \frac{x_i}{y} = \frac{w_i x_i}{p \ y} \qquad (12.3)$$

where $f_i = \partial y / \partial x_i$. Therefore, the monotonicity condition can be equivalently stated as $S_i > 0$. Since $p > 0$ and $w_i > 0$, the input share is a positive fraction. Researchers should check the qualitative nature of the term in parentheses *a posteriori* against the estimated parameters at each data point. If the term is positive, monotonicity is confirmed.

Convexity of the translog function requires that its bordered Hessian must be negative semidefinite, i.e. $d^2 y \leq 0$ or $(-1)^n |\overline{H}_n| > 0$. In order to evaluate $|\overline{H}_n|$, we must know both the first- and second-order derivatives of equation (12.1) for each input. The first-order derivatives have already been presented in equation (12.2). The second-order derivatives are

$$f_{ii} = \frac{y}{x_i^2} [\beta_{ii} + S_i (S_i - 1)] \tag{12.4}$$

$$f_{ij} = \frac{y}{x_i x_j} (\beta_{ij} + S_i S_j) \qquad (i \neq j) \tag{12.5}$$

where $f_{ii} = \partial^2 y / \partial x_i^2$ and $f_{ij} = \partial^2 y / \partial x_i \partial x_j$. For simplicity and explicitness, we consider the translog production function of two inputs x_1 and x_2.

Substituting equations (12.2), (12.4), and (12.5) into the second-order bordered Hessian shown in equation (B.4) in appendix B yields

$$|\overline{H}_2| = \frac{y^3}{x_1^2 x_2^2} [S_1^2 (S_2 - \beta_{22}) + 2\beta_{12} S_1 S_2 + S_2^2 (S_1 - \beta_{11})] > 0 . \tag{12.6}$$

Since the term in the first parentheses is positive, convexity of the translog function requires the bracketed term to be positive. Empirical researchers should ascertain that the bracketed term is positive at each data point by using estimated values of β.

We now turn to the conditions under which the translog function is homothetic and separable. Note that homotheticity and separability assumptions need not automatically be imposed on the function.

For equation (12.1) to be homogeneous of degree one, the translog function must result in $\ln \theta + \ln y$ after each x_i is multiplied by scalar θ. Let us multiply each x_i by θ to obtain

$$f[\ln(\theta x_1), \ln(\theta x_2)] = (a_1 + a_2) \ln \theta$$
$$+ (\beta_{11} + \beta_{12}) \ln \theta \ln x_1 + (\beta_{12} + \beta_{22}) \ln \theta \ln x_2$$
$$+ \tfrac{1}{2} [(\beta_{11} + \beta_{12}) + (\beta_{12} + \beta_{22})] (\ln \theta)^2 + \ln y . \tag{12.7}$$

Equation (12.7) becomes $(\ln \theta + \ln y)$ if the bracketed terms are restricted to

$$a_1 + a_2 = 1 \tag{12.8}$$

$$\beta_{11} + \beta_{12} = \beta_{12} + \beta_{22} = 0 \tag{12.9}$$

$$\beta_{11} + \beta_{12} + \beta_{12} + \beta_{22} = 0 \ . \qquad (12.10)$$

These are the conditions for the translog function to be linearly homogeneous.

We now examine the conditions for the translog to be separable. For our convenience, we consider the translog production function of three inputs x_1, x_2, x_3, among which the third input is separable from inputs x_1 and x_2. The translog production function is weakly separable if inputs x_1 and x_2 are partitioned from the remaining input x_3 such that input x_3 does not affect the marginal rate of technical substitution (MRTS) between inputs x_1 and x_2. The separability conditions are

$$\frac{\partial(f_1/f_2)}{\partial x_3} = \frac{f_2(\partial f_1/\partial x_3) - f_1(\partial f_2/\partial x_3)}{f_2^2} = f_2 f_{13} - f_1 f_{23} = 0 \qquad (12.11)$$

where $f_1 = \partial y/\partial x_1$, $f_2 = \partial y/\partial x_2$, $f_{13} = \partial^2 y/\partial x_1 \partial x_3$, and $f_{23} = \partial^2 y/\partial x_2 \partial x_3$. The relevant derivatives of the translog function are

$$f_1 = \frac{y}{x_1} S_1 \qquad (12.12)$$

$$f_2 = \frac{y}{x_2} S_2 \qquad (12.13)$$

$$f_{13} = \frac{y}{x_1 x_3}(\beta_{13} + S_1 S_3) \qquad (12.14)$$

$$f_{23} = \frac{y}{x_2 x_3}(\beta_{23} + S_2 S_3) \qquad (12.15)$$

where S_i is the same as in equation (12.3) for $i = 1$, 2, and 3, respectively.

Substituting equations (12.12)–(12.15) into equation (12.11), we obtain

$$\beta_{13} S_2 - \beta_{23} S_1 = 0 \ . \qquad (12.16)$$

Since S_1 and S_2 are positive, as explained earlier, separability requires that

$$\beta_{13} = \beta_{23} = 0 \ . \qquad (12.17)$$

If none of the βs in equation (12.17) are zero, we can substitute the S_1 and S_2 equations obtained from equation (12.3) into equation (12.16) to derive the following:

$(a_2 \beta_{13} - a_1 \beta_{23}) + (\beta_{13} \beta_{12} - \beta_{23} \beta_{11}) \ln x_1$

$+ (\beta_{13} \beta_{22} - \beta_{23} \beta_{12}) \ln x_2 + (\beta_{13} \beta_{23} - \beta_{23} \beta_{13}) \ln x_3 = 0 \ .$ (12.18)

Therefore, the translog function is also separable if

$$a_2 \beta_{13} - a_1 \beta_{23} = 0 \tag{12.19}$$

$$\beta_{13} \beta_{12} - \beta_{23} \beta_{11} = 0 \tag{12.20}$$

$$\beta_{13} \beta_{22} - \beta_{23} \beta_{12} = 0 \tag{12.21}$$

yielding

$$\frac{a_1}{a_2} = \frac{\beta_{11}}{\beta_{21}} = \frac{\beta_{12}}{\beta_{22}} = \frac{\beta_{13}}{\beta_{23}} \ . \tag{12.22}$$

Equation (12.17) is referred to as the *linear* separability condition and equation (12.22) as the *nonlinear* separability condition.[3] If neither the linear nor the nonlinear separability conditions applies, it is not valid to assume the value-added specification, which requires the production function to be separable in the form of $[(x_1, x_2), x_3]$, where x_1 is capital, x_2 is labor, and x_3 is any third input such as energy or materials. In this case, estimating any functions derived from the separable translog and computing substitutability between capital and labor while ignoring the third input is improper and misleading.

12.2   Duality, Translog Cost Function, Factor-Share Functions, and Elasticities

In this section, we derive the factor-share functions from the translog cost function, examine various elasticities including the Allen–Uzawa partial elasticities of substitution, and discuss reasons why the translog specification is superior to others. We will note the important roles played by Shephard's duality and Shephard's lemma.

Shephard's duality theory (see appendix J) states that, given cost-minimizing behavior, the underlying technology of production is represented uniquely by a cost function. It is a powerful theory, which enables us to transform an output space into a cost space. On the basis of Shephard's duality, we may write the translog cost function corresponding to the production function as

$$\ln C = \ln a_0 + a_y \ln y + \sum_i a_i \ln w_i + \tfrac{1}{2}\beta_{yy} (\ln y)^2$$

$$+ \tfrac{1}{2} \sum_i \sum_j \beta_{ij} \ln w_i \ln w_j$$

$$+ \sum_i \beta_{iy} \ln y \ln w_i \qquad (i \neq j; i, j = 1, \ldots, n) \qquad (12.23)$$

where C is the total production cost and w_i is the price of input i. The underlying production technology associated with the above cost function is homothetic if $\beta_{iy} = 0$ for all i, linearly homogeneous if $a_y = 1$ and $\beta_{yy} = \beta_{iy} = 0$,[4] and separable (linearly) if $\beta_{ij} = 0$ for all i and j ($i \neq j$) so that all of the cross-product terms of inputs are zero. Note that we do not assume homotheticity and separability *a priori*.

If perfect competition prevails in factor markets, we can treat the ws and y as exogenous. Differentiating equation (12.23) with respect to each of the ws, the left-hand side of the resulting equation is the same as

$$\frac{\partial \ln C}{\partial \ln w_i} = x_i \frac{w_i}{C} \qquad (12.24)$$

by Shephard's lemma (see appendix K), suggesting that

$$\frac{\partial C}{\partial w_i} = x_i . \qquad (12.25)$$

The right-hand side of equation (12.24) therefore represents the total cost share of input x_i, which is the *derived* input demand in monetary terms.

The demand function for input x_i is written as

$$S_i = a_i + \sum_{j=1}^{n} \beta_{ij} \ln w_j + \beta_{iy} \ln y . \qquad (12.26)$$

Equation (12.25) is the same as the left-hand side of equation (12.3) under perfect competition. It is important to note that, unlike the cases in the previous chapters, the factor share (S_i) of the cost is not independent of total output. This is because the translog function does not *a priori* assume homotheticity. The system of equations for all three inputs satisfies the adding-up criterion ($\sum_i S_i = 1$) if the parameters are restricted as $\sum_i a_i = 1$ and $\sum_i \beta_{iy} = 0$, $\sum_j \beta_{ij} = \sum_i \beta_{ij} = 0$, and $\beta_{ij} = \beta_{ji}$,[5] It is also important to ascertain that the fitted results of equation (12.26) ensure that the translog cost function (equation (12.23)) is positive and concave at each observation.

There are two measures of the effects of changes in factor prices on input demands. They are the Allen–Uzawa partial elasticities of substitution and the price elasticities of demand. First, we derive the Allen–Uzawa partial elasticities of substitution in accordance with Uzawa's definitions (see equation (L.6) in appendix L). They are as follows:

$$\sigma_{ii} = \frac{C\,C_i}{C_i\,C_i} \tag{12.27}$$

$$\sigma_{ij} = \frac{C\,C_{ij}}{C_i\,C_j} \quad (i \neq j) \tag{12.28}$$

where

$$C_i = \frac{\partial C}{\partial w_i} = x_i = \frac{C}{w_i}S_i = \frac{C}{w_i}\left(a_i + \sum_{j=1}^{n} \beta_{ij}\ln w_j + \beta_{iy}\ln y\right) \tag{12.29}$$

$$C_{ii} = \frac{\partial^2 C}{\partial w_i^2} = \frac{\partial x_i}{\partial w_i} = \frac{(\beta_{ii} + S_i^2 - S_i)C}{w_i^2} \tag{12.30}$$

$$C_{ij} = \frac{\partial^2 C}{\partial w_i \partial w_j} = \frac{\partial x_i}{\partial w_j} = \frac{(\beta_{ij} + S_i S_j)C}{w_i w_j} \quad (i \neq j)\,. \tag{12.31}$$

Substituting equations (12.29), (12.30) and (12.31) into equations (12.27) and (12.28), we obtain

$$\sigma_{ii} = \frac{\beta_{ii} + S_i(S_i - 1)}{S_i^2} \tag{12.32}$$

$$\sigma_{ij} = 1 + \frac{\beta_{ij}}{S_i S_j} \quad (i \neq j)\,. \tag{12.33}$$

Although there is a perfect symmetry between the translog production function and the translog utility function in their functional form, the argument for the former is w_i and the argument for the latter is p_i/m. Also, the former is differentiated with respect to w_i, whereas the latter is differentiated with respect to p_i instead of p_i/m. If the value of σ_{ij} calculated from the estimated value of β_{ij} is greater than zero, inputs x_i and x_j are substitutes for each other. If it is less than zero, they are complements.

The own- and cross-price elasticities of input demand (defined on the left-hand side below) are

$$\epsilon_{ii} = \frac{\partial x_i}{\partial w_i}\frac{w_i}{x_i} = \sigma_{ii} S_i \tag{12.34}$$

$$\epsilon_{ij} = \frac{\partial x_i}{\partial w_j} \frac{w_j}{x_i} = \sigma_{ij} S_j \quad (i \neq j) \qquad (12.35)$$

$$\epsilon_{ji} = \frac{\partial x_j}{\partial w_i} \frac{w_i}{x_j} = \sigma_{ij} S_i \quad (i \neq j) .^6 \qquad (12.36)$$

Observe that $\sigma_{ij} = \sigma_{ji}$, although $\epsilon_{ij} \neq \epsilon_{ji}$. The Allen–Uzawa cross-partial elasticities of substitution are the same because of the Slutsky symmetry imposed on the translog, i.e. $\beta_{ij} = \beta_{ji}$. Also, note that the value of ϵ require values of σ which, in turn, require estimated values of β.

None of the Allen–Uzawa partial elasticities of substitution are restricted to a constant number. Rather, they vary with the input shares. This is because the translog cost function given in equation (12.23) need not be homothetic and separable. Without separability, the translog production function can accommodate a wide range of substitutabilities. If, however, the underlying production structure is separable, so that all of the relevant cross-product terms of inputs vanish from equation (12.23), then the corresponding Allen–Uzawa cross-partial elasticity of substitution is unity and remains so for any pair of inputs. This returns us to the Cobb–Douglas form.[7]

12.3 Empirical Remarks

There are numerous empirical research studies into the translog production function. Table 12.1 provides a survey of selected studies on factor substitution in the context of the translog function. As shown in the table, different authors use different assumptions, specifications, and data, and obtain different results. However, the type of function under consideration in these studies is generally the same – a uniform set of input-share equations. The standard procedure taken by researchers is to form a system of seemingly unrelated equations with equation (12.26). Since $\Sigma_i S_i = 1$ under the adding-up criterion, the parameters are restricted as indicated in section 12.2. The system is then generally estimated by Zellner's iterative efficient method.

I examine the work done by Berndt and Wood (1975). They focus on the cross-substitution possibilities between energy and nonenergy inputs to characterize the structure of technology in US manufacturing. Berndt and Wood scrutinize the estimated results of elasticities of

Table 12.1 Overview of selected studies on factor substitution

Author	Country and industry	Data and observations[a]	Assumptions and production or cost function	Test on VA separability[b]	Type of equation and method of estimation	Main results
Berndt and Christensen (1973b)	US manufacturing	Time series 1929–68	Linear homogeneous and separable $[f(K_i,K_j,L),X]$	NA	SUE 13SLS IZEF	$(K_i{:}K_j)$, $(K_i$ or $K_j{:}L)$ = substitutes
Hudson and Jorgenson (1974)	US 9 industrial sectors	Time series 1947–71	Homogeneous and separable $[K,L,E,M]$	NA	SUE MMDE	$(K{:}E)$ = complements $(L{:}E)$ = substitutes
Berndt and Wood (1975)	US manufacturing	Time series 1947–71	Linear homogeneous and separable $[K,L,E,M]$	VAS under LSR	SUE 13SLS	$(K{:}L)$, $(K{:}M)$, $(L{:}E)$, $(L{:}M)$, $(E{:}M)$ = substitutes $(K{:}E)$ = complements
Humphrey and Moroney (1975)	US 2-digit manufacturing	Cross section 1963	Linear homogeneous and separable $[f(K,L,N),I]$	NA	SUE IZEF	$(K{:}L)$, $(K{:}N)$, $(L{:}N)$ = substitutes
Griffin and Gregory (1976)	Cross-country (9) manufacturing	Pooled data in 1955, 1960, 1965 and 1969	Homothetic and separable $[Y,\phi(P_K,P_j,P_i),\ P_M,\ t]$	VAS	SUE IZEF	$(K{:}L)$, $(K{:}E)$, $(L{:}E)$ = substitutes in L-R $(K{:}E)$ = complements in S-R
Halvorsen (1977)	US 2-digit manufacturing	Cross section 1971	Linear homogeneous and separable $[E,\ 4$ energy costs$]$	NA	SUE IZEF	$(E_i{:}E_j)$ = substitutes
Fuss (1977a)	Canada manufacturing	Pooled data 1961–71	Homothetic and separable $[K,L,M,E(6)]$	NA	SUE ZEF EIV	$(K{:}L)$, $(K{:}M)$, $(L{:}E)$, $(L{:}M)$, $(E_i{:}E_j)$ = substitutes

$$[f(K, L_i, L_j, E(3)), X]$$

Study	Region / data	Period	Functional form / separability	Separability[b]	Type and method	Results[a]
Pindyck (1979)	Cross-country (10)	Pooled data 1963–73	$[f(K, L_i, L_j, E(3)), X]$	NA	SUE IZEF	$(K{:}L)$, $(K{:}E)$, $(L{:}E)$ = substitutes $(E_i{:}E_j)$ = mixed results
Field and Grebenstein (1980)	US 2-digit manufacturing	Cross section 1971	Homothetic and separable $[f(KML, E(4)), M]$	NA	SUE IZEF	$(K_i{:}E)$ = complements $(K_j{:}E)$ = substitutes
Hazilla and Kopp (1984)	US 34 producing sector	Time series 1958–74	Linear homogeneous and separable $[f(K_i, K_j, L, E), M]$	NA	SUE IZEF	$(E{:}K)$, $(E{:}L)$, $(E{:}I)$ = mixed results
Chung (1987)	US manufacturing	Time series 1947–71	Homothetic and separable $[K(\cdot), L(\cdot), E(\cdot), M(\cdot)]$ — Non-homogeneous and separable $[K, L, E, M]$	VAS under LSR and NSR	SE DTM IZEF	$(K{:}L)$, $(K{:}E)$, $(K{:}M)$, $(L{:}E)$, $(L{:}M)$, $(E{:}M)$ = substitutes

Type of equation: SUE, seemingly unrelated equations; SE, single equation.

Method of estimation: EIV, efficient instrumental variable method; I3SLS, iterative three-stage least squares method; IZEF, Zellner's iterative efficient method; MMDE, Malinvaud's minimum distance estimator method; ZEF, Zellner's efficient method; NIV, non-linear instrumental variable technique; DTM, Durbin's two-stage method

Variable: K, capital; K_i, capital i (i = equipment or structures in the case of Berndt and Christensen; physical capital or working capital in the case of Field and Grebenstein); K, quasi-fixed capital; L, labor; L_i, labor i (i = production workers or nonproduction workers in the case of Halvorsen and Ford); E, energy; E_i, energy i (i = coal, liquid petroleum, fuel oil, natural gas, electricity, and motor gasoline in the case of Fuss; electricity, fuel oil, and gas in the case of Halvorsen and Ford; oil, gas, coal, and electricity in the case of Pindyck); F, fuel; M, materials; N, natural resources; N_i, natural resources i (nonfuel minerals); I, nonresource intermediate inputs; L-R, long run; S-R, short run.

Separability: VAS, value-added separability; LSR, linear separability restrictions; NSR, nonlinear separability restrictions; NA, not available.

[a]In general, a cross-section analysis yields long-run effects, whereas a time-series analysis yields short-run effects.

[b]This column takes no account of other separability tests.

Source: Chung, J.W. 1987: On the estimation of factor substitution in the translog model, Review of Economics and Statistics, LXIX, August, 409–17.

substitution in relation to one another as well as to the value-added specification.

Berndt and Wood use time-series data (1947–71) to estimate the factor share functions for four inputs – capital (K), labor (L), energy (E), and materials (M) – by means of iterative three-stage least squares (I3SLS). To begin with, the authors test the positivity and concavity conditions of the translog cost function for each observation. They conclude that the function is well behaved for the estimation period. Estimated elasticities suggest the following.

1   Energy and labor are substitutable ($\sigma_{EL} = 0.65$) with cross-price elasticities $\epsilon_{EL} = 0.03$ and $\epsilon_{LE} = 0.18$.
2   Energy and capital are complementary ($\sigma_{EK} = -3.2$) with cross-price elasticities $\epsilon_{EK} = -0.15$ and $\epsilon_{KE} = -0.18$.
3   Capital and labor are substitutable ($\sigma_{KL} = 1.01$) with cross-price elasticities $\epsilon_{KL} = 0.28$ and $\epsilon_{LK} = 0.06$.
4   Demand for energy is responsive to a change in its own price ($\epsilon_{EE} = -0.47$) as are capital ($\epsilon_{KK} = -0.48$), labor ($\epsilon_{LL} = -0.45$), and materials ($\epsilon_{MM} = -0.22$).

There is a consensus among economists on substitutability between any pair of inputs other than between capital and energy. Views on capital and energy substitutability are divided. Hudson and Jorgenson (1974) and Fuss (1977a) suggest that capital and energy are complements, whereas Griffin and Gregory (1976), Pindyck (1979), and Chung (1987) find them to be substitutes.

Next, Berndt and Wood investigate the value-added specification. They estimate the input demand equations from the translog cost function, imposing a linear restriction condition and a nonlinear restriction condition. The χ^2 statistic leads to the conclusion that the data do not satisfy the separability conditions for the value-added specification. Berndt and Wood have also tested the value-added specification with the Leontief aggregation condition and the Hicks aggregation condition. The two results also consistently reject separability. The results imply that, in the absence of value-added specification, past investment and factor demand studies for US manufacturing which were based on the value-added specification are unreliable.

Berndt and Wood conclude by presenting some policy implications. Given $\sigma_{EE} < 0$ and $\sigma_{KE} < 0$, and $\sigma_{LE} > 0$, the competitive market price of energy (i.e. the price without ceiling) decreases the energy and capital intensities of output and increases the labor intensity of output. Berndt and Wood note that by 1980 almost all price controls on energy were removed.[8] Given $\sigma_{KE} < 0$, investment incentives, such as investment tax credits and accelerated depreciation allowances that reduce the price of capital services, increase demand for capital and energy. Therefore offering investment incentives is a less attractive policy than energy conservation.

12.4 Summary

The translog production function currently enjoys widespread popularity among economists. We can use Shephard's duality and Shephard's lemma to derive the factor-share functions. The translog function does not require the assumptions of homotheticity and separability. Hence, the factor shares are not independent of output, unlike the case of production functions in the earlier chapters, and the Allen–Uzawa elasticities of substitution are not constant and equal for any pair of inputs. These results demonstrate the superiority of the translog specification. If, of course, the translog does take a homothetic and separable form, it reverts to the Cobb–Douglas function.

Berndt and Wood claim that the estimated translog cost function satisfies positivity and concavity conditions, so it is well behaved. They suggest that capital and energy are complementary. That implies that investment incentives, such as investment tax credits and accelerated depreciation allowances, increase demand for energy. They also suggest that the value-added specification is invalid.

Appendix

A12.1   Derivation of the Factor-Share Functions

The linear homogeneous translog production function with capital (K) and labor (L) is

$$\ln C = \ln a_0 + a_K \ln P_K + a_L \ln P_L + \tfrac{1}{2}\beta_{KK} (\ln P_K)^2$$
$$+ \beta_{KL} \ln P_K \ln P_L + \tfrac{1}{2}\beta_{LL} (\ln P_L)^2 + \ln y \qquad (1)$$

where P_K is the price of capital and P_L is the price of labor.
The total cost-share functions of capital and labor are

$$\frac{\partial C}{\partial P_K}\frac{P_K}{C} = \frac{P_K K}{C} = S_K = a_K + \beta_{KK}\ln P_K + \beta_{KL}\ln P_L \qquad (2)$$

$$\frac{\partial C}{\partial P_L}\frac{P_L}{C} = \frac{P_L L}{C} = S_L = a_L + \beta_{KL}\ln P_K + \beta_{LL}\ln P_L . \qquad (3)$$

A12.2   The Allen–Uzawa Partial Elasticity of Substitution

The Allen–Uzawa partial elasticities of substitution are

$$\sigma_{KK} = \frac{C(\partial^2 C/\partial P_K^2)}{(\partial C/\partial P_K)(\partial C/\partial P_K)} = \frac{\beta_{KK} + S_K(S_K - 1)}{S_K^2} \qquad (4)$$

$$\sigma_{LL} = \frac{C(\partial^2 C/\partial P_L^2)}{(\partial C/\partial P_L)(\partial C/\partial P_L)} = \frac{\beta_{LL} + S_L(S_L - 1)}{S_L^2} \qquad (5)$$

$$\sigma_{KL} = \sigma_{LK} = \frac{C(\partial^2 C/\partial P_K\partial P_L)}{(\partial C/\partial P_K)(\partial C/\partial P_L)} = 1 + \frac{\beta_{KL}}{S_K S_L} . \qquad (6)$$

A12.3   The Own- and Cross-Price Elasticities of Demand

The elasticities of input demand are as follows.

Own-Price Elasticities

$$\epsilon_{KK} = \frac{\partial K}{\partial P_K}\frac{P_K}{K} = \frac{\partial(\partial C/\partial P_K)}{\partial P_K}\frac{P_K}{K} = \left[(\beta_{KK} + S_K^2 - S_K)\frac{C}{P_K^2}\right]\frac{P_K}{K} = \sigma_{KK}S_K \qquad (7)$$

$$\epsilon_{LL} = \frac{\partial L}{\partial P_L}\frac{P_L}{L} = \frac{\partial(\partial C/\partial P_L)}{\partial P_L}\frac{P_L}{L} = \left[(\beta_{LL} + S_L^2 - S_L)\frac{C}{P_L^2}\right]\frac{P_L}{L} = \sigma_{LL}S_L . \qquad (8)$$

Cross-Price Elasticities

$$\epsilon_{KL} = \frac{\partial K}{\partial P_L}\frac{P_L}{K} = \frac{\partial(\partial C/\partial P_K)}{\partial P_L}\frac{P_L}{K} = \left[(\beta_{KL} + S_K S_L)\frac{C}{P_K P_L}\right]\frac{P_L}{K} = \sigma_{KL}S_L \qquad (9)$$

$$\epsilon_{LK} = \frac{\partial L}{\partial P_K}\frac{P_K}{L} = \frac{\partial(\partial C/\partial P_L)}{\partial P_K}\frac{P_K}{L} = \left[(\beta_{KL} + S_K S_L)\frac{C}{P_K P_L}\right]\frac{P_K}{L} = \sigma_{KL}S_K .$$

(10)

Notes

1 The Leontief aggregation condition requires factors other than capital and labor and output to move in fixed proportions, i.e. fixed proportions of E/y and M/y, where E is energy, M is materials, and y is output. The Hicksian aggregation condition requires prices of factors other than capital and labor and the price of output to move in fixed proportions, i.e. fixed proportions of p_E/p and p_M/p, where p_E is the price of energy, p_M is the price of materials, and p is the price of output.
2 Arrow (1972) and Green (1964) justify the value-added specification in terms of separability.
3 Berndt and Christensen (1973a, b) and Blackorby et al. (1977) derive the two separability conditions.
4 See Fuss (1977a, p. 92).
5 Hanoch (1975) classifies these restrictions as: Cournot aggregation ($\Sigma_j\beta_{ij} = 0$), Engle aggregation ($\Sigma_i\beta_{ij} = 0$), Slutsky symmetry ($\beta_{ij} = \beta_{ji}$), and identifiability of the distribution parameters ($\Sigma\ a_i = 1$).
6 See equations (7)–(10) in the appendix to this chapter.
7 Global regularity of the flexible functional forms, including the translog function discussed in this chapter and the generalized Leontief function to be discussed in chapter 15, have recently been examined from the perspective of an applied general equilibrium setting. For detailed arguments, see Caves and Christensen (1980), Jorgenson and Slesnik (1985), and Perroni and Rutherford (1989).
8 Only natural gas still has limited controls at present.

Recommended Reading

Arrow, K.J. 1972: The measurement of real value added. University Institute for Mathematical Studies in the Social Studies, Stanford, Technical Report, No. 60, June.
Berndt, E.R. and Christensen, L.R. 1973: The translog function and the substitution of equipment, structures, and labor in U.S. manufacturing 1929–68. *Journal of Econometrics*, 1, March, 81–113.
—— and Wood, D.O. 1975: Technology, prices, and the derived demand for energy. *Review of Economics and Statistics*, 57, August, 259–68.

Burgess, D. 1975: Duality theory and pitfalls in the specification of technologies. *Journal of Econometrics*, 3, 105–21.

Christensen, L.R., Jorgenson, D.W. and Lau, L.J. 1973: Transcendental logarithmic production function frontiers. *Review of Economics and Statistics*, 55, February, 29–45.

Chung, J.W. 1987: On the estimation of factor substitution in the translog model. *Review of Economics and Statistics*, 64, August, 409–17.

Field, B.C. and Grebenstein, C. 1980: Capital-energy substitution in U.S. manufacturing. *Review of Economics and Statistics*, 62, May, 207–12.

Fuss, M.A. 1977: The demand for energy in Canadian manufacturing. *Journal of Econometrics*, 5, January, 89–116.

—— 1977: The structure of technology over time, 1797–1821. *Econometrica*, 45, 1797–821.

Green, H.A.J. 1964: *Aggregation in Economic Analysis: An Introductory Survey*. Princeton, NJ: Princeton University Press.

Griffin, J.M. and Gregory, P.R. 1976: An intercountry translog model of energy substitution responses. *American Economic Review*, 66, December, 845–57.

Halvorsen, R. 1977: Energy substitution in U.S. manufacturing. *Review of Economics and Statistics*, 59, November, 381–8.

—— and Ford, J. 1979: Substitution among energy, capital, and labor inputs in U.S. manufacturing. In R.S. Pindyck (ed.), *Advances in the Economics of Energy and Resources I*, Greenwich, CT: JAI Press.

Hanoch, G. 1975: Production and demand models with direct or indirect activity. *Econometrica*, 43, May, 395–420.

Hazilla, M. and Kopp, R. 1984: *Industrial Energy-Substitution: Econometric Analysis of U.S. Data, 1958–1974*. Electric Power Research Institute, Palo Alto, CA, EA-3462, Final Report.

Hudson, E.A. and Jorgenson, D.W. 1974: U.S. energy policy and economic growth, 1975–2000. *Bell Journal of Economics and Management Science*, 5, Autumn, 461–514.

Humphrey, D.B. and Moroney, J.R. 1975: Substitution among capital, labor and natural resource products in American Manufacturing. *Journal of Political Economy*, 83, February, 57–82.

Pindyck, R.S. 1979: Interfuel substitution and the industrial demand for energy: an international comparison. *Review of Economics and Statistics*, 61, May, 169–79.

13 The Constant-Elasticity-of-Substitution–Translog Production Function

There is no doubt that the translog production function examined in the previous chapter has many attractive features, including flexible Allen–Uzawa elasticities of substitution. However, as Blackorby et al. (1977) and Denny and Fuss (1977) have indicated, the separable form of the translog restricts its flexibility greatly. So economists continue to search for a more flexible functional form.

This chapter discusses the CES–translog production function suggested by Pollak et al. (1984). Since it combines desired properties of both the CES function and the translog function, it is intuitively correct to expect that the function should display a wider range of substitution possibilities than either the CES or the translog, yet it requires only one more parameter than the translog function. Being a combined form of two accepted production functions, nested testing can be performed by conventional procedures.

Section 13.1 examines limitations of the translog function. Section 13.2 presents the CES–translog cost function. In section 13.3, we derive and examine the factor share functions. We also discuss various elasticities in this section. Section 13.4 discusses empirical results. Finally, section 13.5 summarizes the chapter.

13.1 Limitations of the Translog Production Function

As briefly mentioned at the end of the previous chapter, the separable form of the translog function can be broken down into a Cobb–Douglas function. In this section, we shall examine more specifically how the separability conditions decompose the translog function.

Substituting the linear separability condition, by which the first two inputs are separable from the latter two inputs ($\beta_{13} = \beta_{23} = \beta_{14} = \beta_{24} = 0$), into equation (12.1), we have

$$\ln y = \ln a_0 + \left(\sum_{i=1}^{2} a_i \ln x_i + \frac{1}{2} \sum_{i=1}^{2} \sum_{j=1}^{2} \beta_{ij} \ln x_i \ln x_j \right)$$

$$+ \left(\sum_{i=3}^{4} a_i \ln x_i + \frac{1}{2} \sum_{i=3}^{4} \sum_{j=3}^{4} \beta_{ij} \ln x_i \ln x_j \right) \qquad (i \neq j) . \qquad (13.1)$$

Given arbitrary numbers μ and ν yielding $a_i = \mu g_i$, $\beta_{ii} = \mu g_{ii}$, and $\beta_{ij} = \mu g_{ij}$ for all $i, j = 1,2$ on the one hand and $a_i = \nu h_i$, $\beta_{ii} = \nu h_{ii}$, and $\beta_{ij} = \nu h_{ij}$ for all $i, j = 3$ and 4 on the other hand, it is possible to rewrite equation (13.1) as

$$\ln y = \ln a_0 + \mu \left(\sum_{i=1}^{2} g_i \ln x_i + \frac{1}{2} \sum_{i=1}^{2} \sum_{j=1}^{2} g_{ij} \ln x_i \ln x_j \right)$$

$$+ \nu \left(\sum_{i=3}^{4} h_i \ln x_i + \frac{1}{2} \sum_{i=3}^{4} \sum_{j=3}^{4} h_{ij} \ln x_i \ln x_j \right) \qquad (i \neq j) . \qquad (13.2)$$

Equation (13.1) has been transformed into a *Cobb–Douglas function of translog subaggregates* under the linear separability conditions, implying that the separable form of the translog function can be broken down into a Cobb–Douglas function of translog subaggregates.[1]

If we substitute the nonlinear separability condition

$$\frac{a_1}{a_2} = \frac{\beta_{11}}{\beta_{21}} = \frac{\beta_{12}}{\beta_{22}} = \frac{\beta_{13}}{\beta_{23}} = \frac{\beta_{14}}{\beta_{24}}$$

into equation (12.1), the equation becomes

$$\ln y = \ln a_0 + \sum_i a_i X_i + \sum_i \sum_j b_{ij} \ln X_i \ln X_j \qquad (i \neq j) \qquad (13.3)$$

where $\ln X_i$ is a quadratic function of $\ln x_i$, where $i = 1, 2$, and $\ln X_j$ is a quadratic function of $\ln x_j$, where $j = 3, 4$. In this case, the translog is transformed into a *translog function of Cobb–Douglas subaggregates*.

13.2 The Constant-Elasticity-of-Substitution–Translog Cost Function

Pollak et al. attempt to generalize the translog function. Their CES–translog cost function corresponding to the CES–translog production function is written as follows:

$$\ln C = a_0 + a_y \ln y + \left(\frac{1}{1-\sigma}\right) \ln\left[\sum_i a_i w_i^{1-\sigma}\right]$$

$$+ \frac{1}{2}\sum_i\sum_j \beta_{ij} \ln w_i \ln w_j + \sum_i \beta_{iy} \ln y \ln w_i$$

$$(i \neq j; i, j = 1, \ldots, n) \qquad (13.4)$$

where $\sum_i a_i = 1$, $\beta_{ij} = \beta_{ji}$, $\sum_j \beta_{ij} = \sum_i \beta_{ji} = 0$, and $\sum_i \beta_{yi} = 0$. Note that the third term on the right-hand side including the term in brackets is the CES and part of each of the remaining terms is the quadratic component included in the translog function. If all βs = 0, the CES–translog reduces to the CES. If $\sigma = 1$, it becomes the translog. Therefore, the CES–translog function is a generalization of the CES function on the one hand and the translog on the other hand. Obviously, with only one more parameter (σ), it displays more flexibility than the translog function. In contrast with the CES–translog function, it is interesting to note that the translog function is a generalization of the Cobb–Douglas function because it becomes the Cobb–Douglas for all βs = 0.

The CES–translog production function should be monotonic and strictly quasi-concave at each data point along with the estimated parameters. The function is additive and homothetic only under certain conditions. Given the symmetry between the CES–translog production function and the CES–translog utility function, it is redundant to discuss the properties of the CES–translog production function here. Interested readers should see chapter 7.

13.3 Factor-Share Functions and Elasticities

As usual, Shephard's lemma suggests that we should differentiate the above cost function with respect to factor prices to get the cost-share functions. The result is

$$\frac{\partial C}{\partial w_i} = C\left(\frac{a_i\, w_i^{-\sigma}}{\Sigma_k\, a_k\, w_k^{1-\sigma}} + \sum_j \beta_{ij}\frac{\ln w_j}{w_i}\right) \tag{13.5}$$

yielding

$$S_i = \frac{a_i\, w_i^{1-\sigma}}{\Sigma_k\, a_k\, w_k^{1-\sigma}} + \Sigma_j\, \beta_{ij} \ln w_j \qquad (i, j \in k;\, i \neq j) \tag{13.6}$$

where $S_i = (\partial C/\partial w_i)(w_i/C)$.

To get the Allen–Uzawa elasticities of substitution, we need to differentiate equation (13.4) twice. The results are as follows:

$$\frac{\partial^2 C}{\partial w_i^2} = \frac{S_i^2 C}{w_i^2} + C\Bigg\{ \frac{[-\sigma(\Sigma_j a_j\, w_i^{1-\sigma})w_i^{-1} - (1-\sigma)\, a_i\, w_i^{-\sigma}]a_i\, w_i^{-\sigma}}{(\Sigma_j a_j\, w_j^{1-\sigma})^2}$$

$$+ (\beta_{ii} + \Sigma_j\, \beta_{ij} \ln w_j)\,(-w_i^{-1}\, w_i^{-1})\Bigg\} \qquad (i \in j) \tag{13.7}$$

$$\frac{\partial^2 C}{\partial w_i \partial w_j} = \left[\frac{a_i\, w_i^{\sigma}}{\Sigma_k a_k\, w_k^{-\sigma}} + \left(\sum_k \beta_{ik} \ln w_k\right) w_i^{-1}\right]\frac{\partial C}{\partial w_j}$$

$$+ \left[\frac{-(1-\sigma)\pi_k a_k\, w_k^{-\sigma}}{(\Sigma_k a_k\, w_k^{-\sigma})^2} + \beta_{ij}\, w_i^{-1}\, w_j^{-1}\right] C$$

$$(i, j \in k;\, i \neq j)\,. \tag{13.8}$$

The Allen–Uzawa partial elasticities of substitution are as follows:

$$\sigma_{ii} = \frac{C(\partial^2 C/\partial w_i^2)}{(\partial C/\partial w_i)(\partial C/\partial w_i)} = 1 - \frac{1}{S_i} + \frac{\beta_{ii}}{S_i^2} + \frac{(1-\sigma)\Omega}{S_i^2} \tag{13.9}$$

$$\sigma_{ij} = \frac{C(\partial^2 C/\partial w_i \partial w_j)}{(\partial C/\partial w_i)(\partial C/\partial w_j)} = 1 + \frac{\beta_{ij}}{S_i S_j} - \frac{(1-\sigma)\Omega}{S_i S_j} \tag{13.10}$$

where $\Omega = \Pi_k a_k\, w_k^{1-\sigma}\,(\Sigma_k a_k w_k^{1-\sigma})^{-2}$.

Note that the first three terms on the right-hand side of equation (13.9) and the first two terms on the right-hand side of equation (13.10) are the same as the corresponding Allen–Uzawa elasticities of substitution obtained from the translog production function.

13.4   Empirical Remarks

Pollak et al. (1984) estimate the CES, the translog, and the CES–translog production functions, using a singular system of factor demand equations, and compare the results. They assume that the production technology is homothetic and Hicks-neutral, that factor prices are exogenous, and that factor shares adjust instantaneously to changes in factor prices. They arrange time-series and cross-sectional data from previous studies into eight sets.

The likelihood ratio test indicates the CES–translog to be significantly superior to the CES in all samples and to the translog in all but one sample. The CES–translog values for the elasticity of substitution (σ) estimated with Berndt–Wood's data, Magnus–Woodland's data, and the Cowing's data are 1.00, 0.67, and 2.66, respectively.[2] Note that the translog value of σ is 1. The CES values of σ for the three data sets are 0.59, 0.12 (statistically insignificant), and 0.099 (statistically insignificant), respectively.

As discussed in the previous chapter, there is a consensus among economists on substitutability between inputs other than between capital and energy. Therefore, we limit our focus to the Allen–Uzawa partial elasticity of substitution between capital and energy. The Allen–Uzawa partial elasticities for the translog and the CES–translog models calculated at the first, middle, and the last observation of the sample period for the time-series data (the Berndt–Wood data) are the same and quite stable over time (-3.27 for the middle observation), suggesting that the two are complements. This result is similar to the one presented in the previous chapter. For the cross-sectional data (the Cowing data), however, the Allen–Uzawa partial elasticities of substitution are not consistent. The Allen–Uzawa partial elasticity of substitution between capital and energy is -0.70 for median total cost. Comparing the Allen–Uzawa partial elasticities of substitution shows that for the CES the Allen–Uzawa cross-partial elasticities of substitution are identical for all pairs of factors (see equation (9.30) in chapter 9), are independent of factor prices, and differ substantially from the Allen–Uzawa partial elasticities of substitution for the translog and the CES–translog functions.

Tests for regularity show that while the CES necessarily satisfies globally the regularity conditions (if $\sigma > 0$), the translog and the CES–translog functions often violate these conditions at the extremes and satisfy the conditions near the center of samples.

Based on all of the final estimations, Pollak et al. reject the applicability of the CES because of its highly restrictive nature in analyzing the Allen–Uzawa partial elasticities of substitution. They suggest that the CES–translog function closely resembles the translog but cautiously assert that the CES–translog may prove a suitable replacement for the translog only if other data and other estimation procedures can justifiably support their conclusions.

Westbrook and Buckley (1990) is an additional reference for readers who are interested in applications. Based on the CES–translog function, they develop the cost function for a three-input transportation model to assess the competitive relationship between truck and rail transportation in the United States. Their estimated values of elasticities of substitution confirm strong intermodal competition in the transportation of fresh fruits and vegetables and support deregulation of the transportation industry.

13.5   Summary

The CES–translog production function is the sophisticated, flexible function in use at present. It is the functional form of the CES and the translog functions combined together. The CES–translog function permits a wider range of variations for the Allen–Uzawa partial elasticities of substitution than any of the production functions discussed so far. However, the CES–translog also collapses to the CES or to the translog under certain conditions.

Pollak et al. and a recent study suggest that the CES–translog function is a significant improvement over both the CES and the translog functions in terms of the likelihood ratio test statistic. Among various Allen–Uzawa partial elasticities of substitution that they estimated with time-series data, it is notable that they too found capital and energy to be complementary. For cross-sectional data, however, the results are not consistent.

Appendix

In this appendix, we assume that there are two inputs, capital and labor.

A13.1   The Cost-Share Functions

Given the total cost function below,

$$\ln C = a_0 + a_y \ln y + \frac{1}{1-\sigma} \ln(a_K P_K^{1-\sigma} + a_L P_L^{1-\sigma})$$

$$+ \tfrac{1}{2}[\beta_{KK} (\ln P_K)^2 + \beta_{LL} (\ln P_L)^2 + 2\beta_{KL} \ln P_K \ln P_L]$$

$$+ \beta_{yK} \ln y \ln P_K + \beta_{yL} \ln y \ln P_L \tag{1}$$

where P_K is the price of capital and P_L is the price of labor, the first- and second-order partial derivatives of the function with respect to factor prices are

$$\frac{\partial C}{\partial P_K} = C\left[\frac{a_K P_K^{-\sigma}}{a_K P_K^{1-\sigma} + a_L P_L^{1-\sigma}} + (\beta_{KK} \ln P_K + \beta_{KL} \ln P_L)\frac{1}{P_K}\right] \quad (2)$$

$$\frac{\partial C}{\partial P_L} = C\left[\frac{a_L P_L^{-\sigma}}{a_K P_K^{1-\sigma} + a_L P_L^{1-\sigma}} + (\beta_{KL} \ln P_K + \beta_{LL} \ln P_L)\frac{1}{P_L}\right]. \quad (3)$$

Shephard's lemma tells us that $\partial C/\partial P_K = K$ and $\partial C/\partial P_L = L$. Multiplying through equations (2) and (3) by P_K/C and P_L/C, respectively, yields the cost-share functions (equivalently, the cost-minimizing factor demand function):

$$S_K = \frac{a_K P_K^{1-\sigma}}{a_K P_K^{1-\sigma} + a_L P_L^{1-\sigma}} + \beta_{KK} \ln P_K + \beta_{KL} \ln P_L + \beta_{yK} \ln y \quad (4)$$

$$S_L = \frac{a_L P_L^{1-\sigma}}{a_K P_K^{1-\sigma} + a_L P_L^{1-\sigma}} + \beta_{KL} \ln P_K + \beta_{LL} \ln P_L + \beta_{yL} \ln y \quad (5)$$

where

$$S_K = \frac{\partial C}{\partial P_K}\frac{P_K}{C}$$

$$S_L = \frac{\partial C}{\partial P_L}\frac{P_L}{C}.$$

A13.2 The Allen–Uzawa Partial Elasticities of Substitution

For the Allen–Uzawa partial elasticities of substitution, it is necessary to get second-order partial derivatives of the total cost function.

$$\frac{\partial^2 C}{\partial P_K^2} = \frac{S_K^2 C}{P_K^2} + \left\{\frac{a_K P_K^{-\sigma}[-\sigma P_K^{-1}(a_K P_K^{1-\sigma} + a_L P_L^{1-\sigma}) - (1-\sigma)a_K P_K^{-\sigma}}{(a_K P_K^{1-\sigma} + a_L P_L^{1-\sigma})^2}\right.$$

$$\left. + [\beta_{KK} - (\beta_{KK} \ln P_K + \beta_{KL} \ln P_L)]\frac{1}{P_K^2}\right\}C \quad (6)$$

$$\frac{\partial^2 C}{\partial P_L^2} = \frac{S_L^2 C}{P_L^2} + \left\{\frac{a_L P_L^{-\sigma}[-\sigma P_L^{-1}(a_K P_K^{1-\sigma} + a_L P_L^{1-\sigma}) - (1-\sigma)a_L P_K^{-\sigma}]}{(a_K P_K^{1-\sigma} + a_L P_L^{1-\sigma})^2}\right.$$

$$\left. + [\beta_{LL} - (\beta_{KL} \ln P_K + \beta_{LL} \ln P_L)]\frac{1}{P_L^2}\right\}C \quad (7)$$

$$\frac{\partial^2 C}{\partial P_K \partial P_L} = \left[\frac{a_K P_K^{-\sigma}}{a_K P_K^{-\sigma} + a_L P_L^{-\sigma}} + (\beta_{KK} \ln P_K + \beta_{KL} \ln P_L) \frac{1}{P_K} \right] \frac{\partial C}{\partial P_L}$$

$$+ \left[\frac{-a_K P_K^{-\sigma} a_L (1 - \sigma) P_L^{-\sigma}}{(a_K P_K^{-\sigma} + a_L P_L^{-\sigma})^2} + \beta_{KL} \frac{1}{P_K} \frac{1}{P_L} \right] C . \qquad (8)$$

Substituting equations (2), (3) and (6)–(8) into Allen–Uzawa's definitions for the partial elasticities of substitution (13.9) and (13.10), we obtain

$$\sigma_{KK} = 1 - \frac{1}{S_K} + \frac{\beta_{KK}}{S_K^2} + \frac{(1 - \sigma)\Omega}{S_K^2} \qquad (9)$$

$$\sigma_{LL} = 1 - \frac{1}{S_L} + \frac{\beta_{LL}}{S_L^2} + \frac{(1 - \sigma)\Omega}{S_L^2} \qquad (10)$$

$$\sigma_{KL} = 1 + \frac{\beta_{KL}}{S_K S_L} - \frac{(1 - \sigma)\Omega}{S_K S_L} \qquad (11)$$

where $\Omega = a_K P_K^{1-\sigma} a_L P_L^{1-\sigma} (a_K P_K^{1-\sigma} + a_L P_L^{1-\sigma})^{-2}$.

Notes

1 See Denny and Fuss (1977). Chung (1987) shows that, if the translog function is assumed to be separable, it is not necessary to employ the conventional approach to measure the Allen–Uzawa partial elasticities of substitution. His alternative approach requires only to estimate the total cost function truncated into a form expressed in terms of input shares.
2 The Berndt–Wood data are time series of capital, labor, energy, and materials for US manufacturing industries; the Magnus–Woodland data are time series of four energy inputs (coal, oil, natural gas, and electricity) for Dutch manufacturing; and the Cowing data are cross-sectional samples of capital, labor, energy, and materials for US steam electric power generation.

Recommended Reading

Blackorby, C., Primont, D. and Russell, R.R. 1977: On testing separability restrictions with flexible functional forms. *Journal of Econometrics*, 5, January, 195–209.
Denny, M. and Fuss, M. 1977: The use of approximation analysis to test for separability and the existence of consistent aggregates. *American Economic Review*, 67, June, 404–18.

Pollak, R.A., Sickles, R.C. and Wales, T.J. 1984: The CES–translog: specification and estimation of a new cost function. *Review of Economics and Statistics*, 66, November, 602–7.

Westbrook, M.D. and Buckley, P.A. 1990: Flexible functional forms and regularity: assessing the competitive relationship between truck and rail transportation. *Review of Economics and Statistics*, LXXII, November, 623–30.

14 The Leontief Production Function

The Leontief production function describes the simplest production technology that permits fixed proportions of inputs to determine output. It is a mathematical representation of Wassily Leontief's input–output table, which has been used widely for interindustry analysis. The table provides detailed information on flows of various macroeconomic aggregates. Many LDCs have used it for development planning. The table is based on the general equilibrium theory of Léon Walras (*Elements d'économie politique pure*, 1874), and its origin extends back to François Quesnay (*Tableau économique*, 1758). However, the theory and technique for interindustry analysis by means of the input–output table were not developed extensively until much later by Wassily Leontief (1936, 1947, 1953a). Leontief made a significant contribution even in the area of international trade with his input–output analysis. The so-called Leontief paradox, which refutes the Heckscher–Ohlin theory of factor proportions, has sparked a series of controversies among trade economists for several decades. Koopmans (1951) has contributed to input–output analysis by developing the linear programming techniques. Other important contributions are Dorfman et al. (1958) and Chenery and Clark (1962).

Section 14.1 discusses a condensed version of the input–output table and shows how outputs to meet final demand are determined. It also discusses a linear programming interpretation of the input–output table. Section 14.2 derives the output frontier and the corresponding factor–price frontier. The two linear versions are often used to discuss the Heckscher–Ohlin theory. Section 14.3 derives the Leontief production function from the table. In section 14.4, our concern is the cost function corresponding to the Leontief production function. We will discuss the zero substitutability between inputs in this section. Section 14.5 is concerned with empirical results; however, no empirical study has ever been done directly for the Leontief production/cost function. Section 14.6 summarizes the chapter.

14.1 The Input–Output Table

For simplicity, assume that there are just two industries, each of which produces only one output (i.e. absence of joint products), and that there are just two primary factors – capital and labor. The typical input–output table looks like table 14.1. Each row indicates the amount of output 1 or 2 that is distributed to industries 1 and 2 for their intermediate use (quadrant II) as well as the final use (quadrant I) broken down into household consumption, private investment, government spending, and net exports. On the other hand, each column represents outputs 1 and 2, and primary inputs K and L used for

Table 14.1 Input–output table

	Purchases by			
	Intermediate use			
Sales of	*Industry 1*	*Industry 2*	*Final use*	*Total sales*
Industry 1	x_{11}	x_{12}	c_1	y_1
	(II)		(I)	
Industry 2	x_{21}	x_{22}	c_2	y_2
	K_1	K_2	K_c	K
Primary inputs	(III)		(IV)	
	L_1	L_2	L_c	L
Total purchases	y_1	y_2	c	y

Source: Leontief, W.W. 1953: *The Structure of American Economy, 1919–1939*, New York: Oxford University Press, p. 140; Chenery, H.B. and Clark, P.G. 1962: *Interindustry Economics*, New York: Wiley, p. 16.

producing output 1 or output 2 (quadrants II and III). Note that some of the primary factors are used directly by the final demand sector, e.g. government employment (quadrant IV). Elements of any row are measured in the same physical units and thus are additive across the row. Therefore, it is possible to convert the table into a set of mathematical equations. The equations are

$$y_1 = x_{11} + x_{12} + c_1 \tag{14.1}$$

$$y_2 = x_{21} + x_{22} + c_2 \tag{14.2}$$

$$K = K_1 + K_2 + K_c \tag{14.3}$$

$$L = L_1 + L_2 + L_c \tag{14.4}$$

where y_i is the total output i ($i = 1, 2$), x_{ij} is the output i distributed to industry j as an intermediate input ($j = 1, 2$), K_j, K_c are the primary factors K distributed to industry j ($j = 1, 2$) and the final consumption sector, L_j, L_c are the primary factors L distributed to industry j ($j = 1, 2$) and the final consumption sector, and c_i is the final consumption of output i.

Assume further that each industry uses a fixed amount of each input to produce its output and that $K_c = L_c = 0$. The amount of output i and the amount of primary factors used as input producing output j are

$$\frac{x_{ij}}{y_j} = a_{ij} \tag{14.5}$$

$$\frac{K_j}{y_j} = a_{Kj} \tag{14.6}$$

$$\frac{L_j}{y_j} = a_{Lj} \tag{14.7}$$

where a_{ij} is the input coefficient (the Leontief coefficient), a_{Kj} is the capital coefficient, and a_{Lj} is the labor coefficient. Note that coefficients a are assumed to be fixed and the numerical range for their constant values is restricted to $0 \le a \le 1$. We substitute equations (14.5)–(14.7) into equations (14.1)–(14.4) to rewrite the latter equations as follows:

$$(1 - a_{11}) y_1 - a_{12} y_2 = c_1 \tag{14.8}$$

$$-a_{21} y_1 + (1 - a_{22}) y_2 = c_2 \tag{14.9}$$

$$a_{K1} y_1 + a_{K2} y_2 = K \tag{14.10}$$

$$a_{L1} y_1 + a_{L2} y_2 = L \ . \tag{14.11}$$

Given c_1 and c_2, we can obtain solutions for y_1 and y_2 from the first two equations and then substitute the values for y_1 and y_2 into the latter two equations to determine the amounts of primary factors K and L that the two industries demand. Amounts of outputs required to meet the final demand and amounts of primary factors demanded to produce that particular set of outputs are, respectively, as follows:

$$y = (I - A)^{-1} c \tag{14.12}$$

$$F = By \tag{14.13}$$

where

$$y = \begin{bmatrix} y_1 \\ y_2 \end{bmatrix} \quad (I - A)^{-1} = \begin{bmatrix} 1 - a_{11} & -a_{12} \\ -a_{21} & 1 - a_{22} \end{bmatrix}^{-1} \quad c = \begin{bmatrix} c_1 \\ c_2 \end{bmatrix}$$

$$F = \begin{bmatrix} K \\ L \end{bmatrix} \quad B = \begin{bmatrix} a_{K1} & a_{K2} \\ a_{L1} & a_{L2} \end{bmatrix} \ .$$

Solutions for equations (14.8) and (14.9) exist if the square matrix $I - A$ in equation (14.12) is not singular, requiring, given y and $c > 0$, its determinant $|I - A| > 0$. In other words, all principal minors of the determinant must be positive, i.e.

$$1 - a_{11} > 0 \quad \begin{vmatrix} 1 - a_{11} & -a_{12} \\ -a_{21} & 1 - a_{22} \end{vmatrix} > 0 \ . \tag{14.14}$$

Inequality (14.14) suggests that two linear schedules for equations (14.8) and (14.9) must intersect each other in the first quadrant in order to yield the solutions. This inequality is called the Hawkins–Simon condition. It implies that, given the nonnegative final consumption vector, there exists a corresponding nonnegative gross output vector. The Leontief system is viable only under this condition.[1]

A linear programming interpretation of the Hawkins–Simon condition is interesting. Given the standard form for the linear programming (the objective function of the society involved with output y_1 and y_2, the structural constraints imposed on the primary inputs K and L, and the nonnegativity condition for y_1 and y_2), the typical linear programming problem is to determine the optimal outputs y_1 and y_2 to meet the final demands within society's production possibility frontier defined by the constraints (equations (14.10) and (14.11)). As long as the two schedules for equations (14.8) and (14.9) intersect each other within the production possibility frontier, the final demands are attainable and, in addition, are expandable to yield the *basic feasible* solutions for the outputs at the boundary points or lines (the basic theorem of linear programming), one of which is the optimal output bundle. It is noted that the Hawkins–Simon condition and the basic theorem of linear programming are also applicable for determining the nonnegative factor price vector corresponding to the nonnegative commodity price vector. In the linear programming, the profit maximization problem to determine the nonnegative output vector is referred to as the *primal* problem and the cost minimization problem to determine the nonnegative factor price vector is referred to as the *dual* problem. The solutions to the dual problem are the shadow prices. The shadow prices give the change in the value of the objective function with respect to the change in each input included in the constraint. The shadow price in the profit maximization context is equivalent to the marginal imputed value of each input. As long as the marginal imputed value of each input is greater than the marginal cost of the input, the firm increases its use of the input.

14.2   The Output Frontier and Factor-Price Frontier

The linear system which consists of equations for the primary inputs only, equations (14.10) and (14.11), yields the output frontier and the corresponding factor-price frontier. It is notable that the system of equations is often used by trade economists to illustrate the two-sector Heckscher–Ohlin model.[2] The above two equations can be rewritten as

$$y_2 = \frac{K}{a_{K2}} - \frac{a_{K1}}{a_{K2}} y_1 \tag{14.15}$$

$$y_2 = \frac{L}{a_{L2}} - \frac{a_{L1}}{a_{L2}} y_1 . \tag{14.16}$$

They are the capital constraint (AE) and the labor constraint (CD), respectively, in figure 14.1. The frontier of the trapezium OABC is the output frontier or the product transformation curve. Point B is the full-employment output point at which the economy uses all available factors K and L. The absolute value of the slope of the labor constraint

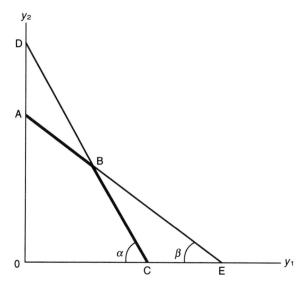

Figure 14.1 Output frontier.

(α) is larger than that of the capital constraint (β) by assumption. The slopes can be rearranged as

$$\frac{a_{L1}}{a_{K1}} > \frac{a_{L2}}{a_{K2}} . \tag{14.17}$$

Inequality (14.17) implies that good y_1 is relatively labor intensive and good y_2 is relatively capital intensive.

The factor-price version corresponding to the above output version of equations (14.10) and (14.11) is

$$p_1 = a_{K1} r + a_{L1} w \tag{14.18}$$

$$p_2 = a_{K2} r + a_{L2} w . \tag{14.19}$$

Rearranging terms in equations (14.18) and (14.19) yields, respectively, the factor-price frontier under perfect competition

$$r = \frac{p_1}{a_{K1}} - \frac{a_{L1}}{a_{K1}} w \tag{14.20}$$

$$r = \frac{p_2}{a_{K2}} - \frac{a_{L2}}{a_{K2}} w . \tag{14.21}$$

They are shown in figure 14.2. The frontier of the trapezium including full-employment point A is the factor-price frontier under perfect competition.

It is important to note that parameter restrictions imposed in this figure, $\alpha' > \beta'$, are consistent with those in the earlier figure, $\alpha > \beta$ (not identical in their values, respectively), implying that good y_1 is labor intensive whereas good y_2 is capital intensive. Given the production technology in the absence of factor-intensity reversal, i.e. α' and β' being fixed, the wage rate increases, *ceteris paribus*, from the level corresponding to point A to the level corresponding to point B when the price of the labor-intensive good increases from p_1 to p_1' as the result of protective trade policy. The positive correlation between p_1 and w is the famous Stolper–Samuelson theorem discussed in chapter 8.

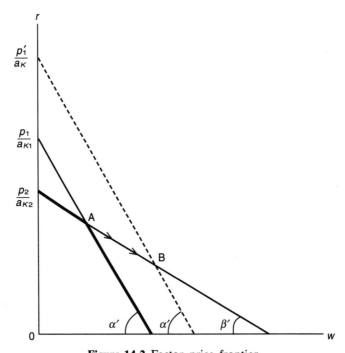

Figure 14.2 Factor–price frontier.

14.3   The Leontief Production Function

Entries in each column of table 14.1 are not necessarily measured in the same physical units and therefore may not be additive. Nonetheless, items in a column are inputs required to produce the total output of the corresponding industry; hence, a column gives one specific point on the isoquant of the corresponding industry. As Leontief assumes, however, an industry always chooses the minimal amount of each input necessary to produce the output, leaving quantities of the input beyond the minimal amount idle. The minimal amounts of inputs required jointly to produce outputs y_1 and y_2 are $x_{11} = a_{11}y_1$, $x_{21} = a_{21}y_1$, $K_1 = a_{K1}y_1$, $L_1 = a_{L1}y_1$ and $x_{12} = a_{12}y_2$, $x_{22} = a_{22}y_2$, $K_2 = a_{K2}y_2$, $L_2 = a_{L2}y_2$, respectively. Production functions for y_1 and y_2 at the minimum input position for all intermediate inputs x_{ij} and primary inputs K, L are then written as

$$y_1 = \min\left(\frac{x_{11}}{a_{11}}, \frac{x_{21}}{a_{21}}, \frac{K_1}{a_{K1}}, \frac{L_1}{a_{L1}}\right) \tag{14.22}$$

$$y_2 = \min\left(\frac{x_{12}}{a_{12}}, \frac{x_{22}}{a_{22}}, \frac{K_2}{a_{K2}}, \frac{L_2}{a_{L2}}\right). \tag{14.23}$$

Equations (14.22) and (14.23) are called the Leontief production function. It is also called the fixed proportion production function because the coefficients a are assumed to be fixed.

For simplicity, let us consider the relationship between an output y and two primary inputs K and L. The isoquants are shown in figure 14.3. To produce y^a, for example, the firm may combine any amount of K with the minimum amount of L or any amount of L with the minimum amount of K. Obviously, the production function yields the L-shaped isoquant. Unlike the case of the neoclassical isoquant, the differential calculus breaks down at the right-angled point. As observed, the isoquant is sloped downward and convex to the origin. Note that angle a is the slope of the isocost line and angle β is the slope of production activity A_1. The former is the wage–rental ratio associated with isocost line BC and the latter is the capital–labor ratio (or the capital intensity) associated with activity A_1. Given the isocost line, point E_1 is the optimal point, yielding K^* and L^*, the least-cost factor combination required to produce amount y^a. All the other points on the isoquant corresponding to y^a are wasteful combinations of the two

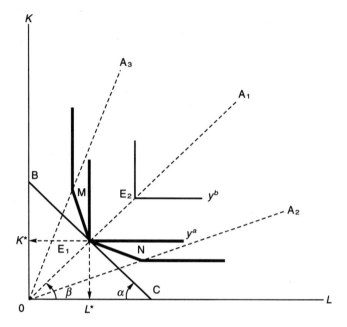

Figure 14.3 Leontief isoquant.

factors and hence are ignored by the firm on the ground of inefficiency. The equation for the expansion path for activity A_1 is then written

$$K = \beta L \qquad (14.24)$$

where β is the capital coefficient/labor coefficient for activity A_1. Also note that a larger output such as y^b requires larger quantities of both inputs. Therefore, the Leontief production function is a homogeneous function but rules out decreasing returns to scale.

Suppose that the firm has two other production activities, A_2 and A_3. Note that their capital–labor ratios are different from that of A_1. If the three production processes are jointly used, they are to be combined linearly. To combine processes A_1 and A_2, the total usage of capital and labor is:

$$K = \lambda K_1^* + (1 - \lambda) K_2^* \qquad (14.25)$$

$$L = \lambda L_1^* + (1 - \lambda) L_2^* \qquad (14.26)$$

where K_1^* and K_2^* are the capital used by A_1 and A_2, L_1^* and L_2^* are the labor used by A_1 and A_2, and $0 < \lambda < 1$. Likewise, activities A_1 and A_3 can be combined together. However, combinations of activities A_2 and A_3 are inefficient since the same output is produced with smaller usages of K and L by A_1. Consequently, the complete isoquant comprised of all three activities is the pair of line segments ME_1N. If the firm has an indefinite number of activities, the isoquant becomes smooth. In this sense, the Leontief production function is a special case of the neoclassical production function.

The fixed coefficient production function implies zero substitution between inputs, if an output is produced by only one particular activity. The Leontief production function uses two primary inputs, capital (K) and labor (L), always in the same proportion, irrespective of factor prices. Given the minimum-cost input point E_1, the corresponding capital–labor ratio is always β. There is no such percentage change in the capital–labor ratio in response to a percentage change in the wage–rental ratio. Recalling the formula for the elasticity of substitution (σ) from equation (8.14) in chapter 8, we know that its numerator is zero and thus the elasticity is zero.

It is interesting to contrast briefly the Leontief production function with the so-called Harrod production function which is the other extreme. The isoquant of the Harrod function is a straight line with a negative slope, so there are an infinite number of capital–labor ratios (the slopes of rays) along the isoquant. If the isoquant coincides with the isocost line, the elasticity of substitution is infinitely large because the input price ratio (the slope of the isocost line) remains constant, and thus the percentage change in the wage–rental ratio is always zero, even if the capital–labor ratio changes by a certain percentage.

14.4   The Leontief Cost Function

In this section, we again assume two primary inputs. Suppose that the firm produces y units of output. No matter what the input prices may be, the amounts of inputs used by the firm are $a_K y$ and $a_L y$ at point E_1, where a_K is the capital coefficient and a_L is the labor coefficient.[3]

The cost function corresponding to the Leontief production function is

$$C = \sum_i w_i(a_i\, y) \qquad (i = K, L) \qquad (14.27)$$

where w_i is the price of factor i. This cost function implies that the firm employs minimum amounts of inputs K and L to produce y units of output and pays price w_i for each unit of input. We should be cautious about relying on Shephard's lemma to derive input demand functions. But the cost-minimizing input demand function is supposed to be

$$x_i = a_i y \; . \tag{14.28}$$

The above result has already been seen in equations (14.6) and (14.7). The corresponding cost-share function is

$$\frac{w_i x_i}{C} = a_i \frac{w_i}{p} \; . \tag{14.29}$$

In the absence of factor substitutions of the Leontief function, the Allen–Uzawa cross-partial elasticity of substitution is zero.[4]

14.5   Empirical Remarks

Leontief's input–output table has been a widely used tool for interindustry analysis. Leontief himself has extensively used it to investigate factor proportions of US exports and imports and has proposed the Leontief paradox. He also used it to analyze economic effects of an arms cut, the future of the world economy, and many other topics. To analyze US energy policy, Hudson and Jorgenson (1974) employ the input–output table incorporated with the translog econometric modeling. Although the input–output table itself represents the Leontief production technology, it is not appropriate to discuss any empirical results of the input–output table in this section. No empirical study has ever been done directly for the Leontief production function or the factor-share function.

14.6   Summary

The input–output table is an analytical tool for interindustry analysis. Under a set of assumptions listed in section 14.1, it determines a nonnegative output vector for a nonnegative final demand vector. The Leontief system is viable only under the Hawkins–Simon condition.

The table yields the Leontief production function, which is often called the fixed coefficient production function. The isoquant is L-shaped. Irrespective of input prices, the firm always employs two inputs at the right-angled point, leaving all the other amounts of the inputs idle. The production function does not permit any substitution between any pair of inputs. The Allen–Uzawa cross-partial elasticity is zero.

The Leontief production function has customarily been the subject of theoretical rather than empirical study. Although there are numerous applications of the input–output table and the table reflects the Leontief production function, they are irrelevant to this chapter.

Notes

1 For the Hawkins–Simon condition, see Dorfman et al. (1958, p. 215).
2 See Jones (1965, pp. 557–72).
3 See equations (14.6) and (14.7).
4 Equation (14.28) represents demand for factor i at the vertex, where the function is not differentiable. However, we know that *no* substitution takes place at this point.

Recommended Reading

Chenery, H.B. and Clark, P.G. 1962: *Interindustry Economics*. New York: Wiley.

Dorfman, R., Samuelson, P.A. and Solow, R.M. 1958: *Linear Programming and Economic Analysis*. New York: McGraw-Hill.

Jones, R.W. 1965: The structure of simple general equilibrium models. *Journal of Political Economy*, LXXIII, December, 557–72.

Koopmans, T.C. (ed.), 1951: *Activity Analysis of Production and Allocation*. Cowles Commission Monography No. 13, New York: Wiley.

Leontief, W.W. 1936: Composite commodities and the problem of index numbers. *Econometrica*, 4, 39–59.

—— 1953: *The Structure of American Economy, 1919–1939*. New York: Oxford University Press.

—— 1953: Domestic production and foreign trade: the American capital position re-examined. *Proceedings of the American Society*, 97, 331–49.

15 The Generalized Leontief Production Function

The Leontief production function discussed in the previous chapter has been generalized in various ways. Diewert (1971) initially made the generalization and his function is most widely known. Other forms of the generalized Leontief production function are technology- or scale-augmented versions of Diewert's function. Additional references for Diewert's function include Parks (1971), Woodland (1975), Fuss (1977b), Berndt and Khaled (1979), Diewert and Wales (1987), Morrison (1988), and Nakamura (1990).

Pollak et al. (1984) and Behrman et al. (1992) extend Diewert's version further. Pollak et al. combine the CES production function with Diewert's generalized Leontief production function; the result is called the CES-generalized Leontief production function. Hall (1973) and Shumway et al. (1988) apply the generalized Leontief function to multi-input and multi-output relationships. However, this book will not examine such relationships because they go beyond its scope.

Section 15.1 examines the Diewert function and its differences from the Leontief function. Section 15.2 derives the factor share function and the Allen–Uzawa partial elasticities of substitution associated with the Diewert function. Section 15.3 discusses briefly the CES-generalized Leontief function. Section 15.4 examines empirical results obtained by Parks and Morrison, Nakamura, and Behrman et al. Section 15.5 summarizes the chapter.

15.1 Differences between the Leontief Production Function and the Diewert Production Function

Let us begin with Diewert's cost function

$$C(w, y) = f(y) \sum_{i=1}^{n} \sum_{j=1}^{n} \beta_{ij} \sqrt{w_i} \sqrt{w_j} \qquad (i, j = 1, \ldots, n; i \neq j) \quad (15.1)$$

where C is cost, y is output (set $f(y) = 1$), and w_i is the price of input i.[1] It is important to note that the cost function with only the first-order terms included in equation (15.1), requiring $\beta_{ij} = 0$ $(i \neq j)$, is precisely the Leontief cost function (equation (14.27)).

By Shephard's lemma, the cost-minimizing demand for factor i is equivalent to $x_i = \partial C / \partial w_i$ which is

$$x_i = \beta_{ii} + \beta_{ij} \frac{\sqrt{w_j}}{\sqrt{w_i}} \qquad (i \neq j) \qquad (15.2)$$

where x_i is the demand for factor i.

For the purpose of illustration, assume two inputs, 1 and 2. Equation (15.2) yields

$$\frac{\sqrt{w_2}}{\sqrt{w_1}} = \frac{x_1 - \beta_{11}}{\beta_{12}} = \frac{\beta_{12}}{x_2 - \beta_{22}} \qquad (15.3)$$

which is the relationship between the given output and the cost-minimizing factor combinations. The contour generated by equation (15.3) is supposed to be the isoquant.[2] Equation (15.3) is rewritten as

$$(x_1 - \beta_{11})(x_2 - \beta_{22}) = \beta_{12}^2 . \qquad (15.4)$$

We will examine equation (15.4) in conjunction with the following restrictions on parameters. They are two of the four restrictions that Diewert examined:[3]

$$\text{case 1: } \beta_{12} = 0, \beta_{11} \geq 0, \beta_{22} \geq 0$$

$$\text{case 2: } \beta_{12} > 0, \beta_{11} > 0, \beta_{22} > 0 .$$

The two cases above are sufficient for us to observe the difference between the Leontief function and the Diewert function. The major difference between the two cases is whether or not $\beta_{12} = 0$.

In case 1, the left-hand side of equation (15.4) equals zero, requiring that

$$x_1 = \beta_{11} \tag{15.5}$$

and

$$x_2 = \beta_{22} . \tag{15.6}$$

Equations (15.5) and (15.6) yield a vertical line segment β_{11} and a horizontal line segment β_{22}, respectively, in the space, where x_1 is on the horizontal axis and x_2 is on the vertical axis.[4] Given the demand for x_1 is β_{11}, any amount of input x_2 beyond $x_2 = \beta_{22}$, though redundant, makes the isoquant become a vertical straight line. Given the demand for x_2 is β_{22}, any amount of input x_1 beyond $x_1 = \beta_{11}$, though redundant, makes the isoquant become a horizontal straight line. Combining the two segments produces a right-angled Leontief isoquant ABC, as shown in figure 15.1.

In case 2, equation (15.4) yields a smoothly convex isoquant. The hypobola is shown as a solid line in figure 15.1. It is Diewert's generalized Leontief isoquant. The isoquant is negatively sloped and is convex to the origin because it is characterized as

$$\frac{\partial x_2}{\partial x_1} = - \frac{\beta_{12}^2}{(x_1 - \beta_{11})^2} < 0 \tag{15.7}$$

$$\frac{\partial^2 x_2}{\partial x_1^2} = \frac{2\beta_{12}^2}{(x_1 - \beta_{11})^3} > 0 .[5] \tag{15.8}$$

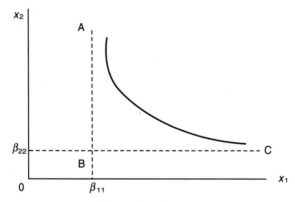

Figure 15.1 Generalized Leontief isoquant.

Note that the curvature of the isoquant depends on the magnitude of β_{12}.

15.2 Factor-Share Functions and Elasticities

Let us now derive the factor-share function of the total cost and also derive the Allen–Uzawa elasticities of substitution for the generalized Leontief production function.

Given the cost-minimizing demand for factor i derived in the previous section (equation (15.2)), we multiply both sides of equation (15.2) by w_i/C to obtain the share function

$$S_i = \frac{\beta_{ii} w_i + \beta_{ij} \sqrt{w_i} \sqrt{w_j}}{\sum_{i=1}^{n} \sum_{j=1}^{n} \beta_{ij} \sqrt{w_i} \sqrt{w_j}} \qquad (i \neq j) . \tag{15.9}$$

The Allen–Uzawa partial elasticities of substitution require to differentiate equation (15.1) partially twice. The second-order partial derivatives are

$$\frac{\partial^2 C}{\partial w_i^2} = -\tfrac{1}{2} \beta_{ij} \frac{\sqrt{w_j}}{\sqrt{w_i}} \qquad (i \neq j) \tag{15.10}$$

$$\frac{\partial^2 C}{\partial w_i \partial w_j} = \tfrac{1}{2} \beta_{ij} \frac{1}{\sqrt{w_i}} \frac{1}{\sqrt{w_j}} \qquad (i \neq j) . \tag{15.11}$$

Substituting equations (15.2), (15.10), and (15.11) into equation (L.6) in appendix L yields the Allen–Uzawa partial elasticities of substitution. They are:

$$\sigma_{ii} = -\frac{1}{2S_i} + \frac{\beta_{ii} w_i}{2S_i^2 \sum_i \sum_j \beta_{ij} \sqrt{w_i} \sqrt{w_j}} \qquad (i \neq j) \tag{15.12}$$

$$\sigma_{ij} = \frac{\beta_{ij} \sqrt{w_i} \sqrt{w_j}}{2S_i S_j \sum_i \sum_j \beta_{ij} \sqrt{w_i} \sqrt{w_j}} \qquad (i \neq j) . \tag{15.13}$$

15.3 The Constant-Elasticity-of-Substitution–Generalized Leontief Production Function

As chapter 13 mentioned briefly, Pollak et al. (1984) extended the generalized Leontief cost function further. They combined the CES form of the cost function with the generalized Leontief cost function, requiring an additional parameter (σ) to play a role in the function. The function is written as

$$C(\mathbf{w}, y) = y\left(\sum_i a_i\, w_i^{(1-\sigma)}\right)^{1/(1-\sigma)} + y\sum_i \sum_j \beta_{ij}\, \sqrt{w_i}\, \sqrt{w_j}$$

$$(i \neq j) \qquad (15.14)$$

where $\beta_{ij} = \beta_{ji}$ for all i and j and y is the output (restricted to 1). The cost-minimizing demand for factor i ($\partial C/\partial w_i$) derived from this function is

$$x_i = \frac{a_i}{w_i^{\sigma}}\left(\sum_k a_k\, w_k^{1-\sigma}\right)^{\sigma/(1-\sigma)} + \left(\beta_{ii} + \beta_{ij}\frac{\sqrt{w_j}}{\sqrt{w_i}}\right) \qquad (i \neq j) \quad (15.15)$$

Note that the CES-generalized Leontief cost function and factor demand functions reduce to those of the generalized Leontief when $\sigma = 0$. In this case, the term $a_i + \beta_{ii}$ in equation (15.15) corresponds to β_{ii} in equation (15.2). If all βs $= 0$, the functions reduce to those of the CES form.

The Allen–Uzawa cross-partial elasticities of substitution are computed as follows:

$$\sigma_{ij} = \frac{\sigma\, \Pi_i\, a_i\, w_i^{1-\sigma}(\Sigma_i a_i\, w_i^{1-\sigma})^{\sigma/(1-\sigma)-1} + \frac{1}{2}\beta_{ij}\sqrt{w_i}\sqrt{w_j}}{S_i\, S_j\left[(\Sigma_i a_i\, w_i^{1-\sigma})^{1/(1-\sigma)} + \Sigma_i \Sigma_j \beta_{ij}\sqrt{w_i}\sqrt{w_j}\right]}. \qquad (15.16)$$

15.4   Empirical Remarks

Parks (1971) has conducted the first econometric study on the generalized Leontief production function. Using time-series data for Swedish manufacturing for the period 1870–1950, he estimates the Allen–Uzawa partial elasticity of substitution. He finds evidence that there is significant substitutability between intermediate inputs and labor.

Recently, Morrison (1988) has also estimated the generalized Leontief factor share model. I discuss Morrison's work in detail because it generalizes previous work.[6] Morrison applies the generalized Leontief-restricted cost function of four inputs (capital, labor, energy, and materials) to an analysis of factor demand patterns in Japanese and US manufacturing and characterizes short- and long-run price elasticities of demand. Morrison's variant of cost function permits an inclusion of one quasi-fixed input (capital) or two quasi-fixed inputs (capital and labor) in the static as well as the dynamic context. The traditional generalized Leontief cost function is a functional form in the square root of factor prices. Morrison extends it to allow for fixed inputs. This section discusses only the static one quasi-fixed input case. Morrison uses time-series data for 1952–81 for US manufacturing and 1955–81 for Japanese manufacturing. She assumes constant returns to scale and strong separability between outputs in the two different countries. She employs an iterative three-stage least squares procedure. Morrison finds that the short-run own-price elasticity for labor is substantially larger for Japan than for the United States (−0.88 for Japan as opposed to −0.435 for the United States). She reports that the long-run elasticity differs little from the short-run elasticity. Labor and materials are substitutes for both Japan and the United States and are substitutable to a greater degree in Japan (0.741 for Japan and 0.398 for the United States). She finds similar relationships for labor and energy (0.070 for Japan and 0.037 for the United States). Labor and capital are complements for both countries (−0.058 for Japan and −0.036 for the United States). Morrison concludes that the overall pattern provides evidence of considerable flexibility of demand responses of labor in Japan and that this flexibility may have helped Japan recover more quickly from problems such as the energy crises of the 1970s.

Additional references are Nakamura (1990), who applies a new nonhomothetic form of the generalized Leontief cost function to a pooled data set for the Japanese iron and steel industries; Behrman et al. (1992), who apply the constant elasticity of transformation, constant elasticity of substitution, generalized Leontief function (CET–CES–GL function) to Indian agriculture. Nakamura reports that the nonhomothetic version performs satisfactorily. Behrman et al. claim that the CET–CES–GL function, which adds only one more parameter than the generalized Leontief function, ensures curvature properties of the estimated multiple-output technology over a large sample region of the price–quantity space and demonstrates a higher degree of flexibility than the generalized Leontief function.

15.5   Summary

This chapter has examined the Diewert production function, which is often referred to as the generalized Leontief production function. As usual, we have focused on the factor share functions and the Allen–Uzawa elasticities of substitution.

The Diewert function, which reduces to the Leontief function under the special condition, permits considerable flexibility. The main difference between the two functions is that the Allen–Uzawa cross-partial elasticity of substitution of the Leontief function is zero whereas the Allen–Uzawa cross-partial elasticity of substitution of the Diewert function is a variable. The factor demand model allows considerable freedom in the variation of substitution parameters.

The Diewert function is increasingly popular. It has recently been generalized further. One version is the CES-generalized Leontief function and the other is the CET–CES generalized Leontief function. They are more flexible than the generalized Leontief function.

Parks presents estimated values of the Allen–Uzawa partial elasticities of substitution based on the data for Swedish manufacturing. He suggests that there is significant substitutability between intermediate inputs and labor. Recently, Morrison has estimated factor demand functions derived from the generalized Leontief-restricted cost function of four inputs to analyze demand patterns in Japanese and US manufacturing. The cost function includes quasi-fixed inputs. Estimated values of short-run and long-run elasticities show that demand for labor is more flexible in Japan. Morrison believes that Japan's higher flexibility helped it recover more quickly than other countries from global shocks such as the oil crises in the 1970s.

Notes

1   A generalized McFadden cost function and a generalized Barnett cost function are comparable with the generalized Leontief cost function. See McFadden (1978b), Barnett (1985), Barnett and Lee (1985), and Diewert and Wales (1987) for details.
2   See Baumol (1977, p. 371).
3   There are two other cases that Diewert (1971) examines. In case 3, we move the origin to the right beyond point β_{11} on the horizontal axis of figure 15.1 to have $\beta_{11} < 0$. In case 4, we move the origin upward and rightward

beyond point B to have $\beta_{11} < 0$ and $\beta_{22} < 0$. Given $\beta_{12} > 0$ as for case 2, isoquants for cases 3 and 4 are part of the isoquant for case 2.

4 If the output is restricted to one, equation (14.28) is the same as equations (15.5) and (15.6).

5 Equation (15.8) implies the concavity of the total production surface, requiring that the bordered Hessian $|\bar{H}_2|$ is positive.

6 Morrison's generalized Leontief restricted cost function is an extension of the Diewert–Fuss–Parks–Woodland–Diewert/Wales version.

Recommended Reading

Barnett, W.A. and Lee, Y.W. 1985: The global properties of the minflex Laurent, generalized Leontief, and translog flexible functional forms. *Econometrica*, 53, November, 1421–37.

Behrman, J.R., Lovell, C.A.K., Pollak, R.A. and Sickles, R.C. 1992: The CET–CES-generalized Leontief variable profit function: an application to Indian agriculture. *Oxford Economic Papers*, 44, 341–54.

Berndt, E.R. and Khaled, M.S. 1979: Parametric productivity measurement and choice among flexible functional forms. *Journal of Political Economy*, 87, 1120–45.

Diewert, W.E. 1971: An application of the Shepard duality theorem: a generalized Leontief production function. *Journal of Political Economy*, 79, 481–507.

—— and Wales, T.J. 1987: Flexible functional forms and global curvature conditions. *Econometrica*, 55, 43–68.

Hall, R.E. 1973: The specification of technology with several kinds of output. *Journal of Political Economy*, 81, 878–92.

McFadden, D. 1978: General linear profit function. In M. Fuss and D. McFadden (eds), *Production Economics: A Dual Approach to Theory and Applications*, volume 1, Amsterdam: North-Holland, 269–86.

Morrison, C. 1988: Quasi-fixed inputs in U.S. and Japanese manufacturing: a generalized Leontief restricted cost function approach. *Review of Economics and Statistics*, 70, May, 275–87.

Nakamura, S. 1990: A nonhomothetic generalized Leontief cost function based on pooled data. *Review of Economics and Statistics*, LXXII, November, 649–55.

Parks, R.W. 1971: Price responsiveness of factor utilization in Swedish manufacturing, 1870–1950. *Review of Economics and Statistics*, May, 129–39.

Pollak, R.A., Sickles, R.C. and Wales, T.J. 1984: The CES–translog: specification and estimation of a new cost function. *Review of Economics and Statistics*, 66, November, 602–7.

Shumway, R.R., Saez, R.R. and Gottret, P.E. 1988: Multi-product supply and input demand in U.S. agriculture. *American Journal of Agricultural Economics*, 70, 330–7.

184 *Production Functions*

Westbrook, M.D. and Buckley, P.A. 1990: Flexible functional forms and regularity: assessing the competitive relationship between truck and rail transportation. *Review of Economics and Statistics*, LXXII, November, 623–30.
Woodland, A.D. 1977: Joint outputs, intermediate inputs, and international trade theory. *International Economic Review*, 18, 517–34.

Appendices

These appendices summarize some essential concepts, definitions, and theorems that occur in this book. The summaries are for quick reference. I assume that readers already are somewhat familiar with the mathematical concepts involved.

Appendix A   Monotonicity

Given a differentiable function $f(x)$ with x_i and $x_j \in x$, it is a *monotonically increasing function* if $f(x_j) \geq f(x_i)$ for $x_j > x_i$. The function is a *monotonically decreasing function* if $f(x_j) \leq f(x_i)$ for $x_j > x_i$. If a weak inequality, either $\geq$ or $\leq$, is replaced by a strict inequality, $>$ or $<$, respectively, the function is called a *strictly monotonic* (either increasing or decreasing) function. In general, the sign of the first-order derivative determines the type of monotonicity. If $\partial f / \partial x_i > 0$, the function f is monotonically increasing. If $\partial f / \partial x_i < 0$, the function f is monotonically decreasing.

Appendix B   Concavity and Convexity

A concave function has the shape of an igloo. A convex function has the shape of an inverted igloo. For any two points on the surface, if a point on the straight line connecting the two points lies below a point on the surface right up the straight line other than the two points on the same surface, the function is *strictly concave*. If the point lies on or below the surface, the function is called *concave*. If the height of a point on the arc is strictly greater than the lower end-points of the arc, the function is called *strictly quasi-concave*. If the height of a point on the arc is at least as great as the height of the lower end-point of the arc, the function is called *quasi-concave*.

Given a differentiable function $y = f(x_1, x_2)$, it is strictly concave for x_1 and x_2 if the second-order total differential is everywhere *negative definite*, i.e. $d^2y < 0$ (concave if it is *negative semidefinite*, i.e. $d^2y \leq 0$). Specifically, a strict concavity is

$$d^2y = f_{11}(dx_1)^2 + 2f_{12}\,dx_1dx_2 + f_{22}(dx_2)^2 < 0 \qquad (B.1)$$

where $f_{11} = \partial^2 f/\partial x_1^2, f_{22} = \partial^2 f/\partial x_2^2$, and $f_{12} = \partial^2 f/\partial x_1 \partial x_2$. Equation (B.1) is equivalent to principal minors of the Hessian determinant, $|H|$, that alternate their signs such that

$$|H_1| = f_{11} < 0 \qquad |H_2| = \begin{vmatrix} f_{11} & f_{12} \\ f_{21} & f_{22} \end{vmatrix} > 0, ..., (-1)^n|H_n| > 0\,.$$

$$(B.2)$$

Recall that the stationary point determined by the first-order condition is the unconstrained maximum if the function is concave downward. Also recall that the second-order conditions for the maximum are

$$f_{11} < 0 \quad \text{and} \quad f_{11}f_{22} > (f_{12})^2 \qquad (B.3)$$

which is the same as equation (B.2). For a strictly concave function, the second-order condition for the maximum must be upheld.

In contrast, *strict quasi-concavity* prevails if, for the augmented objective function z and constraint g, we have $d^2z < 0$ subject to $dg = 0$ (quasi-concave if $d^2z \leq 0$ subject to $dg = 0$). Equivalently, we have

$$|\bar{H}_1| = \begin{vmatrix} 0 & f_1 \\ f_1 & f_{11} \end{vmatrix} < 0 \qquad |\bar{H}_2| = \begin{vmatrix} 0 & f_1 & f_2 \\ f_1 & f_{11} & f_{12} \\ f_2 & f_{21} & f_{22} \end{vmatrix} > 0, ..., (-1)^n|\bar{H}_n| > 0$$

$$(B.4)$$

where $f_1 = \partial f/\partial x_1 > 0$, $f_2 = \partial f/\partial x_2 > 0$. Although the conditions for strict quasi-concavity are similar to the second-order conditions for a constrained maximum, the principal minors of the bordered Hessian ($|\bar{H}|$) for a maximum begin with the second-order bordered Hessian. In general, the concavity condition is the natural extension of the second-order maximum condition for a maximum.

Strict convexity and *convexity* require us to reverse both strict and weak inequalities ($<$ or $>$ and $\leq$ or $\geq$) of the Hessian determinants for *strict concavity* and *concavity*, respectively, whereas *strict quasi-convexity* and *quasi-convexity* require us to reverse the strict inequalities and weak inequalities of the bordered Hessian determinants for *strict quasi-concavity* and *quasi-concavity*.

It is important for readers to note that the concave total utility (or production) *surface* yields the convex indifference *curve* (or isoquant). The condition for convexity of an indifference curve is that its slope has a positive rate of change, i.e.

$$\frac{\mathrm{d}^2 x_2}{\mathrm{d} x_1^2} = -\frac{1}{f_2^3}(f_{11}f_2^2 - 2f_{12}f_1f_2 + f_{22}f_1^2) > 0 \qquad \text{(B.5)}$$

where $\mathrm{d}x_2/\mathrm{d}x_1 = -f_1/f_2 < 0$, which implies that the indifference curve is negatively sloped. Inequality (B.5) requires the parenthesized term on its right-hand side to be negative. The negative parenthesized term is the same as the condition for a strictly quasi-concave function, $|\overline{H}_2|$ (inequality (B.4)).

It is also important for readers to keep in mind that both the concave utility surface and the convex utility surface yield convex indifference curves. Unlike the case of indifference curves generated from the concave utility surface, however, an indifference curve generated from the convex utility surface represents a higher utility if it lies below and to the left of another. Obviously, the optimization in connection with the convex utility surface is a minimization problem of a convex decreasing function (see appendix G).

Appendix C   Homogeneity and Homotheticity

Given a production function

$$y = f(x_1, x_2, \ldots, x_n) \qquad \text{(C.1)}$$

it is *homogeneous* of degree k if scalar multiplication of the xs in the function yields

$$f(\theta x_1, \theta x_2, \ldots, \theta x_n) = \theta^k f(x_1, x_2, \ldots, x_n) \qquad \text{(C.2)}$$

where θ is a scalar. If $k = 1$ in the above relationship, the given function is linearly homogeneous in $x_1, \ldots, x_n$. Linearly homogeneous functions have many special economic features. Among them are that their expansion paths are linear and that Euler's theorem applies to them. It is also well known that the *classical* demand function, as a homogeneous function of degree zero, satisfies the homogeneity condition (see appendix E) which implies that there is no money illusion.

Homotheticity is a generalized concept of homogeneity. Function F is homothetic if it is a monotonically increasing function of function f, expressed as a composite function in the form

$$z = F[f(x_1, x_2, ..., x_n)] \qquad (C.3)$$

where function f is homogeneous of degree k. It is important to note that the slope of the curvature of function F and the slope of the curvature of function f are the same at any given point, i.e.

$$\frac{\partial F/\partial x_i}{\partial F/\partial x_j} = \frac{\partial f/\partial x_i}{\partial f/\partial x_j} \qquad (i \neq j) . \qquad (C.4)$$

Equation (C.4) implies that function F is characterized by function f. Then it is possible to suggest that a homothetic production function produces a linear expansion path; that the optimal input ratio on the linear expansion path is independent of output levels; that, for constant input prices, the relative factor shares of output are also independent of output levels; and hence that, given Euler's theorem, the output shares (the cost shares in the dual context) of inputs are independent of the output. For the same reason, a homothetic utility function gives the expenditure shares that are independent of the total budget.

Appendix D   Additivity and Separability

Given a function

$$y = f(x_1, x_2, ..., x_n) \qquad (D.1)$$

it is *strongly additive* if

$$\frac{\partial^2 y}{\partial x_i \, \partial x_j} = 0 \qquad (i \neq j) \qquad (D.2)$$

and is *strongly separable* (from x_k) if

$$\frac{\partial[(\partial y/\partial x_i)/(\partial y/\partial x_j)]}{\partial x_k} = 0 \qquad (i \neq j \neq k) . \qquad (D.3)$$

Equation (D.3) can be rewritten as

$$\frac{\partial y}{\partial x_j}\frac{\partial^2 y}{\partial x_i\,\partial x_k} - \frac{\partial y}{\partial x_i}\frac{\partial^2 y}{\partial x_i\,\partial x_j\,\partial x_k} = 0 \ . \tag{D.4}$$

As we can see in equations (D.2) and (D.3), separability is a more general concept than additivity.

Given a function partitioned into branches 1 and 2,

$$y = F[f(x_{11},x_{12}), g(x_{21},x_{22})] \tag{D.5}$$

where f is a sub-function representing branch 1 and g is another sub-function representing branch 2, the function is *weakly additive* if equation (D.2) holds for $i \in f$ and $j \in g$ and is *weakly separable* if equation (D.3) holds for i and $j \in f$ and $k \in g$.

If a function is additive and homothetic, the partial elasticities of substitution between any pair of commodities (inputs) must be constant. We will discuss this feature in appendix L.

Appendix E Four Classical Properties of Consumer Demand

The four *classical* properties of consumer demand are general features of a demand function. They are restrictions on the income slope and the price slopes. Let us assume that the derived demand functions for two goods 1 and 2 are

$$x_1 = f(p_1, p_2, m) \tag{E.1}$$

$$x_2 = g(p_1, p_2, m) \tag{E.2}$$

where x_1 is good 1, x_2 is good 2, p_1 is the price of good 1, p_2 is the price of good 2, and m is income. The four conditions that the demand functions must fulfill to qualify as "classical" demand functions are as follows.

1 Engel Aggregation Condition

$$p_1\frac{\partial x_1}{\partial m} + p_2\frac{\partial x_2}{\partial m} = 1 \ . \tag{E.3}$$

Multiplying each of the two terms on the left-hand side of equation (E.3) by $[(x_1/m)\,(m/x_1)]$ and $[(x_2/m)\,(m/x_2)]$ yields

$$S_1 \, \epsilon_{1m} + S_2 \, \epsilon_{2m} = 1 \tag{E.4}$$

where S_1 is the expenditure share of good 1, i.e. $p_1 x_1/m$; S_2 is the expenditure share of good 2, i.e. $p_2 x_2/m$; ϵ_{1m} is the income elasticity of demand for good 1; and ϵ_{2m} is the income elasticity of demand for good 2. The last equation clearly suggests that the average income elasticity weighted by budget shares is 1 and hence implies that, for example, a 5 percent increase in income causes a 5 percent increase in the average demand for the two goods.

2   Cournot Aggregation Condition

$$p_1 \frac{\partial x_1}{\partial p_1} + p_2 \frac{\partial x_2}{\partial p_1} = -x_1 \, . \tag{E.5}$$

Dividing equation (E.5) by $x_1 m$ and multiplying the second term of the left-hand side of the equation by $(p_1/x_2)(x_2/p_1)$ gives

$$S_1 \, \epsilon_{11} + S_2 \, \epsilon_{21} = -S_1 < 0 \tag{E.6}$$

where ϵ_{11} is the own-price elasticity of demand for good 1 with respect to the price of good 1 and ϵ_{21} is the cross-price elasticity of demand for good 2 with respect to the price of good 1. Similarly, we can have

$$S_1 \, \epsilon_{12} + S_2 \, \epsilon_{22} = -S_2 < 0 \tag{E.7}$$

where ϵ_{12} is the cross-price elasticity of demand for good 1 with respect to the price of good 2 and ϵ_{22} is the own-price elasticity of demand for good 2 with respect to the price of good 2. Note that the first term of equation (E.6) is negative, whereas its second term is either positive (if the two goods are substitutes) or negative (if they are complements). The equation suggests that the average percentage response in the demand for two goods to an increase in price of good 1 is negative, implying that, when the price of good 1 increases, the demand for good 2 *decreases* or at least cannot rise as strongly as the average response to be positive.

3   Symmetry Condition

Given the Slutsky equations (F.24) and (F.27), it is possible to derive

$$\left. \frac{\partial x_1}{\partial p_2} \right|_{u \, = \, \text{constant}} = \left. \frac{\partial x_2}{\partial p_1} \right|_{u \, = \, \text{constant}} \tag{E.8}$$

which is therefore the same as

$$\frac{\partial x_1}{\partial p_2} + \frac{\partial x_1}{\partial m} x_2 = \frac{\partial x_2}{\partial p_1} + \frac{\partial x_2}{\partial m} x_1 . \tag{E.9}$$

For equation (E.8), see equations (F.25) and (F.27) in the subsequent section. The sum of the two terms on the left-hand side of equation (E.9) is the substitution effect in connection with x_1 adjusted with respect to a variation in p_2. The right-hand side as a whole is the substitution effect in connection with x_2 adjusted with respect to variation in p_1. Multiply the first term on the left-hand side of equation (E.9) by $(p_2/x_1)(x_1/p_2)$, the second term by $(x_1/m)(m/x_1)$, the first term on the right-hand side of the same equation by $(p_1/x_2)(x_2/p_2)$, and the second term by $(x_2/m)(m/x_2)$ to get

$$\frac{1}{S_2} \epsilon_{12} + \epsilon_{1m} = \frac{1}{S_1} \epsilon_{21} + \epsilon_{2m} . \tag{E.10}$$

Samuelson (1947, p. 107) calls the symmetry condition the reciprocal *integrability condition*. For implication of equation (E.10), see appendix F.

4   Homogeneity Condition

Given the classical demand function (equation (E.1)), which is homogeneous of degree zero, the following condition holds:

$$\frac{\partial x_1}{\partial p_1} p_1 + \frac{\partial x_1}{\partial p_2} p_2 = - \frac{\partial x_1}{\partial m} m . \tag{E.11}$$

Dividing both sides of equation (E.11) by x_1 transforms the equation into one written in terms of elasticities, i.e.

$$\epsilon_{11} + \epsilon_{12} + \epsilon_{1m} = 0 . \tag{E.12}$$

Similarly, we have

$$\epsilon_{21} + \epsilon_{22} + \epsilon_{2m} = 0 . \tag{E.13}$$

Equations (E.12) and (E.13) imply that equi-proportional simultaneous increases in income and in the prices of the two goods leave the quantity of good 1 demanded unchanged. This particular feature is what we mean by the *absence of money illusion*, which occurs because the demand function is homogeneous of degree zero.

Appendix F   The Slutsky Equation: Derivation and Implications

The Slutsky equation is the basis for studies of consumer behavior and production. This appendix is concerned with the behavior of a consumer; however, it is directly applicable to the behavior of a producer.

The rational consumer maximizes his utility

$$u = f(x_1, x_2) \tag{F.1}$$

subject to the budget constraint

$$m = p_1 x_1 + p_2 x_2 \tag{F.2}$$

where x_1 is good 1, x_2 is good 2, m is income, p_1 is the price of good 1, and p_2 is the price of good 2. Following the method of Lagrange, write the augmented objective function as

$$\mathcal{L}(x_1, x_2; \lambda) = f(x_1, x_2) = \lambda\,(m - p_1 x_1 - p_2 x_2) \tag{F.3}$$

where λ is the Lagrangian multiplier. The first-order conditions for a maximum are

$$\frac{\partial \mathcal{L}}{\partial x_1} = f_1 - \lambda p_1 = 0 \tag{F.4}$$

$$\frac{\partial \mathcal{L}}{\partial x_2} = f_2 - \lambda p_2 = 0 \tag{F.5}$$

$$\frac{\partial \mathcal{L}}{\partial \lambda} = m - p_1 x_1 - p_2 x_2 = 0 \tag{F.6}$$

where $f_1 = \partial u / \partial x_1$ and $f_2 = \partial u / \partial x_2$.

Differentiating equations (F.4)–(F.6) partially with respect to m, we get the effect of a change in income on demand for x_1 (the income effect). First we assume $dp_1/dm = dp_2/dm = 0$ to have

$$f_{11}\frac{\partial x_1}{\partial m} + f_{12}\frac{\partial x_2}{\partial m} - p_1\frac{\partial \lambda}{\partial m} = 0 \tag{F.7}$$

$$f_{21}\frac{\partial x_1}{\partial m} + f_{22}\frac{\partial x_2}{\partial m} - p_2\frac{\partial \lambda}{\partial m} = 0 \tag{F.8}$$

$$-p_1\frac{\partial x_1}{\partial m} - p_2\frac{\partial x_2}{\partial m} = -1 \tag{F.9}$$

where $f_{11} = \partial^2 u/\partial x_1^2$, $f_{12} = f_{21} = \partial^2 u/\partial x_1 \partial x_2$, and $f_{22} = \partial^2 u/\partial x_2^2$. Solving equations (F.7)–(F.9) for $\partial x_1/\partial m$ by means of Cramer's rule, we get

$$\frac{\partial x_1}{\partial m} = \frac{\begin{vmatrix} 0 & f_{12} & -p_1 \\ 0 & f_{22} & -p_2 \\ -1 & -p_2 & 0 \end{vmatrix}}{\begin{vmatrix} f_{11} & f_{12} & -p_1 \\ f_{21} & f_{22} & -p_2 \\ -p_1 & -p_2 & 0 \end{vmatrix}} = -\frac{\begin{vmatrix} f_{12} & -p_1 \\ f_{22} & -p_2 \end{vmatrix}}{|\bar{H}_2|} . \tag{F.10}$$

Note that the denominator of equation (F.10) is the same bordered Hessian as the second-order conditions for utility to be at a maximum; hence the value of the bordered Hessian is positive.

To get the effect of a change in p_1 on demand for x_1 (the price effect), differentiate equations (F.4)–(F.6) partially with respect to p_1 to get

$$f_{11}\frac{\partial x_1}{\partial p_1} + f_{12}\frac{\partial x_2}{\partial p_1} - p_1\frac{\partial \lambda}{\partial p_1} = \lambda \tag{F.11}$$

$$f_{21}\frac{\partial x_1}{\partial p_1} + f_{22}\frac{\partial x_2}{\partial p_1} - p_2\frac{\partial \lambda}{\partial p_1} = 0 \tag{F.12}$$

$$p_1\frac{\partial x_1}{\partial p_1} + p_2\frac{\partial x_2}{\partial p_1} = -x_1 . \tag{F.13}$$

We assume that $dp_2/dp_1 = dm/dp_1 = 0$. By Cramer's rule, we get

$$\frac{\partial x_1}{\partial p_1} = \frac{\begin{vmatrix} \lambda & f_{12} & -p_1 \\ 0 & f_{22} & -p_2 \\ x_1 & -p_2 & 0 \end{vmatrix}}{\begin{vmatrix} f_{11} & f_{12} & -p_1 \\ f_{21} & f_{22} & -p_2 \\ -p_1 & -p_2 & 0 \end{vmatrix}} = \lambda\frac{\begin{vmatrix} f_{22} & -p_2 \\ -p_2 & 0 \end{vmatrix}}{|\bar{H}_2|} + x_1\frac{\begin{vmatrix} f_{12} & -p_1 \\ f_{22} & -p_2 \end{vmatrix}}{|\bar{H}_2|} . \tag{F.14}$$

Note that the second term on the right-hand side of equation (F.14), excluding x_1, is the same as equation (F.10). Given the utility level (the same indifference curve, i.e. $u = \bar{u}$), however, it vanishes. Differentiating equation (F.1) totally yields

$$d\bar{u} = 0 = f_1\, dx_1 + f_2\, dx_2 \tag{F.15}$$

which can be rewritten as

$$p_1 \, dx_1 + p_2 \, dx_2 = 0 \qquad \text{(F.16)}$$

by means of the first-order conditions (equations (F.4) and (F.5)). Convert equation (F.16) by dividing through it by dp_1, to have

$$p_1 \frac{dx_1}{dp_1} + p_2 \frac{dx_2}{dp_1} = 0 \, . \qquad \text{(F.17)}$$

The left-hand side of equation (F.17) is the same as the left-hand side of equation (F.13), implying that $x_1 dp_1 = 0$. Clearly, the second term of equation (F.14) becomes zero and hence its first term is the own-price effect, i.e. $\partial x_1 / \partial p_1$, when $u = \bar{u}$. Therefore equation (F.14) along with equation (F.10) can be rewritten as

$$\frac{\partial x_1}{\partial p_1} = \left. \frac{\partial x_1}{\partial p_1} \right|_{u = \bar{u}} - x_1 \left. \frac{\partial x_1}{\partial m} \right|_{p = \bar{p}} \qquad \text{(F.18)}$$

which is called the *Slutsky equation*. The term on its left-hand side is referred to as the *total effect*. It is broken down into the *Hicks–Allen net substitution effect* (the first term on the right-hand side) and the *income effect* (the second term on the right-hand side). It is important to keep in mind that the total effect is the slope of the demand curve. The net substitution effect is always negative and the income effect is negative (but $\partial x_1 / \partial m > 0$) if x_1 is a normal good, so that the total effect is negative and hence the slope of the demand curve is negative. If, however, x_1 is an inferior good ($\partial x_1 / \partial m < 0$), the income effect is positive. If the positive income effect is so strong that it dominates the negative substitution effect, the total effect will be positive. In this case, the demand curve will slope upward, contradicting the classical law of demand.

The net substitution effect is the slope of the compensated demand curve. If price p_1 increases, the consumer must be *compensated* by an increase in income sufficient to permit him to purchase the initial quantity. For a higher p_1, the compensated demand should be greater than the uncompensated demand. Therefore, the compensated *inverse* demand curve lies to the right of the ordinary *inverse* demand curve (except at the initial point where price p_1 is lower) and is thus steeper than the ordinary (uncompensated) *inverse* demand curve (flatter than the ordinary demand curve), provided the commodity in question is not an inferior good. Equation (F.18) confirms this relationship. If good x_1 is a normal good, two negative numbers on the right-hand side of the equation add up to a negative number on the left-hand side. Thus the absolute value of the negative number for the net substitution effect is smaller than that for the total effect. Note that if p_1 decreases the compensated inverse demand curve lies to the left of the ordinary inverse demand curve and is again steeper than the ordinary inverse demand curve.

It is useful to express equation (F.18) in terms of elasticities. Multiplying both sides of the equation by p_1/x_1 and multiplying the last term on the right-hand side by m/m yields

$$\epsilon_{11} = \epsilon_{11}|_{u = \bar{u}} - S_1 \epsilon_{1m} \tag{F.19}$$

where $S_1 = p_1 x_1/m$ is the budget share of x_1. Equation (F.19) implies that the compensated demand is less elastic than the ordinary demand curve.

The cross-price effect is obtained by differentiating equations (F.4)–(F.6) partially with respect to p_2. Assuming that $dp_1/dp_2 = dm/dp_2 = 0$, we get

$$f_{11}\frac{\partial x_1}{\partial p_2} + f_{12}\frac{\partial x_2}{\partial p_2} - p_1\frac{\partial \lambda}{\partial p_2} = 0 \tag{F.20}$$

$$f_{21}\frac{\partial x_1}{\partial p_2} + f_{22}\frac{\partial x_2}{\partial p_2} - p_2\frac{\partial \lambda}{\partial p_2} = \lambda \tag{F.21}$$

$$p_1\frac{\partial x_1}{\partial p_2} + p_2\frac{\partial x_2}{\partial p_2} = -x_2 \tag{F.22}$$

yielding

$$\frac{\partial x_1}{\partial p_2} = \frac{\begin{vmatrix} 0 & f_{12} & -p_1 \\ \lambda & f_{22} & -p_2 \\ x_2 & -p_2 & 0 \end{vmatrix}}{\begin{vmatrix} f_{11} & f_{12} & -p_1 \\ f_{21} & f_{22} & -p_2 \\ -p_1 & -p_2 & 0 \end{vmatrix}} = -\lambda \frac{\begin{vmatrix} f_{12} & -p_1 \\ -p_2 & 0 \end{vmatrix}}{|\overline{H}_2|} + x_2 \frac{\begin{vmatrix} f_{12} & -p_1 \\ f_{22} & -p_2 \end{vmatrix}}{|\overline{H}_2|}. \tag{F.23}$$

The second term on the right-hand side of equation (F.23), excluding x_2, is equivalent to $-(\partial x_1/\partial m)$ (see equation (F.10)) and thus yields the income effect. Again, the sign of the income effect is indeterminate. Given the utility level, however, the term for the income effect vanishes because, as equations (F.13) and (F.16) give $-x_1 dp_1 = 0$, we know that the term $-x_2 dp_2$, which comes from equation (F.22), equals zero.

This enables us to understand what the first term on the right-hand side of equation (F.23) is. Equation (F.23) can be restated as

$$\frac{\partial x_1}{\partial p_2} = \frac{\partial x_1}{\partial p_2}\bigg|_{u=\bar{u}} - x_2 \frac{\partial x_1}{\partial m}\bigg|_{p=\bar{p}} . \tag{F.24}$$

The sign of the first term on the right-hand side of equation (F.23) is not known, in general. If it is positive and thus the corresponding term in equation (F.24) is positive, demand for x_1 increases as the price p_2 increases, so long as the consumer remains on the same indifference curve. For this reason, the first term of equation (F.24) is called the (net) cross substitution effect. Two goods x_1 and x_2 are *net* substitutes. The sign of the total effect depends on whether or not the positive substitution effect dominates a negative income effect if x_1 is a normal good. If the total effect is positive, goods x_1 and x_2 are *gross* substitutes. If it is negative, they are *gross* complements.

It is interesting to note that the substitution effect is symmetrical for all goods, i.e.

$$\frac{\partial x_1}{\partial p_2}\bigg|_{u=\bar{u}} = \frac{\partial x_2}{\partial p_1}\bigg|_{u=\bar{u}} . \tag{F.25}$$

Through similar procedures to get equation (F.23), we obtain

$$\frac{\partial x_2}{\partial p_1} = \frac{\begin{vmatrix} f_{11} & \lambda & -p_1 \\ f_{21} & 0 & -p_2 \\ -p_1 & x_1 & 0 \end{vmatrix}}{\begin{vmatrix} f_{11} & f_{12} & -p_1 \\ f_{21} & f_{22} & -p_2 \\ -p_1 & -p_2 & 0 \end{vmatrix}} = -\lambda \frac{\begin{vmatrix} f_{21} & -p_2 \\ -p_1 & 0 \end{vmatrix}}{|\bar{H}_2|} - x_1 \frac{\begin{vmatrix} f_{11} & -p_1 \\ f_{21} & -p_2 \end{vmatrix}}{|\bar{H}_2|} \tag{F.26}$$

and hence

$$\frac{\partial x_2}{\partial p_1} = \frac{\partial x_2}{\partial p_1}\bigg|_{u=\bar{u}} - x_1 \frac{\partial x_2}{\partial m}\bigg|_{p=\bar{p}} . \tag{F.27}$$

Observe that the element in the first row and the first column of the first term on the right-hand side of equations (F.23) and (F.26) are identical by Young's theorem. Given the same determinant and the constant Lagrangian multiplier in these two terms, we know that the values of these two substitution effects are the same. This relationship is the symmetry condition (see appendix E).

Finally, we obtain the elasticity representation of equation (F.24) by multiplying through equation (F.24) by p_2/x_1 and multiplying the second term on the right-hand side of the equation by m/m. The result is

$$\epsilon_{12} = \epsilon_{12}|_{u=\bar{u}} - S_2\,\epsilon_{1m} \qquad (F.28)$$

where $S_2 = (p_2 x_2/m)$ is the budget share of good 2. Similarly, we have

$$\epsilon_{21} = \epsilon_{21}|_{u=\bar{u}} - S_1\,\epsilon_{2m}\,. \qquad (F.29)$$

The symmetry condition suggests that

$$\epsilon_{12}|_{u=\bar{u}} = \epsilon_{21}|_{u=\bar{u}}\,. \qquad (F.30)$$

This feature implies, for example, that if demand for x_1 increases at the rate of 10 percent as the price p_2 increases by 1 percent, demand for x_2 increases at the rate of 10 percent as the price p_1 increases by 1 percent.

Appendix G   Duality between Direct Utility Function and Indirect Utility Function

Consider the conventional utility function

$$u = f(x_1, x_2) \qquad (G.1)$$

and the budget constraint

$$m = p_1 x_1 + p_2 x_2\,. \qquad (G.2)$$

We call the utility function above the *direct* utility function. Note that the function is expressed in terms of goods. We can express the budget constraint transformed into

$$1 = \frac{p_1}{m} x_1 + \frac{p_2}{m} x_2 \qquad (G.3)$$

where p_i/m is called the *normalized price*.

The first-order conditions for utility maximization are

$$\frac{\partial u}{\partial x_1} - \lambda\frac{p_1}{m} = 0 \qquad (G.4)$$

$$\frac{\partial u}{\partial x_2} - \lambda\frac{p_2}{m} = 0 \qquad (G.5)$$

$$1 - \frac{p_1}{m} x_1 - \frac{p_2}{m} x_2 = 0 . \tag{G.6}$$

The demand functions derived from equations (G.4)–(G.6) take the form

$$x_1 = x_1\left(\frac{p_1}{m}, \frac{p_2}{m}\right) \tag{G.7}$$

$$x_2 = x_2\left(\frac{p_1}{m}, \frac{p_2}{m}\right) . \tag{G.8}$$

Alternatively, the homogeneity feature associated with the classical demand function (e.g. equations (E.1) and (E.2) which are homogeneous of degree zero) enables us to have

$$x_1 = m^{r=0} x_1\left(\frac{p_1}{m}, \frac{p_2}{m}\right) \tag{G.9}$$

$$x_2 = m^{r=0} x_2\left(\frac{p_1}{m}, \frac{p_2}{m}\right) . \tag{G.10}$$

Substituting the demand functions back into the utility function yields the utility function expressed in terms of normalized prices, i.e.

$$u = f\left[x_1\left(\frac{p_1}{m}, \frac{p_2}{m}\right), \; x_2\left(\frac{p_1}{m}, \frac{p_2}{m}\right)\right] = g\left(\frac{p_1}{m}, \frac{p_2}{m}\right) . \tag{G.11}$$

Equation (G.11) is called the *indirect* utility function. Note that the direct utility function is independent of prices and income, whereas the indirect utility function is independent of quantities of goods. As the result of substitution of the negative relationship between demand for a good and its price in the direct utility function, the indirect utility surface is strictly quasi-convex. An indifference curve corresponding to the indirect utility function is convex but represents a higher preference if it is closer to the origin. Therefore, optimizing with the direct utility function is a problem of *maximizing* under the assumption of given prices and income, whereas optimizing with the indirect utility function is a problem of *minimizing* under the assumption of given quantities.

Appendix H   Roy's Identity

Roy's identity defines the optimal demand for a good as the negative of the ratio of the partial derivatives of the indirect utility function with respect to the price of that particular good and with respect to income.

Given the indirect utility function and the budget constraint (equations (G.11) and (G.3) in appendix G), the total derivatives of the equations with respect to p_1 are, respectively,

$$\frac{\partial u}{\partial p_1} = \frac{\lambda}{m}\left[p_1\frac{\partial x_1}{\partial(p_1/m)} + p_2\frac{\partial x_2}{\partial(p_1/m)}\right] \qquad (H.1)$$

$$-x_1 m = \left[p_1\frac{\partial x_1}{\partial(p_1/m)} + p_2\frac{\partial x_1}{\partial(p_1/m)}\right]. \qquad (H.2)$$

Combining equations (H.1) and (H.2) yields the demand functions

$$x_1 = -\frac{\partial u/\partial p_1}{\lambda} \qquad (H.3)$$

where $\lambda = \partial u/\partial m$. Similarly, we can have

$$x_2 = -\frac{\partial u/\partial p_2}{\lambda}. \qquad (H.4)$$

Equations (H.3) and (H.4) are Roy's identity. Equation (H.3) enables us to derive the budget share function (also called the expenditure share function)

$$S_1 = \frac{p_1 x_1}{m} = -\frac{(\partial u/\partial p_1)\,p_1}{(\partial u/\partial m)\,m}\frac{1/u}{1/u} = -\frac{\partial \ln u/\partial \ln p_1}{\partial \ln u/\partial \ln m}. \qquad (H.5)$$

Similarly, we have

$$S_2 = \frac{p_2 x_2}{m} = -\frac{\partial \ln u/\partial \ln p_2}{\partial \ln u/\partial \ln m}. \qquad (H.6)$$

It is now straightforward to derive the budget share function if we have the indirect utility function in a logarithmic form.

Equations (H.3) and (H.4) are demand for x_1 and x_2, measured in terms of physical units. In contrast, equations (H.5) and (H.6) are consumer's budget shares allocated to goods 1 and 2 and thus are demands for x_1 and x_2, measured in dollar amounts.

Appendix I   The Shephard–Samuelson Theorem

Consider the production function and cost equation with two inputs:

$$y = f(x_1, x_2) \tag{I.1}$$

$$C = w_1 x_2 + w_2 x_2 \tag{I.2}$$

where y is output, C is the total cost, x_1 is input 1, x_2 is input 2, w_1 is the price of input 1, and w_2 is the price of input 2. For simplicity, we disregard the fixed input.

The augmented objective function for the cost minimization is

$$\mathcal{L}(x_1, x_2; \lambda) = w_1 x_1 + w_2 x_2 + \lambda [\bar{y} - f(x_1, x_2)] \tag{I.3}$$

where λ is the Lagrangian multiplier and $\bar{y}$ is fixed output. The first-order conditions for cost minimization are

$$w_1 = \lambda \frac{\partial f}{\partial x_1} \tag{I.4}$$

$$w_2 = \lambda \frac{\partial f}{\partial x_2} . \tag{I.5}$$

Substituting equations (I.4) and (I.5) into equation (I.2) yields

$$C = \lambda \frac{\partial f}{\partial x_1} x_1 + \lambda \frac{\partial f}{\partial x_2} x_2 \tag{I.6}$$

which can be rewritten as

$$C = \lambda \left(\frac{\partial f}{\partial x_1} x_1 + \frac{\partial f}{\partial x_2} x_2 \right) . \tag{I.7}$$

Note that by Euler's theorem, the term in parentheses on the right-hand side of equation (I.7) equals output if the production function above is linearly homogeneous. Therefore we have

$$C = \lambda y \tag{I.8}$$

yielding

$$\lambda = \frac{C}{y} = AC . \tag{I.9}$$

where AC is the average cost.

On the other hand, totally differentiating equations (I.1) and (I.2) gives

$$dy = \frac{\partial f}{\partial x_1}dx_1 + \frac{\partial f}{\partial x_2}dx_2 \qquad (I.10)$$

$$dC = w_1\,dx_1 + w_2\,dx_2 . \qquad (I.11)$$

Substituting equations (I.4) and (I.5) into equation (I.11), and dividing equation (I.11) by equation (I.10), yields

$$\frac{dC}{dy} = MC = \frac{\lambda[(\partial f/\partial x_1)dx_1 + (\partial f/\partial x_2)dx_2]}{(\partial f/\partial x_1)dx_1 + (\partial f/\partial x_2)dx_2} = \lambda \qquad (I.12)$$

where MC is the marginal cost. Equations (I.9) and (I.12) suggest that

$$\lambda = MC = AC = p \qquad (I.13)$$

where p is price. Equation (I.13) is called the *Shephard–Samuelson theorem*.

Note that equation (I.13) is firm's long-run profit condition under perfect competition. The equation constitutes the microeconomic foundation for the cost-push price dynamics (inflation).

Appendix J   Shephard's Duality

Shephard's duality is the duality existing between the production function and the cost function. What this duality suggests is that, given a production function, we can always derive a cost function that reflects the same production technology. It is similar to the duality existing between the direct utility function and indirect utility function, discussed in appendix G.   Given the two-input production function and cost equation of appendix I

$$y = f(x_1, x_2) \qquad (J.1)$$

$$C = w_1 x_1 + w_2 x_2 \qquad (J.2)$$

the expansion path function or the marginal rate of technical substitution (MRTS) condition is

$$\frac{f_1(x_1, x_2)}{f_2(x_1, x_2)} = MRTS(x_1, x_2) = \frac{\partial y/\partial x_1}{\partial y/\partial x_2} = \frac{w_1}{w_2} . \qquad (J.3)$$

Solving equations (J.2) and (J.3) with respect to x_1 and x_2 gives

$$x_1 = x_1(w_1, w_2, C) \tag{J.4}$$

$$x_2 = x_2(w_1, w_2, C) . \tag{J.5}$$

We can substitute equations (J.4) and (J.5) into equation (J.1) to get

$$C = C(w_1, w_2, y) . \tag{J.6}$$

Let us compare equations (J.1) and (J.6). Normalizing output ($y = 1$), there exists a duality between the production function and the corresponding cost function. The duality we can observe is called *Shepherd's duality*.

Appendix K Shephard's Lemma

Given the same production function (I.1) and cost equation (I.2) as in the previous section, i.e.

$$y = f(x_1, x_2) \tag{K.1}$$

$$C = w_1 x_1 + w_2 x_2 \tag{K.2}$$

the total derivative of equation (K.2) with respect to the price of input 1 gives

$$\frac{\partial C}{\partial w_1} = x_1 + w_1\frac{\partial x_1}{\partial w_1} + x_2\frac{\partial w_2}{\partial w_1} + w_2\frac{\partial x_2}{\partial w_1} \tag{K.3}$$

where $\partial w_2/\partial w_1 = 0$ by assumption. Note that factor prices vary and thus a comparative static analysis is possible with respect to them.

The first-order conditions for *minimizing* the total cost are

$$w_1 = \lambda\frac{\partial f}{\partial x_1} \tag{K.4}$$

$$w_2 = \lambda\frac{\partial f}{\partial x_2} . \tag{K.5}$$

Equations (K.4) and (K.5) are the same as equations (I.4) and (I.5). Substituting equations (K.4) and (K.5) into equation (K.3) yields

$$\frac{\partial C}{\partial w_1} = x_1 + \lambda\left(\frac{\partial \bar{y}}{\partial x_1}\frac{\partial x_1}{\partial w_1} + \frac{\partial \bar{y}}{\partial x_2}\frac{\partial x_2}{\partial w_1}\right) . \tag{K.6}$$

Note that the position of the isoquant is fixed under the cost minimization principles (hence $f = \bar{y}$) and that the term in parentheses is zero. Equation (K.6) reduces to

$$\frac{\partial C}{\partial w_1} = x_1 . \tag{K.7}$$

Equation (K.7) is *Shephard's lemma*. It suggests that the first-order differentiation of the cost function with respect to an input price yields the *cost-minimizing* demand function for the input corresponding to that input price. Given the definition of factor share, i.e.

$$\frac{\partial C}{\partial w_i} \frac{w_i}{C} \equiv S_i \tag{K.8}$$

it is necessary to convert equation (K.7) into the equation for cost share of input 1. Multiplying both sides of equation (K.7) by w_1/C yields

$$\frac{\partial C}{\partial w_1} \frac{w_1}{C} = S_1 = \frac{w_1 x_1}{C} . \tag{K.9}$$

Equation (K.9) suggests that, if we have the cost function in a logarithmic form, a partial derivative of the cost function with respect to the price of an input gives the cost-share function of that input. Similarly, we have

$$\frac{\partial C}{\partial w_2} = x_2 \tag{K.10}$$

for the demand function for input 2 and

$$\frac{\partial C}{\partial w_2} \frac{w_2}{C} = S_2 = \frac{w_2 x_2}{C} \tag{K.11}$$

for the cost-share function of input 2.

Appendix L Allen–Uzawa Partial Elasticity of Substitution

The formula for the Allen partial elasticity of substitution presented here applies to both the utility function and the production function.
   Given either the utility function or the production function,

$$Z = Z(z_1, ..., z_n) \tag{L.1}$$

where Z is utility or output and z_i is good i or factor i.

Allen (1938) suggested a formula to compute the partial elasticity of substitution of the pair of goods or inputs z_i and z_j. The formula is

$$\sigma_{ij} = \frac{\sum_{h=1}^{n} z_h \, (\partial Z/\partial z_h)|\overline{H}_{ij}|}{z_i z_j |\overline{H}_n|} \tag{L.2}$$

where

$$|\overline{H}_n| = \begin{vmatrix} 0 & \dfrac{\partial Z}{\partial z_1} & \cdots & \dfrac{\partial Z}{\partial z_n} \\[2mm] \dfrac{\partial Z}{\partial z_1} & \dfrac{\partial^2 Z}{\partial z_1^2} & \cdots & \dfrac{\partial^2 Z}{\partial z_1 \partial z_n} \\ \vdots & & & \\ \dfrac{\partial Z}{\partial z_n} & \dfrac{\partial^2 Z}{\partial z_n \partial z_1} & \cdots & \dfrac{\partial^2 Z}{\partial z_n^2} \end{vmatrix}$$

and $|\overline{H}_{ij}|$ is the cofactor of the ijth element in the determinant $|\overline{H}|$. Note that the Allen partial elasticity of substitution is symmetrical as the result of the symmetric cofactor, i.e. $\sigma_{ij} = \sigma_{ji}$ for $|\overline{H}_{ij}| = |\overline{H}_{ji}|$. Its value can be positive or negative. Since Allen discusses the formula in detail, it is unnecessary to discuss it here. But it is important to contemplate the partial elasticity of substitution in the Slutsky context. Note that the cofactor/bordered Hessian terms included in the net substitution effect in equations (F.23) and (L.2) are the same. Therefore, it is immediately clear that the Allen partial elasticity of substitution is an element of the net substitution effect. Allen shows that

$$\epsilon_{ij} = S_j \, (\sigma_{ij} - \epsilon_{im}) \qquad (i \neq j) . \tag{L.3}$$

If $\sigma_{ij} > 0$, goods (or inputs) i and j are *net* substitutes (not gross substitutes). If $\sigma_{ij} < 0$, they are *net* complements.

Equation (3.42) in chapter 3 and equation (L.3) enable us to have

$$\epsilon_{ik} = S_k \, (\sigma_{ik} - \epsilon_{im}) = S_k \, (\sigma_{jk} - \epsilon_{jm}) = \epsilon_{jk} \qquad (i \neq j \neq k) \tag{L.4}$$

Since $\epsilon_{im} = \epsilon_{jm}$ (equation (3.44)), we have

$$\sigma_{ik} = \sigma_{jk} . \tag{L.5}$$

Equation (L.5) shows that, if the utility function or the production function is *additive*, the Allen partial elasticities of substitution are equal for all pairs of commodities or inputs for k.

Uzawa (1962) proved that equation (L.2) is equivalent to

$$\sigma_{ij} = \frac{C(\partial^2 C/\partial w_i \partial w_j)}{(\partial C/\partial w_i)(\partial C/\partial w_j)} \tag{L.6}$$

where C is the total cost and w_i is the factor price. For the proof, see chapter 10. Equation (L.6) is called the *Allen–Uzawa partial elasticity of substitution*. If $i = j$, the result is called the Allen–Uzawa *own*-partial elasticity of substitution. If $i \neq j$, it is called the Allen–Uzawa *cross*-partial elasticity of substitution. Uzawa also proved that the Allen–Uzawa cross-partial elasticities of substitution (equation (L.5)) for all k ($k = 1, 2, \ldots, n$) are equal to the elasticity of substitution (σ) if the production function is *homothetic*.

Therefore, if the utility function or the production function is *additive and homothetic*, the Allen–Uzawa partial elasticities of substitution are equal and constant for all pairs of commodities or inputs.

Recommended Reading

Allen, R.G.D. 1938: *Mathematical Analysis for Economists*. London: Macmillan.

Hicks, J.R. 1932: *Value and Capital*, second edition. Oxford: Clarendon Press.

Samuelson, P.A. 1947: *Foundations of Economic Analysis*. Cambridge, MA: Harvard University Press.

Shephard, R.W. 1970: *Theory of Cost and Production Functions*. Princeton, NJ: Princeton University Press.

Epilogue

There have been considerable extensions and applications of utility and production theory over time. Some important parts of utility theory are the theory of intertemporal choice (I. Fisher, 1954; Hirshleifer, 1970), choice under uncertainty (von Neumann and Morgenstern, 1947; Friedman and Savage, 1948; Arrow, 1970), macroeconomic perspectives on household consumption (Modigliani and Brumberg, 1954; Friedman, 1957), and the axiomatic approach to utility theory (Debreu, 1959). In production theory, notable areas are technical change (Solow, 1957, 1962; Salter, 1960; Kennedy, 1964; Diamond, 1965; Fei and Ranis, 1965; F. Fisher, 1965; Samuelson, 1965b; Drandakis and Phelps, 1966), production, uncertainty, and information cost (Alchian, 1950; Stigler, 1961; Leibenstein, 1966; Alchian and Demsetz, 1972; Leijonhvud, 1981; Heiner, 1983), the multiproduct case (Hall, 1973), and Laurent expansions or third-order polynomials (Barnett, 1985). Many other areas often presuppose utility and production functions. Among them are the social welfare function in welfare economics (Samuelson, 1956) and public-choice theory (Buchanan and Tullock, 1962). Readers should keep in mind that this book focuses only on the development of the main functions of utility and production and their features and arguments.

References

Alchian, Armen A. 1950: Uncertainty, evolution and economic theory. *Journal of Political Economy*, 58, June, 211–21.

—— 1953: The meaning of utility measurement. *American Economic Review*, 43, March, 26–50.

—— and Demsetz, H. 1972: Production, information costs, and economic efficiency. *American Economic Review*, 62, December, 777–95.

Allen, R.G.D. 1938: *Mathematical Analysis for Economists*. London: Macmillan.

—— and Bowley, A. 1935: *Family Expenditure*. London: P.S. King.

Arrow, K.J. 1960–1: Additive logarithmic demand functions and the Slutsky relations. *Review of Economic Studies*, 23, 176–81.

—— 1970: *Essays in the Theory of Risk Bearing*. Chicago, IL: Maskham.

—— 1972: The measurement of real value added. University Institute for Mathematical Studies in the Social Studies, Stanford, Technical Report, No. 60, June.

——, Chenery, H.B., Minhas, B.S. and Solow, R.M. 1961: Capital–labor substitution and economic efficiency. *Review of Economics and Statistics*, 63, August, 225–50.

Barnett, W.A. 1979: Theoretical foundations for the Rotterdam model. *Review of Economic Studies*, XLVI, January, 109–30.

—— 1985: The minflex–Laurent translog flexible functional form. *Journal of Econometrics*, 30, 33–4.

—— and Lee, Y.W. 1985: The global properties of the minflex Laurent, generalized Leontief, and translog flexible functional forms. *Econometrica*, 53, November, 1421–37.

Barten, A.P. 1964: Consumer demand functions under conditions of almost additive preferences. *Econometrica*, 32, 1–38.

—— 1968: Estimating demand equations. *Econometrica*, 36, 213–51.

—— and Böhm, V. 1982: Consumer theory. In K.J. Arrow and M.D. Intriligator (eds), *Handbook of Mathematical Economics*, volume II, Amsterdam: North-Holland, 381–429.

Basmann, R.L. 1968: Hypothesis formulation in quantitative economics: a contribution to demand analysis. In J. Quirk and H. Zarley (eds), *Papers in Quantitative Economics*, Lawrence, KS: University Press of Kansas, 143–202.

Baumol, W.J. 1977: *Economic Theory and Operation Analysis*, fourth edition. Englewood Cliffs, NJ: Prentice-Hall.

Becker, G. 1971: *Economic Theory*. New York: Alfred A. Knopf.

Behrman, J.R., Lovell, C.A.K., Pollak, R.A. and Sickles, R.C. 1992: The CET–CES–generalized Leontief variable profit function: an application to Indian agriculture. *Oxford Economic Papers*, 44, April, 341–54.

Bergson, A. 1936: Real income, expenditure proportionality, and Frisch's "new method". *Review of Economic Studies*, 4, 33–52.

Berndt, E.R. and Christensen, L.R. 1973a: The internal structure of functional relationships: separability, substitution, and aggregation. *Review of Economic Studies*, 40, July, 403–10.

—— and —— 1973b: The translog function and the substitution of equipment, structures, and labor in U.S. manufacturing 1929–68. *Journal of Econometrics*, 1, March, 81–113.

—— and Khaled, M.S. 1979: Parametric productivity measurement and choice among flexible functional forms. *Journal of Political Economy*, 87, 1120–45.

—— and Wood, D.O. 1975: Technology, prices, and the derived demand for energy. *Review of Economics and Statistics*, 57, August, 259–68.

Blackorby, C., Primont, D. and Russell, R.R. 1977: On testing separability restrictions with flexible functional forms. *Journal of Econometrics*, 5, January, 195–209.

Bowles, S. 1970: The aggregation of labor inputs in the study of growth and planning: experiments with a two-level CES function. *Journal of Political Economy*, 78, 68–81.

Bronfenbrenner, M. and Douglas, P.H. 1939: Cross-section studies in the Cobb–Douglas production function. *Journal of Political Economy*, 47, December, 761–85.

Brown, A. and Deaton, A. 1972: Surveys in applied economics: models of consumer behavior. *Economic Journal*, 82, December, 1145–234.

Brown, J.A.C. 1954: The consumption of food in relation to household composition and income. *Econometrica*, 22, 444–60.

Brown, M. 1966: *On the Theory and Measurement of Technological Change*. Cambridge: Cambridge University Press.

—— and de Cani, J.S. 1963: Technological change and the distribution of income. *International Economic Review*, 4, September, 289–309.

—— and Conrad, A.H. 1967: The influence of research and education on CES production relations. In M. Brown (ed.), *The Theory and Empirical Analysis of Production*, New York: Columbia University Press.

Brown, M. and Heien, D. 1972: The S-branch utility tree: a generalization of the linear expenditure system. *Econometrica*, 40, July, 737–47.

Buchanan, J.M. and Tullock, G. 1962: *The Calculus of Consent*. Ann Arbor, MI: University of Michigan Press.

Burgess, D. 1975: Duality theory and pitfalls in the specification of technologies. *Journal of Econometrics*, 3, 105–21.

Caves, D.W. and Christensen, L.R. 1980: Global properties of flexible functional forms. *American Economic Review*, 70, 422–32.

Caves, R. 1960: *Trade and Economic Structure: Models and Methods*, Cambridge, MA: Harvard University Press.

Chambers, R.G. 1988: *Applied Production Analysis*. Cambridge: Cambridge University Press.

Chenery, H.B. and Clark, P.G. 1962: *Interindustry Economics*. New York: Wiley.

Chetty, V.K. 1969: On measuring the nearness of near-Moneys. *American Economic Review*, LIX, June, 270–81.

Chipman, J.S. 1971: Introduction to part II. In J.S. Chipman, L. Hurwicz, M.K. Richter, and H.F. Sonnenschein (eds), *Preferences, Utility, and Demand*, New York: Harcourt Brace Jovanovich, 321–31.

Christensen, L.R. 1977: Estimating U.S. consumer preferences for meat with a flexible utility function. *Journal of Econometrics*, 5, January, 37–53.

—— and Manser, M.E. 1976: Cost-of-living indexes for U.S. meat and produce, 1947–1971. In N.E. Terleckjy (ed.), *Household and Production*, New York: Columbia University Press.

——, Jorgenson, D.W. and Lau, Lawrence J. 1973: Transcendental logarithmic production function frontiers. *Review of Economics and Statistics*, 55, February, 29–45.

——, —— and —— 1975: Transcendental logarithmic utility functions. *American Economic Review*, LXV, June, 367–83.

Chung, J.W. 1980: Tarde liberalization and factor prices: an application to the U.S. manufacturing sector. *Journal of Policy Modeling*, 2, January, 101–20.

—— 1987: On the estimation of factor substitution in the translog model. *Review of Economics and Statistics*, 64, August, 409–17.

—— 1988: The CES–translog utility function and consumer expenditure system: theory and application. Paper presented at 1988 North American Winter Meetings of the Econometric Society, New York, December.

Cobb, C.W. and Douglas, P.H. 1928: A theory of production. *American Economic Review*, 18, 139–65.

Deaton, A.S. 1973: Additive preferences and Pigou's law. Paper presented at the European Meetings of the Econometric Society in Oslo, August.

—— 1974a: A reconsideration of the empirical implications of additive preferences. *Economic Journal*, 84, June, 338–47.

—— 1974b: The analysis of consumer demand and the United Kingdom. 1900–1970. *Econometrica*, 42, 341–67.

—— and J. Muellbauer 1980a: *Economics and Consumer Behavior*. Cambridge: Cambridge University Press.

—— and —— 1980b: An almost ideal demand system. *American Economic Review*, 70, June, 312–26.

Debreu, G. 1959: *Theory of Value*. New York: Wiley.

Denny, M. and Fuss, M. 1977: The use of approximation analysis to test for separability and the existence of consistent aggregates. *American Economic Review*, 67, June, 404–18.

Dhrymes, P.J. 1963: A comparison of productivity behavior in manufacturing and service industries. *Review of Economics and Statistics*, 45, 64–9.

—— 1965: Some extensions and tests for the CES class of production functions. *Review of Economics and Statistics*, XLVII, November, 357–66.

—— 1967: On a class of utility and production functions yielding everywhere differentiable demand functions. *Review of Economic Studies*, 34, October, 399–408.

—— and Kurz, M. 1964: Technology and scale in electricity generation. *Econometrica*, 32, July, 287–315.

Diamond, P.A. 1965: Disembodied technical change in a two-sector model. *Review of Economic Studies*, XXXII, 161–8.

Diewert, W.E. 1971: An application of the Shepard duality theorem: a generalized Leontief production function. *Journal of Political Economy*, 79, 481–507.

—— 1976: Exact and superlative index numbers. *Journal of Econometrics*, 4, 116–45.

—— 1982: Duality approaches to microeconomic theory. In K.J. Arrow and M.D. Intriligator (eds), *Handbook of Mathematical Economics*, volume II, Amsterdam: North-Holland, 535–99.

—— and Wales, T.J. 1987: Flexible functional forms and global curvature conditions. *Econometrica*, 55, 43–68.

Dorfman, R., Samuelson, P.A. and Solow, R.M. 1958: *Linear Programming and Economic Analysis*. New York: McGraw-Hill.

Douglas, P.H. 1948: Are there laws of production? *American Economic Review*, 38, 1–41.

—— 1967: Comments on the Cobb–Douglas production function. In M. Brown (ed.), *The Theory and Empirical Analysis of Production*, New York: Columbia University Press, 15–22.

Drandakis, E.M. and Phelps, E.S. 1966: A model of induced invention, growth, and distribution. *Economic Journal*, LXXVI, 823–40.

Eisner, R. and Nadiri, M.I. 1968: Investment behavior and neoclassical theory. *Review of Economics and Statistics*, 50, August, 369–82.

Fei, J.C. and Ranis, G. 1965: Innovational intensity and factor bias in the theory of growth. *International Economic Review*, VI, 182–98.

Ferguson, C.E. 1963: Cross-section production functions and the elasticity of substitution in American manufacturing industry. *Review of Economics and Statistics*, 45, 305–13.

—— 1965: Time-series production functions and technological progress in American manufacturing industry. *Journal of Political Economy*, April, 135–47.

—— 1969: *The Neoclassical Theory of Production and Distribution*. Cambridge: Cambridge University Press.

Field, B.C. and Grebenstein, C. 1980: Capital-energy substitution in U.S. manufacturing. *Review of Economics and Statistics*, 62, May, 207–12.

Fisher, F. 1965: Embodied technical change and the existence of an aggregative capital stock. *Review of Economic Studies*, XXXII, 263–88.

Fisher, I. 1954: *The Theory of Interest*. New York: Keelley and Millman.

Friedman, M. 1949: The Marshallian demand curve. *Journal of Political Economy*, LVII, December, 463–95.

—— 1957: *A Theory of the Consumption Function*. New York: NBER.

—— and Savage, L.J. 1948: The utility analysis of choices involving risk. *Journal of Political Economy*, 56, August, 279–304.

Frisch, R. 1932: *New Methods of Measuring Marginal Utility*. Tübingen.

—— 1936: Annual survey of general economic theory: the problem of index numbers. *Econometrica*, 4, 1–38.

—— 1954: Linear expenditure functions, an expository article. *Econometrica*, 22, 505–10.

—— 1959: A complete scheme for computing all direct and cross demand elasticities in a model with many sectors. *Econometrica*, 27, 177–95.

Fuchs, V.R. 1963: Capital labor substitution, a note: *Review of Economics and Statistics*, November, 436–8.

Fuss, M.A. 1977a: The demand for energy in Canadian manufacturing. *Journal of Econometrics*, 5, January, 89–116.

—— 1977b: The structure of technology over time, 1797–1821. *Econometrica*, 45, November, 1797–1821.

——, McFadden, D. and Mundlak, Y. 1978: A survey of functional forms in the economic analysis of production. In M. Fuss and D. McFadden (eds), *Production Economics: A Dual Approach to Theory and Applications*, volume I, Amsterdam: North-Holland Publishing Company.

Geary, R.C. 1949–50: A note on "a constant utility index of the cost of living". *Review of Economic Studies*, 65–6.

Goldberger, A.S. 1967: Functional form and utility: a review of consumer demand theory. Social Systems Research Institute, University of Wisconsin, Workshop Paper SFMP 6703, October, 1–122.

Goldman, S.M. and Uzawa, H. 1964: A note on separability in demand analysis. *Econometrica*, 32, 387–98.

Gorman, W.M. 1959: Separable utility and aggregation. *Econometrica*, 27, 469–81.

Green, H.A.J. 1964: *Aggregation in Economic Analysis: An Introductory Survey*. Princeton, NJ: Princeton University Press.

Griffin, J.M. and Gregory, P.R. 1976: An intercountry translog model of energy substitution responses. *American Economic Review*, 66, December, 845–57.

Griliches, Z. 1967: Production functions in manufacturing: some preliminary results. In M. Brown (ed.), *The Theory and Empirical Analysis of Production*, New York: Columbia University Press.

—— 1980: Returns to research and development expenditures in the private sector. In J. Kendrick and B. Vaccara (eds), *New Developments in Productivity Measurement and Analysis*, Chicago, IL: NBER.

—— and Ringstad, V. 1971: *Economies of Scale and the Form of the Production Function*. Amsterdam: North-Holland.

Hall, R.E. 1973: The specification of technology with several kinds of output. *Journal of Political Economy*, 81, 878–92.

Halvorsen, R. 1977: Energy substitution in U.S. manufacturing. *Review of Economics and Statistics*, 59, November, 381–8.

—— and Ford, J. 1979: Substitution among energy, capital, and labor inputs in U.S. manufacturing. In R.S. Pindyck (ed.), *Advances in the Economics of Energy and Resources I*, Greenwich, CT: JAI Press.

Hanoch, G. 1975: Production and demand models with direct or indirect activity. *Econometrica*, 43, May, 395–420.

Hazilla, M. and Kopp, R. 1984: *Industrial Energy Substitution: Econometric Analysis of U.S. Data, 1958–1974*, Electric Power Research Institute, Palo Alto, CA, EA-3462, Final Report.

Heien, D.M. 1972: Demographic effects and the multiperiod consumption function. *Journal of Political Economy*, 80, January/February, 125–38.

Heiner, R. 1983: The origin of predictable behavior. *American Economic Review*, 73, September, 560–95.

Henderson, J.M. and Quandt, R.E. 1980: *Microeconomic Theory*, third edition. New York: McGraw-Hill.

Hicks, J.R. 1932: *The Theory of Wages*. London: Macmillan.

—— 1956: *A Revision of Demand Theory*. Oxford: Oxford University Press.

—— 1965: *Value and Capital*, second edition. Oxford: Clarendon Press.

Hirschleifer, J. 1970: *Interest and Capital*. Englewood Cliffs, NJ: Prentice-Hall.

Hotelling, H. 1932: Edgeworth's taxation paradox and the nature of demand and supply functions. *Journal of Political Economy*, 40, October, 577–616.

Houthakker, H.S. 1957: An international comparison of household expenditure patterns, commemorating the centenary of Engel's law. *Econometrica*, 25, October, 532–51.

—— 1960: Additive preferences. *Econometrica*, 28, April, 244–57.

—— and Taylor, L.D. 1970: *Consumer Demand in the United States 1929–70*, second edition. Cambridge, MA: Harvard University Press.

Hudson, E.A. and Jorgenson, D.W. 1974: U.S. energy policy and economic growth, 1975–2000. *Bell Journal of Economics and Management Science*, 5, Autumn, 461–514.

Hulten, C.R. 1973: Divisia index numbers. *Econometrica*, 41, November, 1017–26.

Humphrey, D.B. and Moroney, J.R. 1975: Substitution among capital, labor and natural resource products in American manufacturing. *Journal of Political Economy*, 83, February, 57–82.

Hurwicz, L. 1971: On the problem of integrability of demand functions. In J.S. Chipman, L. Hurwicz, M.K. Richter, and H.F. Sonnenschein (eds), *Preferences, Utility, and Demand*, New York: Harcourt Brace Jovanovich, 174–214.

Intriligator, M.D. 1965: Embodied technical change and productivity in the United Kingdom, 1929–1958. *Review of Economics and Statistics*, XLVII, February, 65–70.

—— 1971: *Mathematical Optimization and Economic Theory*. Englewood Cliffs, NJ: Prentice Hall.

Jones, R.W. 1965: The structure of simple general equilibrium models. *Journal of Political Economy*, LXXIII, December, 557–72.

Jorgenson, D. and Slesnik, D. 1985: General equilibrium analysis of economic policy. In J. Piggot and J. Whalley (eds), *New Developments in Applied General Equilibrium Analysis*, Cambridge: Cambridge University Press.

Katzner, D.W. 1970: *Static Demand Theory*. New York: Macmillan.

Kaul, T.K. and Sengupta, J.K. (eds), 1991: *Economic Models, Estimation, and Socioeconomic Systems*, Essays in Honor of Karl A. Fox. Amsterdam: Elsevier Science.

Kendrick, J. and Sato, R. 1963: Factor prices, productivity, and economic growth. *American Economic Review*, 53, 974–1003.

Kennedy, C. 1964: Induced bias in innovation and the theory of distribution. *Economic Journal*, LXXIV, 541–7.

Klein, L.R. and Rubin, H. 1947–8: A constant utility index of the cost of living. *Review of Economic Studies*, 15, 84–7.

Kmenta, J. 1967: On estimation of the CES production function. *International Economic Review*, 8, June, 180–9.

Koopmans, T.C. (ed.) 1951: *Activity Analysis of Production and Allocation*, Cowles Commission Monograph, No. 13, New York: Wiley.

Kurz, M. and Manne, A.S. 1963: Engineering estimates of capital–labor substitution in metal industry. *American Economic Review*, 53, September, 662–81.

Lancaster, K.J. 1966: A new approach to consumer theory. *Journal of Political Economy*, 74, April, 132–57.

Lau, L.J. 1969: Duality and the structure of utility functions. *Journal of Economic Theory*, 1, 374–96.

—— and Mitchell, B.M. 1970: A linear logarithmic expenditure system: an application to U.S. data. *Program and Abstracts of Papers*, Second World Congress of Econometric Society, Cambridge, England.

—— and Yotopoulos, P.A. 1971: A test for relative efficiency and an application to Indian agriculture. *American Economic Review*, 61, 94–109.

Lee, J.W. 1970: Determinants of the changes in the relative factor share. *Review of Economics and Statistics*, LII, August, 331–6.

Lee, T.H. 1972: On measuring the nearness of near-moneys: comment. *American Economic Review*, LXII, March, 217–20.

Leibenstein, H. 1966: Allocative efficiency vs. X-efficiency. *American Economic Review*, 56, June, 392–415.

Leijonhufvud, A. 1981: *Information and Coordination*. New York: Oxford University Press.

Leontief, W.W. 1936: Composite commodities and the problem of index numbers. *Econometrica*, 4, 39–59.

—— 1947: Introduction to a theory of the internal structure of functional relationships. *Econometrica*, 15, October, 361–73.

—— 1953a: *The Structure of American Economy, 1919–1939*. New York: Oxford University Press.

—— 1953b: Domestic production and foreign trade: the American capital position re-examined. *Proceedings of the American Philosophical Society*, 97, 331–49.

—— 1966: *Input–Output Economics*. New York: Oxford University Press.

——, Morgan, A., Polenske, K., Simpson, D. and Tower, E. 1965: Economic impact – industrial and regional – of an arms cut. *Review of Economics and Statistics*, XLVII, August, 217–41.

Lerner, A.P. 1933: Notes on the elasticity of substitution: the diagrammatical representation. *Review of Economic Studies*, I, 68–71.

Leser, C.E.V. 1941: Family budget data and price elasticities of demand. *Review of Economic Studies*, IX, 40–59.

—— 1963: Forms of Engel functions. *Econometrica*, 31, 694–703.

Machlup, F. 1935: The commonsense of the elasticity of substitution. *Review of Economic Studies*, 30, 202–13.

McFadden, D. 1963: Constant elasticity of substitution production function. *Review of Economic Studies*, 30, 73–83.

—— 1978a: Cost, revenue and profit functions. In M. Fuss and D. McFadden (eds), *Production Economics: A Dual Approach to Theory and Applications*, volume 1, Amsterdam: North-Holland, 3–109.

—— 1978b: General linear profit function. In M. Fuss and D. McFadden (eds), *Production Economics: A Dual Approach to Theory and Applications*, volume 1, Amsterdam: North-Holland, 269–86.

—— 1978c: Estimation techniques for the elasticity of substitution and other production parameters. In M. Fuss and D. McFadden (eds), *Production Economics: A Dual Approach to Theory and Applications*, volume 2, Amsterdam: North-Holland, 73–123.

McKinnon, R.I. 1962: Wages, capital costs, and employment in manufacturing: a model applied to 1947–58 U.S. data. *Econometrica*, 30, July, 501–21.

Miles, M. 1978: Currency substitution, flexible exchange rates, and monetary interdependence. *American Economic Review*, 68, 428–36.

Minhas, B. 1963: *An International Comparison of Factor Costs and Factor Use.* Amsterdam: North-Holland.

Modigliani, F. and Brumberg, R. 1954: Utility analysis and the consumption function. In K. Kurihara (ed.), *Post Keynesian Economics*, New Brunswick, NJ: Rutgers, 388–436.

Moroney, J.R. 1967: Cobb–Douglas production functions and returns to scale in U.S. manufacturing industry. *Western Economic Journal*, VI, December, 39–51.

—— and Wilbratte, B.J. 1976: Money and money substitutes: a time series analysis of household portfolios. *Journal of Money, Credit and Banking*, VIII, May, 181–98.

Morrison, C. 1988: Quasi-fixed inputs in U.S. and Japanese manufacturing: a generalized Leontief restricted cost function approach. *Review of Economics and Statistics*, 70, May, 275–87.

Mukerji, V. 1963: A generalized SMAC function with constant ratios of elasticities of substitution. *Review of Economic Studies*, 30, 233–6.

Mundlak, Y. 1964: Transcendental multiproduct production functions. *International Economic Review*, 5, September, 273–84.

Muth, R.F. 1966: Household production and consumer demand functions. *Econometrica*, 34, 699–708.

Nadiri, M.I. 1972: An alternative model of business investment spending. *Brookings Paper on Economic Activity*, 3, 547–83.

—— 1982: Producers theory. In K.J. Arrow and M.D. Intriligator (eds), *Handbook of Mathematical Economics*, volume II, Amsterdam: North-Holland, 431–90.

Nakamura, S. 1990: A nonhomothetic generalized Leontief cost function based on pooled data. *Review of Economics and Statistics*, LXII, November, 649–55.

Nerlove, M. 1963: Return to scale in electricity supply. In C.F. Christ (ed.), *Measurement in Economics: Studies in Mathematical Economics and Econometrics in Memory of Yehuda Grunfeld*, Stanford, CA: Stanford University Press.

—— 1965: *Estimation and Identification of Cobb–Douglas Production Functions*. Chicago, IL: Rand McNally.

—— 1967: Recent empirical studies of the CES and related production function. In M. Brown (ed.), *The Theory and Empirical Analysis of Production*, New York: Columbia University Press.

Neumann, J., von and Morgenstern, O. 1947: *Theory of Games and Economic Behavior*, second edition. Princeton, NJ: Princeton University Press.

Parks, R.W. 1969: Systems of demand equations: an empirical comparison of alternative functional forms. *Econometrica*, 37, 611–29.

—— 1971: Price responsiveness of factor utilization in Swedish manufacturing, 1870–1950. *Review of Economics and Statistics*, 53, May, 129–39.

Pearce, I.F. 1961: An exact method of consumer demand analysis. *Econometrica*, 29, 499–516.

—— 1964: *A Contribution to Demand Analysis*. Oxford: Oxford University Press.

Perroni, C. and Rutherford, T. 1989: The stability and flexibility of functional forms for applied general equilibrium analysis. Paper presented at the NBER Applied General Equilibrium Workshop at San Diego, California, August.

Phlips, L. 1983: *Applied Consumption Analysis*. Amsterdam: North-Holland.

Pindyck, R.S. 1979: Interfuel substitution and the industrial demand for energy: an international comparison. *Review of Economics and Statistics*, 61, May, 169–79.

Pollak, R.A. 1971a: Additive utility functions and linear Engel curves. *Review of Economic Studies*, 38, October, 401–14.

—— 1971b: The theory of the cost of living index. Research Discussion Paper No. 11, Research Division, Office of Prices and Living Conditions, U.S. Bureau of Labor Statistics, June.

—— 1972: Generalized separability. *Econometrica*, 40, 431–54.

—— and Wales, T.J. 1969: Estimation of the linear expenditure system. *Econometrica*, 37, October, 611–28.

Pollak, R.A., Sickles, R.C. and Wales, T.J. 1984: The CES–translog: specification and estimation of a new cost function. *Review of Economics and Statistics*, 66, November, 602–7.

Powell, A.A. 1974: *Empirical Analytics of Demand Systems*. Lexington, MA: D.C. Heath.

Prais, S.J. and Houthakker, H.S. 1971: *The Analysis of Family Budgets*. New York: Cambridge University Press.

Robinson, J. 1933: *The Economics of Imperfect Competition*. London: Macmillan.

Rossiter, R. and Lee, T.H. 1984: Statistical tests of relative substitutabilities of near-monies over time. *Journal of Macroeconomics*, 6, Summer, 249–64.

Salter, W.E.G. 1960: *Productivity and Technical Change*. Cambridge: Cambridge University Press.

Samuelson, P.A. 1947: *Foundations of Economic Analysis*. Cambridge, MA: Harvard University Press.

—— 1948: Some implications of "linearity." *Review of Economic Studies*, 15, 88–90.

—— 1953–4: Prices of factors and goods in general equilibrium. *Review of Economic Studies*, 21, 1–20.

—— 1956: Social indifference curves. *Quarterly Journal of Economics*, LXX, 1–22.

—— 1965a: A theory of induced innovations along Kennedy–Weizsäcker lines. *Review of Economics and Statistics*, XLVII, 343–56.

—— 1965b: Using full duality to show that simultaneously additive direct and indirect utilities implies unitary price elasticity of demand. *Econometrica*, 33, 781–96.

—— 1969: Corrected formulation of direct and indirect additivity. *Econometrica*, 37, 355–9.

Sato, K. 1967: A two-level constant-elasticity of substitution production function. *Review of Economic Studies*, 34, 201–18.

—— 1972: Additive utility functions with double-log consumer demand functions. *Journal of Political Economy*, 80, January/February, 102–24.

Schultz, H. 1938: *The Theory and Measurement of Demand*. Chicago, IL: University of Chicago Press.

Seale, J.L. and Theil, H. 1991: Income and price sensitivity in demand systems, part I: income sensitivity and part II: price sensitivity. In T.K. Kaul and J.K. Sengupta (eds), *Economic Models, Estimation, and Socioeconomic Systems*, *Essays in Honor of Karl Fox*, Amsterdam: North-Holland, 141–74.

Shafer, W. and Sonnenschein, H. 1982: Market demand and excess demand functions. In K.J. Arrow and M.D. Intriligator (eds), *Handbook of Mathematical Economics*, Amsterdam: North-Holland, 671–93.

Shephard, R.W. 1970: *Theory of Cost and Production Function*. Princeton, NJ: Princeton University Press.

—— 1981: *Cost and Production Functions*. New York: Springer-Verlag.

Shumway, R.R., Saez, R.R. and Gottret, P.E. 1988: Multi-product supply and input demand in U.S. agriculture. *American Journal of Agricultural Economics*, 70, 330–7.

Solow, R.M. 1955–6: The production function and the theory of capital. *Review of Economic Studies*, 23, 101–8.

—— 1957: Technical change and the aggregate production function. *Review of Economics Statistics*, 39, August, 312–20.

—— 1962: Substitution and fixed proportions in the theory of capital. *Review of Economic Studies*, 29, 207–18.

—— 1964: Capital, labor, and income in manufacturing. In National Bureau of Economic Research, *The Behaviors of Income Shares*, in *Studies in Income and Wealth*, volume 27, Washington, DC: NBER.

—— 1967: Some recent developments in the theory of production. In M. Brown (ed.), *The Theory and Empirical Analysis of Production*. New York: Columbia University Press, 25–50.

Stigler, G.J. 1939: Production and distribution in the short run. *Journal of Political Economy*, 47, June, 305–27.

—— 1950: The development of utility theory. *Journal of Political Economy*, LVIII, 307–27, 373–96.

—— 1961: The economics of information. *Journal of Political Economy*, 69, June, 213–25.

Stone, R. 1954a: *The Measurement of Consumers' Expenditure and Behavior in the United Kingdom, 1920–1938*, volume I. Cambridge: Cambridge University Press.

—— 1954b: Linear expenditure systems and demand analysis: an application to the pattern of British demand. *Economic Journal*, 64, September, 511–27.

—— and Croft-Murray, G. 1959: *Social Accounting and Economic Models*. London: Bowes and Bowes.

—— and Rowe, D.A. 1957: The market demand for durable goods. *Econometrica*, 25, 423–43.

——, Brown, J.A.C. and Rowe, D.A. 1964: Demand analysis and projections for Britain 1900–1970: a study in method. In J. Sandee (ed.), *Europe's Future Consumption*, Amsterdam: North-Holland.

Strotz, R.H. 1959: The utility tree – a correction and future appraisal. *Econometrica*, 27, 482–8.

Theil, H. 1965a: *Linear Aggregation of Economic Relations*. Amsterdam: North-Holland.

—— 1965b: The information approach to demand analysis. *Econometrica*, 33, January, 67–87.

—— 1967: *Economics and Information Theory*. Amsterdam: North-Holland.

Uzawa, H. 1962: Production function with constant elasticities of substitution. *Review of Economic Studies*, 29, 291–9.

—— 1964: Duality principles in the theory of cost and production. *International Economic Review*, 5, 216–20.

Varian, H.R. 1983: Non-parametric tests of consumer behavior. *Review of Economic Studies*, 50(1), 99–110.

—— 1984: *Microeconomic Analysis*, second edition. New York: W.W. Norton.

Wales, T.J. 1971: A generalized linear expenditure model of the demand for non-durable goods in Canada. *Canadian Journal of Economics*, 4, November, 471–84.

Walters, A.A. 1963: Production and cost function: an econometric survey. *Econometrica*, 31(1–2), 1–66.

Westbrook, M.D. and Buckley, P.A. 1990: Flexible functional forms and regularity: assessing the competitive relationship between truck and rail transportation. *Review of Economics and Statistics*, LXXII, November, 623–30.

Wold, H.O.A. and Juréen, L. 1953: *Demand Analysis*. New York: Wiley.

Woodland, A.D. 1975: Substitution of structures, equipment and labor in Canadian production. *International Economic Review*, 16, February, 171–87.

—— 1977: Joint outputs, intermediate inputs, and international trade theory. *International Economic Review*, 18, 517–34.

Working, H. 1943: Statistical laws of family expenditure. *Journal of the American Statistical Association*, 38, 43–56.

Index